D1325961

A NEXTEXT COURSEBOOK

ESSENTIALS OF

Speech COMMUNICATION

Authors

Sharon Franklin   Deborah J. Clark

nextext

Author Affiliates

Sharon Franklin, President, Franklin Tull

Deborah J. Clark, Towson University

Cover and interior illustrations: Eric Larsen

Printed in the United States of America

ISBN 0-618-04829-4

3 4 5 6 7 — QKT — 06 05 04 03 02

Table of Contents

Organizing a Persuasive Speech 189
Problem-Solution Format
Monroe's Motivated Sequence Format
Sequential Format
Labeling Format
Comparison and Contrast Format
Cause-Effect Format

Evaluating Persuasive Speeches 193
Evaluation Methods
The Evaluation Process

CHAPTER 11: OTHER TYPES OF PUBLIC SPEAKING 197

Preparing Other Types of Speeches 198
Evaluate the Situation
Choose and Narrow the Topic
Gather Information
Write and Rehearse the Speech

Speeches about People 199
Speeches of Introduction
Speeches of Presentation
Speeches of Acceptance
Commemorative Speeches

Special Occasion Speeches 209
Keynote Speeches
Commencement Speeches
Dedication Speeches
Speaking to Entertain

Speaking for Business 213
Reports
Proposals
Public Relations Speeches
Sales Presentations

Impromptu Speaking 218
How to Handle an Impromptu Speech

SPEECH LISTS

CHAPTER 1

Contexts of Communication

In this chapter, you will consider:

- **What is communication?**
- **Why do you sometimes misunderstand what people say to you?**
- **How do speaker and listener ensure effective communication?**
- **Why is it important to know your audience?**
- **How does context affect communication?**
- **In what careers are communication skills vital?**

In this chapter, you will learn that communication is almost inescapable. Every day you take part in a huge and pervasive cultural system of giving and getting messages. Messages that are sent through the symbol systems of words and nonverbal behavior can't communicate perfectly and often are misunderstood. So communicating begins with knowing your audience and establishing an appropriate communication relationship between speaker and listener.

As you will discover, communication doesn't occur in a vacuum but in a specific context— a social situation, a place, or a set of circumstances. You communicate very differently with your family, your peer group, at school or work, in the community, to older generations, and to those of a different culture. Being aware of the unique communication features of each context can help you to communicate more effectively.

How important are communication skills? They are vital in every context and in almost all career situations. Mastering communication skills can have a great impact on your future.

What Is Communication?

Communication is almost inescapable. On a typical day you might:

* Wake up to a hit song on the clock-radio.
* Read the news and comics in the morning paper.
* Listen to announcements on the school intercom.
* Raise your hand to answer a teacher's question.
* Talk to friends.
* Read the mail.
* Answer the telephone when it rings.
* Watch the news on television.
* Exchange e-mail.
* Converse with your family.

Nearly everything that happens between individuals communicates something. Every **message** carries information that defines your place in the world. You were born into a world of people, with language and culture all ready for you. You take part in this system of giving and getting messages that tell about what the world is and who you are.

For example, the radio plays music that's popular, comics display what's considered funny, school instructs you in things that society expects you to know, and newspapers and television report events that are considered important. Such messages are communicated to you all day and communicated by you to others.

Messages and Meanings

Humans have devised symbolic systems for sending and receiving messages. We use **verbal** symbols—words—as well as **nonverbal** symbols—gestures, facial expressions, body motions, and tone of voice. By word, action, and dress, whether intentional or not, we communicate who we are and what we think.

Communication is sharing **meaning** by transmitting messages. **Speech communication** is sharing meaning by transmitting verbal messages.

Language is a system of word symbols that lets you reach beyond your primary relationships and make contact with other members of the culture. Language can convey ideas, feelings, and needs. However, language doesn't exist separately from the people who use it.

How Meaning Is Created

Meanings are in message senders—people—not in the messages themselves. Individuals assign meanings to words and intend them in a particular way. Each person has had different experiences that cause him or her to associate certain emotional meanings with words. For example, you may have warm and positive associations with the word *brother,* but another person may not, depending upon his or her experiences.

If meaning were in words, then knowing words would eliminate all misunderstanding. But one person's understanding of a verbal message often differs from that of another. People carry their own personal histories, moods, biases, language, attitudes, and knowledge with them. And as experiences change, meanings change.

For example, no one can take the meaning of the statement "I saw a really great movie" and inject it into your head. Everyone's idea of a "great movie" is different.

To your biology teacher, a "great movie" might be a black-and-white film about microscopic animals. To your science-fiction-loving friend Todd, a "great movie" probably would feature machine-like creatures with absurd problems. To your three-year-old sister, a "great movie" might be about a cute doggie.

Messages and Meanings

This box illustrates statements about how meaning is created.

How Meaning Is Created	Examples
1. Messages are sent and received.	You speak, he speaks. He speaks, you nod.
2. Meanings are in message users (people), not in the messages (words). That is, meanings exist in your head.	He imagines his day at the beach. He talks about the beach. You imagine swimming.
3. Meanings change as experiences change.	When you were small, the beach was huge. Now you're a lifeguard.
4. Shared meanings are never exactly the same.	His perfect beach day—under an umbrella, reading a book. Your perfect beach day—in the water the entire time.
5. Misunderstandings can't be totally avoided but can be anticipated.	Ask "What do you mean by 'a perfect beach day'?"

Verbal Misunderstandings

GOAL

The goal of this activity is to identify and analyze sentences that might be misunderstood.

TASKS

1. Think of sentences that you've sent, received, or overheard today that could have been misunderstood.

2. Make a table with three columns. In column one, list five or six examples of sentences that could be misunderstood. In column two, list all possible meanings that each of these sentences could have had. In column three, list reasons that you think these sentences were confusing.

3. Share your sentences, their potential meanings, and your analysis with the class.

4. Make a list of reasons that sentences often are misunderstood.

OUTCOMES

What were some of the common causes of misunderstandings? In what ways can you improve your own communication to avoid such misunderstandings?

Guitar Lingo

Technical language doesn't just belong to scientists. People who share interests have their own vocabularies that others may not understand. Here's a conversation between two friends who both play electric guitar:

"Can I borrow your pedal this weekend?"

"Why? Isn't yours good?"

"It's a different kind of pedal. It's a wah wah."

"Oh. And you want to go with distortion for some songs?"

"Yeah."

"I thought you guys only did covers."

"Not any more. We got good. We wrote four of our own songs."

Nonverbal Messages

Nonverbal messages also convey emotional meaning. People's facial expressions, gestures, and the way they move their bodies send messages about their moods and attitudes. However, nonverbal messages can easily be misinterpreted. They must be considered in connection with verbal messages. For example, if you saw someone knit her brow and narrow her eyes, you might think she looked angry or confused. But maybe she was squinting to see better. If a nonverbal message is confusing, ask the speaker what he or she means.

Know Your Audience

Regardless of the size of your audience, as a speaker, you must establish a relationship with your listener. Before opening your mouth, do you consider to whom you're talking? For example, do you speak differently to your boss than to your little brother? Do you share different information with your best friend than you share with your parents?

"Know your audience" is a basic communication rule at every level, whether interpersonal, group, public, or mass communication.

Before speaking, consider who is in a dominant role, has higher status, or deserves recognition. If you are sent to the principal's office, you'll acknowledge the principal's authority. You'll also be careful how you speak to a college admissions officer. But if you are asking friends to bring refreshments to a party, you'll behave differently.

Communicators also consider each other's education, culture, beliefs, and current emotional state. If you see a friend sobbing alone in a chair, it wouldn't be a great time to mention that you just got an A on a test. If one of your friends has strong religious beliefs, you probably are careful how you speak around him or her.

Conversation Critique

GOAL

The goal of this activity is to work on improving communication skills as speakers and listeners.

TASKS

1. Form groups of four; then break into pairs.

2. Each pair takes turns conversing while the other pair critiques their conversation. During each turn, one speaker might try to explain a favorite topic to the listener.

3. Critique conversations according to the following. Did each speaker tailor the message to the listener, show respect and sincerity, present information clearly, and ask for feedback? Did the listener know the sender, focus attention, keep an open mind, and ask for clarification when needed?

4. The pairs switch roles and repeat the activity.

OUTCOMES

Which were the most difficult skills to perform? Did speaker and listener agree with the critique?

How to Communicate Effectively	
Good communicators know how to speak and how to listen. Listener and speaker change roles often.	
Speaker's Role	**Listener's Role**
Know the listener (language, education, status, culture, beliefs, emotional state).	Know the speaker (language, education, status, culture, beliefs, emotional state).
Direct information to the listener. For example, if you help a younger cousin with math, use simple words and sentences that he or she understands.	Focus attention on the speaker.
Be sincere and respectful so the listener knows that you want to reach him or her.	Treat the speaker with respect.
Present information clearly.	Keep an open mind.
Get feedback, both verbal and nonverbal.	Ask for clarification, if needed.

Communication in Context

Understanding Context

Communication doesn't occur in a vacuum. Rather it occurs in a **context**—a social situation, place, or set of circumstances—that influences it. Outside of the context, an isolated signal doesn't contain all the information necessary to provide all the intended meaning. The meaning of a signal depends on the situation and the behavior that accompanies it.

Context can change meaning. Take the sentence, "You need help." If you're instructing someone and see he or she is having difficulty, "You need help" might be a sincere offer to assist. If someone is seriously hurt, "You need help" becomes a declaration that you intend to call for first aid. If a friend does something outrageous, "You need help" might be said as a joke.

Communication in Careers

A Well-Tuned Ear

Jim Booth, an auto mechanic in Pennsylvania, says, "I've learned to ask a lot of questions to be sure of good communication—at least when it comes to fixing cars." He adds, "It's always best to give your mechanic as many symptoms as possible." One way to describe a car problem is to mimic the sound of the trouble. "Most people are somewhat inhibited when it comes to mimicking car sounds, but it does help."

A teenage boy brought in a fairly new Chevrolet and said that it had a "clunk" in the front. Jim checked it out and found nothing wrong. The boy picked up the car, then brought it back the next day and said he still heard the clunk. When Jim asked which side, he replied, "Definitely the left side." Jim asked, "The driver's side?" and the boy replied, "No, the passenger's side." Jim muses, "I guess he meant 'left' as you're looking at the car from the front."

Jim road-tested the car but still heard nothing. That evening the boy explained, "It won't do it now. About five minutes after I leave home each morning, it clunks when I turn right."

Jim suggested that they go together and drive his regular route to work. "About five minutes away," Jim says, "we made a right-hand turn and heard a clunk, just as the right front wheel ran over a manhole cover!"

Another car owner came in and said her car sounded "rough." Did she mean grinding noises, clanking, or scraping? Jim started the engine and immediately heard how loud it was. But he wouldn't have called it "rough." "I called her and asked if she meant it was 'loud.'" She did.

Jim says, "It takes concentrated effort to listen properly to people's explanations."

Context also can change the type of communication you receive. For example, what someone tells you on the phone or in your living room probably differs from what he or she would say in a classroom, at a youth group meeting, or at a chance encounter in a store.

Types of Context

A context can be a physical place, such as a classroom, a store, or a home. Context can be social-psychological, including the views you hold or your current mood. It can be a relationship, as with friends, family, or coworkers. It can be cultural, as with the people of your country, generation, region, or city. Or it can be temporal, dealing with time, such as the position in a series or who speaks first. The purpose of the communication and the role of each participant can be crucial to understanding a context.

Here is information about **six** relationship contexts—family, friends and peer group, school and work, community, generational, and multicultural contexts. It's important to know how to communicate effectively in each of these contexts.

❶ Family Context

You first learned to communicate in your family. The quality of a family's communication depends upon the family's culture, the roles of family members, and the emotional connections within the group. Within each family, parents and children often behave in patterned, structured, and predictable ways. Some families are strict and formal, with parents occupying a commanding role. Others are more democratic, with all family members speaking freely.

Dimensions of Context

Contexts can be classified in a number of different ways. Even within a context, other dimensions of context affect communication.

Dimensions	Definition
Physical dimension	Location, physical presence, attractiveness of participants
Social-psychological dimension	Status, values, moods, perceptions, roles, rules, norms
Relationship dimension	Friends, family, coworkers
Cultural dimension	Collection of beliefs, values, attitudes, traditions, taboos, customs, and behaviors passed through generation
Temporal dimension	Time of day, week, season, history, position of the communication in a series

The roles of family members influence their communication. Parents communicate differently than their children. Older brothers and sisters communicate differently than younger siblings. It can be hard to get your family to see you outside of your role. Parents stay locked into a position of authority. The youngest child or children always will be the youngest.

Family communication often is both intimate and emotional. Parents and siblings have patterned emotional reactions to each other. Though some families are always loving and harmonious, it's easy for a household to get locked into behavior patterns of anger and yelling, nagging and withdrawal.

To improve family communication, start by identifying negative communication patterns. Propose improvements, based on what you know about effective communication. Take a fresh look at the people with whom you live, trying to understand them as individuals, outside of their family roles. Get to know them better by asking questions. Your family may not know your thoughts and feelings. Try explaining your feelings to them in a quiet time, outside of an argumentative context.

❷ Friendship and Peer Group Context

Although you don't choose your family, you definitely choose your friends. Friends are the people whose company you enjoy, with whom you build relationships. Friendship involves wishing good for another person for his or her own sake and causing good to happen.

Friendships can begin because of a specific element two individuals have in common—similar personalities, family backgrounds, or interests. Some of our most basic needs—for enjoyment, security, affection, and self-esteem—are fulfilled by friendships.

Many people treat their friends with more respect than their family members. Friends feel comfortable confiding with each other, so they usually communicate in an intimate way. But when problems or misunderstandings come along, it can be difficult to be truly honest. Because they know each other well, friends also can make the mistake of being rude to each other, neglecting each other, and forgetting to respect each other. As with family, it's important to respect your friends' individuality.

❸ School and Work Contexts

In a school or work context, as within the family, everyone has a role to play. These roles influence communication.

In school, the principal, teachers, and counselors have authority over many factors that affect you—your workload, behavior, and rewards and punishment. Your role as a student is to come to school prepared to learn and to help ensure that the environment is a good one for your learning as well as for the learning of others.

At work, the boss also has authority over you. He or she supervises your work, judges your performance, and can promote or fire you. This relationship can affect the amount of information you're willing to share. It goes both ways. Bosses try to preserve some emotional distance from their employees so they can continue to exert authority.

While you're a student or an employee, you should remember that the boss and the teacher have jobs to perform. You are in a subordinate role and need to respect their position and communicate with them appropriately.

❹ Community Context

Communities are networks of people living near each other and interacting together. In the neighborhood where you live, there may be a corner store owned by a neighbor, a school crossing guard stationed at the corner every day, and neighbors in the house next door, in the same apartment building, or across the alley.

Many people in today's fast-paced world complain that they don't know their neighbors' names. Communities where people do know each other— besides being more pleasant places to live—are safer. Neighbors who know you will tell you when your dog jumps over the fence or if a stranger they don't recognize is poking around near your garage.

Communities work well when the people in them communicate in a consistent and friendly manner. Good neighbors watch out for each other, respect each other's privacy, try to keep their own properties neat, and don't disturb everyone with loud noise, especially early in the morning and late at night when others may be asleep.

Everyday COMMUNICATION

Community Survival

When Alex was ten years old, his family moved to the house behind eight-year-old Doug and his family. Both are now in their early twenties. Recently they were walking together along a main street when suddenly Alex collapsed, screaming in pain.

Doug looked around frantically and noticed a passing car. The woman driving it was a neighbor who knew both boys. Doug flagged her down.

They drove Alex to the emergency room—just in time, according to the doctors. Alex had a collapsed lung. The fact that Doug knew his neighbors helped him to save Alex's life.

❺ Generational Context

You and your peer group share experiences. As you grow older, you have memories of events you've lived through together. People born within a 25-year time span comprise a **generation**. Your grandparents' generation may have lived during the Great Depression in the 1930s and World War II in the 1940s. Those events directly affected their lives and the lives of their peer group. Your parents' generation probably came of age during the 1960s and 1970s. If they grew up in the United States, they probably remember watching the first human footsteps on the moon, the turmoil of the Civil Rights movement, the agony of the Vietnam War, and the shocking assassinations of President John F. Kennedy, Dr. Martin Luther King, Jr., and Senator Robert Kennedy. They probably recall the first transistor radios, audiocassette players, and microwave ovens.

When you speak with older generations, you need to be aware that they've experienced the world much differently than you have. Their tastes, needs, and attitudes may be quite different from yours. Their experiences and values, as well as yours, need to be respected. While you may be quite comfortable with computers and the Internet, some members of older generations may still be unfamiliar with this technology and apprehensive about learning it. But you also may be able to bridge the gap by teaching them to use this valuable technology.

❻ Multicultural Context

Communication expresses identities. People in different geographical areas and of different ethnicities or religions may approach relationships differently than you do. For example, North Americans and Northern Europeans value individual expression. But in Asia and Africa, cultures often focus on consensus building, harmony, and the good of the group. In today's shrinking world, where people of widely different backgrounds are more likely to come together in **multicultural** situations, communication is especially important.

In communicating across cultures, it's important to be sensitive to fundamental differences. Be patient and be willing to assume that misunderstandings may occur.

Contexts and Communication Hot Spots		
Context Type	**Description**	**Communication Hot Spot**
Family	Home	Emotions, roles
Friends/Peer Group	Peers, for pleasure, enjoyment	Dealing with conflicts Familiarity allows for neglect Need for mutual respect
School/Work	School, job	Superior-subordinate roles
Community	Neighborhood	Knowing neighbors; helping each other
Generational	Different age groups	Understanding the past; respecting differences
Multicultural	Different cultures	Understanding tradition

Context Role-Play

GOAL

The goal of this activity is to observe how different contexts can affect a message.

TASKS

1. Choose a partner.

2. Take turns role-playing speaker and listener.

3. The speaker chooses a topic, such as littering, love, a recent movie, popular music, or summer plans, and begins a discussion with the listener. The listener chooses a role and role-plays a best friend, a parent, a classmate, a boss, or a stranger.

OUTCOMES

How did the listener's role affect the way the speaker presented the information? What things did the speaker tell his or her "friend" but not the "parent"? Were there things that the speaker said only to a "stranger"? Why?

Levels of Communication

One of the basic principles of communication is to tailor your message to your audience. Your communication should vary depending on to whom you're speaking. Communication occurs on **five** different levels, described below.

❶ Intrapersonal Communication

You do a type of self-talk, or **intrapersonal communication,** when you think to yourself in words. Intrapersonal communication helps you to reason out problems and plan what to say. This is one audience that you should know pretty well.

❷ Interpersonal Communication

Speaking one-to-one—**interpersonal communication**—is probably the form of communication most familiar to you because you do it most often. *Interpersonal* means "between people." Whenever you're engaged in conversation with another person, whether face-to-face or over the phone, it's interpersonal communication. In this type of communication, speaker and listener frequently change roles.

❸ Group Communication

When three or more people—such as family members, neighbors, committees, clubs, or work groups—come together to discuss a specific problem or for a common purpose, they're involved in **group communication**. Usually the focus is decision making. When you're aware of some of the dynamics involved, group communication can move more smoothly.

❹ Public Communication

Most likely, you've given an oral report in class at some point during your school career. This is a form of **public communication**. Individuals speak in public to spread information and ideas.

In public communication, you really need to know your audience. Adapting to and addressing an audience involves some of the same skills as interpersonal and group communication, but it requires more organization and preparation.

❺ Mass Communication

When one person or a group of people communicates with a large audience through a mass medium, such as print, radio, TV, or the Internet, **mass communication** is taking place. Mass communication allows for wide dispersal of a message. The speaker, however, will probably not know who the audience will be, in part because it is so large and probably not in view.

Sidebar

Levels of Communication

These are the various levels of speech communication:

- *Intrapersonal communication*—the internal dialogue you have with yourself.
- *Interpersonal communication*—two people engaging in one-to-one conversations. Sender and receiver speak and listen at the same time and change roles frequently.
- *Group communication*—involves three or more individuals. The purpose of group communication is usually to solve a problem.
- *Public communication*—one or more individuals speaking to an audience.
- *Mass communication*—one or more people communicating with a large number of listeners, usually through a medium such as television, radio, newspaper, posters, the Internet, or magazines.

Communication and Careers

Oral communication, listening ability, and enthusiasm are the three most important factors in helping new college graduates get jobs. Interpersonal and human relations skills are the most important factors in keeping a job. All of which is to say that communication abilities seem to be strong predictors of career success.

According to the American Society for Training and Development (ASTD), employers in the United States spend billions of dollars a year training their managers to speak before audiences and to work in groups. The ASTD also highlights the importance of verbal and nonverbal abilities, listening, interpersonal relationship building, understanding barriers to effective communication, consensus building, compromising, and knowing cultural differences in communication styles.

Where Communication Is Central

Some careers are all about communicating. For example, radio announcers, television reporters, and voice-over talent for commercial advertising all are trained to modulate their voices and to vary the pace and rhythm of their speech so that they never sound monotonous. Many of these professionals have studied drama. Some news announcers write their own copy, so written communication skills are very important, too.

Listening skills are very important for mental health care workers, such as psychiatrists, guidance counselors, psychologists, marriage therapists, and psychiatric social workers. They learn to listen to clients' descriptions of their problems in order to help.

All professions require good verbal communication skills. Teachers organize course material and learn to present it

step-by-step, in ways that are understandable to their students. Doctors need to listen closely to their patients' complaints to arrive at an accurate diagnosis. Then they need to explain complex medical conditions and treatments to their sometimes fearful patients. Trial lawyers must be good communicators, too, since winning cases depends upon their communicating effectively and eloquently with witnesses, judge, and jury. Journalists often interview a variety of people to get information for stories.

Business organizations of all kinds depend on the communication skills of their employees. Office managers have to convince people to work together to complete a job. Workers ask questions so they can perform their work successfully. Sales people listen to customers' needs and then explain why the products they sell will satisfy those needs. Marketers, advertisers, and public relations practitioners find ways to present a business and its product to the public. Consultants study the way that employees and employers interact and find ways for them to improve. Writers, editors, researchers, publishers, graphic artists, and Web site designers develop materials that communicate almost any topic imaginable.

Where Communication Is Needed

Good communication skills matter in trade professions, too. Carpenters, electricians, plumbers, and other tradespeople must communicate well to meet their customers'

needs. They also need to coordinate well with each other. Cabinetmaker Mike Gardner says that professionals "need to be aware of the other trades, and not just finish their work and go away." If they don't ask each other questions to find out the scope of each other's tasks, they risk damaging one another's work. "On construction sites, fights break out over this kind of thing," says Mike.

People who repair televisions, computers, and other appliances may need to explain what went wrong and how the customer can avoid future problems. Computer programmers need to understand the problems a client wants to solve in order to design good software. All those who work with people—from investment bankers to theater ushers—need to be able to listen and to communicate effectively.

Communication Basics

✔ Realize that meanings shift.

✔ Know your audience.

✔ Assess the speaker.

✔ Understand the context.

✔ Anticipate misunderstandings.

When you communicate, you share meaning by sending and receiving messages. Communication connects people in a culture, enabling people both to learn about themselves and to deliver messages about themselves. People communicate through symbols, both verbal and nonverbal. Speech communication occurs on several levels, beginning with oneself and ending with mass communication. Messages can be easily misunderstood, since the meanings of messages are found in those who send them. To communicate effectively, it's important to know your audience and the context.

Individuals exchange messages within a specific situation, or context—a physical place, a social-psychological dimension, a relationship dimension, a cultural dimension, or a temporal dimension. The context in which communication occurs affects the way a message is sent and received.

Communication skills can be improved. Effective communication helps people strengthen their relationships and improve their success in almost any career.

Speech

communication—sharing of meaning by transmitting messages.

context—social situation, place, or set of circumstances affecting communication.

generation—people born within a 25-year time span.

group communication—three or more people communicating, often to solve a problem.

interpersonal communication—communicating with another individual.

intrapersonal communication—internal dialogue with oneself.

mass communication—one person or a small group sending messages to a large number of people, usually using the media.

meaning—one's understanding of a message.

message—information sent and received between people using symbols.

multicultural—coming together of groups with different ways of doing things.

nonverbal—communicating without words.

public communication—one or few people talking to a large group.

speech communication—sharing meaning by transmitting verbal messages.

verbal—using spoken words.

CHAPTER 2

Sending and Receiving

In this chapter, you will consider:

- How carefully do you choose the words that you speak?
- In what ways can facial expressions, gestures, and appearances convey meaning?
- How well can you decipher others' nonverbal communication?
- How much control do you have over the quality of your voice?

The two basic communication tasks are sending and receiving messages. That's what you do when giving out and taking in information. In this chapter, you'll explore the areas of verbal and nonverbal communication, focusing on the verbal symbolism of language and the ways that people use voice, body movements, spatial positions, touch, and appearance to communicate. Finally, you'll learn how perception works, how people speak, and how they listen.

Elements of Communication

Sending the Message

Communication begins with ideas, experiences, or feelings. Information that you wish others to understand is a message that you send. You are the **sender**. Putting your information into words is verbal communication.

Communication is easy; you've been communicating since your first wail in the crib. But communicating a message involves more than speaking. You also communicate through your tone of voice, gestures, and facial expressions. These are some nonverbal ways of communicating. Both verbal and nonverbal communication work to create meaning.

Receiving the Message

Others receive your message, so they are called **receivers**. Your message arrives through their senses—through sight, sound, smell, and touch. These are called **channels** of communication. When you greet your friends, they see your smile, hear your words and the sound of your voice, smell your cologne, and feel your hug or your handshake. These impressions work together to create meaning.

Message receivers let you know whether and how they understood you. Depending upon how they interpret your message, receivers may give you an answer and smile, laugh, or frown. Perhaps they'll leave the room and slam the door or prepare to defend themselves. These are all types of **feedback** to your message.

Elements of Communication

Source: sender, speaker

Message: signals sent between a source and receiver

Receiver: listener or audience that gives feedback (becomes a sender)

Channel: sense that carries the message—ears, eyes, nose, mouth, hands/body (touch)

Context: space, time, setting, situation, field of experience, culture

Noise: interference or barrier to the message that is caused by distracting stimuli (external) or thoughts and feelings (internal)

Context and Noise

Two other elements affect communication. Every message is sent in a specific context—a time, space, setting, or situation. Context changes the way you communicate. For example, you speak differently at a basketball game than at home. The relationship between sender and receiver and the culture also are a part of the context of communication.

Anything that hinders a message is called **noise**. Interference with a message can come from the sender, the receiver, or the outside world. The sender may have chosen imprecise words that obscure the message. Or the receiver may have misunderstood the message. For example, if a sore shoulder makes a sender grimace, the receiver may think he or she is angry. Your physical environment also can hinder your messages. It can be hard to communicate in a crowded, noisy restaurant or on a static-filled phone line.

Symbolism

People send signals to each other with verbal and nonverbal **symbols**. We interpret things and events and apply meaning to them. We see clouds in the sky and wonder whether it might rain. A picture of a cloud on a weather map may symbolize a cloudy day. The word *cloud* symbolizes the white puff of water vapor in the sky. Our use of symbols is vast.

Verbal Symbolism and Language

We all use symbols. Emily has a mental picture of the yellow roses on the wall of her house. She can't show you that picture, but she can use words that stand for that image. You know the color yellow and what a rose is, but your mental picture of yellow roses on a wall won't look exactly like the one Emily envisions.

People have ideas and words in their heads, not rose bushes. The word *rose* is not an actual rose, but a symbol used for this plant. Using symbols can cause confusion. If people don't use the same symbols or agree on the meanings of their symbols, their messages won't be communicated.

When you put ideas into words, you **encode.** When your listener translates your words into ideas, he or she **decodes.** However, words are arbitrary. There's no physical reason that we call those flying feathered creatures *birds* rather that *oiseaux* or *uccelli* or *flapdoodles.* As Shakespeare put it, "a rose by any other name would smell as sweet."

Sidebar

How Words Can Fail You

Here are some ways that words can fail you:

* Your words have different denotative and connotative meanings.
* Your word has multiple meanings.
* The word's meaning has changed.
* The word is imprecise.
* The word is inaccurate.
* The word is inappropriate.

Identifying Communication Elements

GOAL

This activity is designed to help you identify the elements of communication in everyday conversations: sender, message, channel, receiver, context, and noise.

TASKS

1. Form groups of three or four.
2. Select a topic, such as a recent controversy that class members disagree on or a movie that inspired differing opinions.
3. If possible, prepare to tape record your conversation. If you don't have tape recorders, take turns observing the conversation and taking notes.
4. Each group discusses the topic for five minutes and tape records or takes notes on the conversation.
5. Play back the tape or read the notes. Identify senders, messages, channels, receivers, context, and noise.
6. Each group presents its findings to the class and compares lists with each other.

OUTCOMES

How well do your lists compare? Were you aware of sending all of the messages that others say they received? Did you receive what they wanted to send? Why or why not?

Denotation and Connotation

People usually learn word meanings in context, rather than by looking them up in a dictionary. For this reason, individuals can and often do use the same word differently, leading to misunderstandings.

Word meanings change over time. Words have both **denotative** meanings—their dictionary definitions—and **connotative** meanings—the values, attitudes, and emotions that people associate with them. For example, the denotation of *home* is the place where you live. What *home* usually connotes is comfort, security, and peacefulness.

Choosing the Right Words

When you communicate, you use only a tiny fraction of the words in your dictionary. But sometimes choosing a more precise word can clarify your meaning. For example, don't tell your friend that you went out in a *boat*. Instead, use the word *sailboat*, *yacht*, *powerboat*, *catamaran*, or whatever is appropriate.

It's also important to choose words that fit the situation or the audience. If you tell someone about doing a fifty-fifty on a rail, your listener won't understand unless he or she knows skateboarding jargon.

Checklist

How to Choose Words

✓ Be accurate.

✓ Be as specific as possible.

✓ Be concrete.

✓ Be aware of audience.

✓ Be aware of appropriateness.

Nonverbal Symbols

Whenever two people encounter each other, they communicate something, whether or not they understand each other and whether or not they intend to. Some of this communication occurs without words. Along with learning to speak, you've also learned nonverbal ways to communicate.

People have sensations, imaginings, feelings, and thoughts for which there are no simple words or single phrases. Sometimes it's hard to find ways to describe something. People unconsciously communicate how they feel through their appearance and the way they act.

Nonverbal communication includes all the ways that people share messages without words. People show their meanings through their tones of voice. They convey meaning with facial expressions and hand gestures. They communicate through the way they dress and move their bodies.

Verbal and nonverbal communications interplay with and support each other. You don't usually notice how well they go together unless you detect contradictory verbal and nonverbal messages—for instance, if your friend frowns at you and snaps, "Of course, I'm happy!"

When verbal and nonverbal messages seem to conflict, the nonverbal signals often indicate the real meaning. Trial lawyers pay close attention to the nonverbal behavior of witnesses. They have learned to decode such things as eye contact, tone of voice, and body position to detect when a person is lying or when jurors are believing their arguments.

Nonverbal communication must be read in the context of a situation. It usually lasts throughout an entire communication rather than beginning and ending like a sentence. It's usually uncontrolled and happens while a sender is speaking or a receiver is listening, so several channels of communication are open at once.

Sidebar

The Power of Nonverbal Communication

Nonverbal communication has several aspects. It:

* Always communicates something.
* Is tied to the situation.
* Affects the relationship.
* Makes commentary on the content.
* Is continuous.
* Reveals the true meaning of the communication.

Nonverbal communication can be divided into **five** main categories: paralanguage, kinesics (body motions and eye movements), proxemics (spatial distances), haptics (touch), and appearance (how people look).

❶ Paralanguage

Say each of these statements to yourself, placing emphasis on the underlined word:

Carol wants to call Dan.
Carol wants to call Dan.
Carol wants to call Dan.
Carol wants to call Dan.

Notice how the meaning of the same sentences changes when you emphasize different words. **Paralanguage** is a type of nonverbal communication that uses vocal inflection—that is, stressing some words and using different tones of voice—to convey meaning.

People usually convey much of their meaning through paralanguage. Since we're used to hearing people speak expressively, we laugh at cartoon robots because of their stilted, emotionless speech.

Persons for whom English is a second language occasionally will have a different vocal inflection to their sentences, because users of different languages use different paralanguage. For example, English speakers raise the pitch at the end of a sentence that asks a question. Intercultural misunderstandings can occur over such things, and the communicators may not realize the cause.

❷ Kinesics

Kinesics, another type of nonverbal communication, means communicating through body movements. People are influenced by each other's body movements and attribute meanings to them. A person's posture, gestures, facial expression, and way of moving all convey meaning nonverbally. Some nonverbal communication is learned, some is innate.

It's easy to misinterpret a person's kinesics. If a person moves rapidly toward you, you could see this as haste, anger, or aggression. Your decoding can easily be wrong. Nonverbal communication must always be seen in context of the situation. There are **five** main categories of kinesics:

1. **Emblems** are gestures that stand for words. For example, a thumbs-up sign means "OK" in the United States. Emblems are specific to cultures.

2. **Affect displays**, such as frowning, smiling, body tenseness, and posture, communicate emotional meaning.

3. **Regulators** control or moderate another person's speech. Nodding your head encourages the other person to continue talking. Leaning forward and opening your mouth or raising your index finger indicates that you wish to speak.

4. **Adaptors**, such as scratching or moving the hair out of your eyes, are gestures that satisfy a personal need.

5. **Illustrators** are gestures that reinforce your verbal language, like holding your hands apart to indicate a measured distance.

Listen with Your Eyes

Thumb and first finger making circle

In the United States, this means "OK."
In southern France, this means "worthless."
In Mexico, it means an obscenity.
In Japan, it means "money."

V with fingers

In Churchill's England, this meant "victory."
In England today, with the palm toward
your face, it's an obscene gesture.
In many cultures, it means your wife
is unfaithful.

Hiss

To the English, this shows disapproval.
To the Japanese, it shows deference.

Sitting down

In the Fiji Islands, this shows respect to a
superior (like a standing ovation in North
America and Europe).

Hands in pockets

In France, Belgium, Finland, Sweden,
Indonesia, this is impolite.

Eye movements can express a great variety of information, some of which is culturally variable. For example, the length of time acceptable for maintaining eye contact is one to three seconds in England but differs in other cultures. In Italy, if you make eye contact with the driver of a car when you're trying to cross the street, you may never get across. In the United States, people tend not to make eye contact with strangers on public streets. In India, strangers often look directly in your eye as they pass.

Eye movements can:

* Convey intense interest (looking intently at someone).
* Communicate high or low interest, self-consciousness, or nervousness (degree of eye contact).
* Express surprise, fear, disgust (width or narrowness of the lids).
* Cue that the channel of communication is open (open eyes, direct gaze).
* Define the nature of the relationship— positive (attentive glance) or negative (avoidance).
* Communicate power (high level of eye contact when speaking).
* Establish psychological distance (making or breaking eye contact).
* Help others maintain privacy (averted eyes in public).
* Display lack of interest (avoidance of eye contact).
* Convey disrespect (intense attention to someone else).

Five Types of Kinesics Communication		
Body movements that	**Are called**	**These are**
stand for words	emblems (thumbs up)	learned
convey emotional meaning	affect displays (crying)	innate
control or affect another's speech	regulators (tapping foot, looking at watch, sighing)	learned
satisfy a need	adaptors (tying shoe)	innate
accompany, illustrate	illustrators (making finger quote marks, showing how big the fish was)	learned

ACTIVITY

Spotting Kinesic Communication

GOAL

The goal of this activity is to identify various types of kinesic communication: emblems, affect displays, regulators, adaptors, and illustrators.

TASKS

1. As a class, watch a TV conversation between two or three people. This can be an interview or part of a soap opera, drama, or movie. Record part of the conversation, so you can replay it.

2. Take notes on the conversation and the kinesic behavior that accompanied it.

3. Discuss the conversation and identify kinesic communication that you observed. Classify the behavior as emblems, affect displays, regulators, adaptors, and illustrators.

4. Discuss the meanings you saw in this nonverbal communication. Do you think these meanings were intended by the speakers?

5. If desired, replay the taped conversation and see if you agree with one another's interpretations.

OUTCOMES

How different would this scene have been without the kinesic communication? Did some types of kinesic communication seem more crucial than others?

❸ Proxemics

The ways in which we position ourselves in relation to other people also can communicate nonverbally. Spatial communication, known as **proxemics**, conveys cultural preferences as well as a degree of emotional intimacy. As you speak to someone, you can sit close and lean against him or her, sit on the opposite side of the room, or turn your back. Each position communicates your connection to that person at that moment.

Norms for personal space and territory vary in different cultures. For example, North Americans usually stand at arm's length during a conversation. Latin Americans and Mediterraneans stand closer. All stand farther away from strangers than from friends.

Spatial Distance in the United States
Intimate: 0"–18"
Friendly: 18"–24"
Social: 4"–12'
Public: 12"–25'

Spatial Distance Varies by
Culture: Distances in some cultures are closer.
Sex: Women stand closer than men.
Age: Younger people stand closer than older people.
Status: Those with equal status stand closer than those with unequal status. The higher status person approaches the lower status person first.
Content: When discussing personal subjects, people stand closer.

❹ Haptics

Another channel of communication is **haptics**, or touch. Touch is most often associated with emotional intimacy and is common among friends and family.

There are cultural variations in haptics. North Americans often shake hands when they're introduced. A firm handshake communicates confidence and sincerity. In Japan and India, people are more likely to bow. Many people from European and Middle Eastern countries kiss each other on the cheek in greeting.

Just as verbal languages differ all over the world, different cultures have unique nonverbal languages. Because some of these differences are subtle, misunderstandings often arise between people of different cultures. They may not even know why.

In some cultures (sometimes known as contact cultures), hugging and touching is common. In other cultures (noncontact cultures), hugging and touching is less common. When a contact culture person meets a noncontact culture person, misunderstandings are rampant. For example, someone from a contact culture may seem pushy, aggressive, or inappropriately intimate to someone from a noncontact culture. And someone from a noncontact culture may seem cold, distant, or uninvolved to an individual from a contact culture.

In the United States, touch communicates:

* Positive emotions (hug).
* Playfulness (quick tap on the shoulder or hand).
* Control (firm grasp of shoulders or waist).
* Ritual (handshake).
* Performing a task (shampooing).

Sidebar

Some Nonverbal Cultural Differences

Contact Cultures: Southern Europe, Middle East

* Closer distances
* Touch during conversation
* More direct facing
* Longer and more focused eye contact

Noncontact Cultures: Northern Europe, Japan

* Greater distance during interactions
* Little or no touch during conversation
* Less direct facing
* Less eye contact

⑤ Appearance

You've probably had plenty of coaching about appearance, a final area of nonverbal communication. Your parents and society both firmly remind you to watch your grooming and to wear nice clothing. People do judge each other by appearance. Because the lessons on looking good are so pervasive, any deviations from the norm are very obvious. No one would dream of wearing shorts to a job interview, unless it was for a job at the beach.

People draw conclusions about who a person is from his or her appearance—including details of grooming, clothing, race, sex, and age. In fact, all cultures develop stereotypes, or shorthand ways of knowing people by a combination of physical traits. For example, if you see a gray-haired, middle-aged man in a dark suit, you'd probably consider him a person of means who is fairly well off and who works in a business or profession. Of course, this may not be true at all.

Many studies have been done on the relationship between appearance and credibility. Television networks, for instance, have been interested in how news anchors look as they read the news. Studies show that the public is more likely to believe a TV anchor wearing a suit than the same person giving the same information but dressed in blue jeans. As "business casual" dress becomes society's norm, this standard may change.

Think of people whom you know or know about who either fit or defy an appearance stereotype. Do you know an auto mechanic who wears wire-rim glasses?

How about a math teacher with an earring and a tattoo? What kind of messages do these people send?

Perception

Whether you are acting as a sender or receiver, you absorb information about the world through your senses, noting people's actions, appearance, and speech. You mentally organize these sensory data, or **perception**, into memory. You also compare new data with those already stored in your memory. Emotions can influence your memories and impressions.

You use logic to find similarities and then make inferences about people's knowledge, feelings, and attitudes. Experience tells you that certain characteristics often go with each other, so you often make assumptions about people from their isolated actions. For example, the guy who pushed you aside at the water fountain wouldn't be your first choice to call for a homework assignment. Why? You might reason that, because he acted in a self-centered, rude way, he might not be altogether helpful or trustworthy.

In describing literary characters, good fiction writers rely on their readers' abilities to attribute meanings to behavior and appearance and to draw conclusions about the characters' personalities.

Your perceptions about people guide your reactions and influence your communications. Meanwhile, others are making similar inferences about you. To the extent that your judgments are accurate, you will communicate effectively.

Casting *The Sixth Sense*

In a National Public Radio interview, M. Night Shyamalan, the young director of the 1999 movie hit *The Sixth Sense*, described his casting for the movie. Shyamalan interviewed dozens of boys for the character whose secret is that he sees ghosts. "I wanted him to look intelligent, sensitive, but still be vulnerable," Shyamalan said.

He first looked at nonprofessional kids because he wanted someone who acted natural rather than someone who was acting. But before he made the final choice, he decided to look at professional actors. All of the children, whether professional or not, came to their auditions dressed in jeans and T-shirts, "like kids," Shyamalan said. All except for Haley Joel Osment, who showed up dressed in a suit. To Mr. Shyamalan, this communicated respect.

Whether or not the suit cinched it, Haley got the part.

Exploring Nonverbal Communication

GOAL

The goal of this activity is to explore the limits as well as the value of nonverbal communication.

TASKS

1. Form groups of two or three.
2. Each group chooses a topic to communicate nonverbally.
3. In each group, one member, the sender, tries to convey some aspect of that topic, using only nonverbal language—paralanguage, kinesics, proxemics, haptics, and appearance.
4. Receivers take notes, indicating their understanding of the message and reaction to it.
5. Senders and receivers change roles and repeat.

OUTCOMES

How much information could you communicate nonverbally? Were messages ambiguous? Were you frustrated by limits?

Other Factors That Influence Communication

When you are in the process of sending and receiving messages, you also are perceiving the content of the message, the person delivering it or receiving it, and the physical surroundings in which the communication takes place.

Sidebar

Stages of Perception

Your mental process of assigning meaning to sensory messages provides the basis for forming impressions of others. It occurs in three stages:

Stage 1. Sensation (selection)
One of our five senses responds to a stimulus.

Stage 2. Organization
Your brain recodes the sensory data, stores it in memory, and associates it with other sensations.

* You compare, contrast, and identify what you have sensed.
* You group by patterns, proximity, and good form.

Stage 3. Interpretation-Evaluation
You give meaning to the stimulus, depending on culture, past experience, beliefs, and emotions.

In the process of perceiving, you conjure up memories and make associations between what's going on now and what you've learned before. All of these variables influence the communication and can help or hurt it.

Here are some ways in which mental processes can influence perception:

* **Implicit Personality Theory.** People devise or learn rules for characteristics that seem to go together. These vary by individual and by culture. For example, if the driver behind you on the expressway follows too closely, you assume that he or she is angry or aggressive.
* **Self-Fulfilling Prophecy.** People make predictions or hold certain beliefs, and then act as if these are true. For example, if you think that someone dislikes you, you avoid him or her.
* **Primacy-Recency.** What comes first (primacy) or last (most recently) influences perceptions. For example, the first time you met Jeff, he had spilled yogurt on his shirt, so you think he is sloppy.
* **Stereotyping.** People develop fixed impressions of a group of people. These serve as a shorthand, though often inaccurate, means of understanding individuals. For example, the notion that all males enjoy sports is a stereotype.
* **Attribution.** People attempt to explain the motivation of someone's behavior. For example, Meg is always late because she's self-centered.

People interpret data received through their senses to predict future events. Mistakes in perception may result from any of the following variables:

* **Physical Limits.** Even if your vision and hearing are perfect, you can't perceive all the data around you. For example, when you're reading a book in your room, you tune out traffic, heater noise, your hands holding the book, and the chair you're sitting on.

* **The Familiar.** If the stimuli aren't strong enough to be noticed or are difficult to organize, you may not be able to interpret them. For example, how many different types of fonts on signs and billboards do you pass each day?

Testing Your Perceptions

GOAL

The goal of this activity is to test the accuracy of your perceptions of surprising events.

TASKS

1. Form groups of four to five students.

2. Plan to stage an event that will test people's perceptions. For example, you might place an object (such as a large birthday present) in the room somewhere and then remove it; or say something unexpected, then deny it; or wear something unusual (like a wild hat or feathered boa) and remove it at a particular moment. The incident should occur for several minutes. The event needs to have elements of surprise. The rest of the class won't know when your event will occur, though you should let the teacher know your plans.

3. Prepare questions for those who witnessed your event. Some of the questions may be bogus. For example, "What happened to the girl wearing a feather?" when no one wore a feather.

4. Carry out the plan. During a regular class period or sometime during the school day, stage your event.

5. Ask the questions of those who witnessed the event, taking notes on their answers.

6. Evaluate the perceptions of those who witnessed the event.

7. When all groups have staged their events, meet as a class and compare your results.

OUTCOMES

How accurate were the perceptions of the observers? How many different variations were there? Were there times or types of incidents in which perceptions were clearer than in other times or incidents? Why do you think so?

* **The Obvious.** Data may be expected and therefore you will ignore it. If you are familiar with objects, places, and people, you may see things that you expect to see but that aren't actually there. For example, does your English teacher wear the same brown shoes every day?
* **Context.** You might respond differently to a man in a hat and coat if you see him in broad daylight rather than in a dark alley.
* **Emotions and Attitudes.** Your mood of the moment affects what you perceive.
* **Logic.** Ability to reason logically varies among individuals.

Improving the Accuracy of Perceptions

Here are some ways to improve the accuracy of your perceptions:

* **Realize that your perceptions may be inaccurate.** Maybe someone didn't actually say what you thought you heard. Maybe you didn't see what you thought you saw.
* **Avoid snap judgments.** If someone did something nasty, you may decide that he or she is mean and expect him or her to act unkindly in the future. Be patient and be willing to observe that person in a variety of other circumstances before drawing any conclusions.
* **Separate fact from inference.** Inference is drawing a logical conclusion from a set of facts. It's important to reason things out accurately. Try to observe what happens without prejudice.

How We Speak, How We Listen

You have your ideas in place, and your word choice is good. You know the basics of communicating nonverbally. You try to perceive events and people accurately. Now it's time to start talking. Talking is one of those skills that just seem to happen by themselves. But there actually is a lot to it. Talking is a miracle of sorts. It is what separates us from other animals. Humans have a powerful skill in the ability to speak.

The Mechanics of Speech

Speaking begins with breathing. The **diaphragm** is a thick muscle beneath your rib cage. When you breathe in, it expands. Exhale, and it pushes up, forcing air through the **trachea**, or windpipe. This happens naturally, but some people—such as singers and horn players—learn to control their breathing.

As you exhale, you can direct air through the top of the trachea into the **larynx**. The larynx contains your **vocal cords**, which vibrate to make sounds. Your vocal cords' length affects your voice quality. Shorter cords make a higher pitch, and longer cords make a lower pitch.

You can see how vocal cords work with a balloon. If you blow up the balloon and hold its opening between your fingers as you let the air out, you can control the sound by shortening or lengthening the balloon end. The more you shorten it, the shriller the sound.

Pitch, Volume, Rate, and Resonators

Your voice's optimum **pitch**—that is, the level at which it is least strained—is about four notes above the lowest note of your normal speaking voice. You can vary your pitch to make your speaking more expressive and less monotonous.

Volume is the loudness of your voice. The best way to control volume is not by straining your vocal cords but by breathing from your diaphragm to control the air pressure. After sound waves pass through your vocal cords, they pass through your tongue, jaw, and lips, which you move to form words.

The **rate**, or speed, of your speech is affected by your emotions. People speak more quickly when they're nervous or afraid.

Have you ever been inside a cave, a tunnel, or a big empty room? When you talked, the sound inside resonated, or echoed. If the empty room was concrete, like a garage, it resonated more than a wooden or empty room would. Sound resonates in partially enclosed areas like these, sometimes called *cavities.*

When you speak, your voice resonates in the cavities in your head—first in your throat (pharyngal cavity), then in your nose (nasal cavity) and your mouth (oral cavity). The natural size and shapes of these **resonators** ensure different resonance in different people. You also have some control over the resonance of your voice.

Sidebar

How We Speak

Our energy source for speaking is our breathing machinery.

We speak when breathing out. Unexpected changes in inhalation can lead to speech fright.

The vibrator in speech is our vocal cords.

Resonators are the cavities in the head.

Modifiers are the lips, tongue, teeth, jaw, and palate. These can control rate, loudness, pitch, and quality. Nasality, breathiness, and harshness affect quality.

The rate of speech depends on speed and use of pauses.

Articulation determines how things fit together. This is the shaping of sounds into words. One of the most common problems is slurring words.

Speakers can learn to use articulating mechanisms. Common problems are:

* locked jaw
* slack lips
* muffled mouth

Communication Cautions

☑ Choose words carefully.

☑ Pay attention to paralanguage.

☑ Notice other nonverbal signals.

☑ Consider any possible cultural differences.

☑ Think about your perceptions.

☑ Breathe deeply and enunciate your words as clearly as you can.

Communication

in Careers

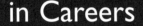

Decoding Nonverbals at Work

Sean Mosby often decodes nonverbal communication in his job. He works as a rehabilitation counselor for adults suffering from major mental illnesses. Because "sometimes people don't talk," the 30-year-old counselor has to determine what they're saying from their body language.

Decoding nonverbal information is a daily practice for Sean. "Clients might tell me they're not smoking, and they'll be sitting and looking at their hands, or crossing their arms and legs real tight. That tells me they're uneasy about what they're saying."

Sean's job is to support clients' activities outside the treatment center and to teach them how to use proper communication and social skills.

"People with illnesses like schizophrenia, manic depression, and drug addictions can be brilliant . . . but not know how to

present themselves," says Sean. "Some have changed from the illness."

Sean also tells them to dress appropriately, not to go out in public with holes in their pants. "They've had this illness but need to be out in public without being stigmatized. Appearance matters a lot. We've all gone out and seen someone who's obviously mentally ill."

Sean attributes some of his sensitivity to nonverbal communication to his upbringing. His parents both were stationed at the U.S. military base in Okinawa, so he lived there until age seven. His father was part Japanese. His parents spoke Japanese at home, though learning English was required at Sean's school.

"I'm bilingual," he says. "That has a big effect on my ability to communicate. I think Americans in general are handicapped that way, not knowing other languages."

Resonator Troubleshooting

Here are some common problems related to controlling the sound of your voice.

* **Throat.** When your throat is tense, your voice resonates high. When your throat is relaxed, it resonates lower.

* **Nose.** If you speak with your mouth partly closed, the nose resonates your vowels and your voice sounds twangy. A stuffed-up nose blocks nasal passages, muffling your voice.
* **Mouth.** Changing the position of tongue, lips, and jaw affects resonance.

Wrap-up

Communication begins when you have ideas, experiences, or feelings to express. You encode them by putting them into words to send as verbal messages. You also encode your emotions in nonverbal messages—your appearance, your spatial position, your touch, and the way you use your voice and move your body, face, and eyes.

Others receive your messages through their senses and assign meaning to them. Receivers may not understand your messages as you intend them to. They filter your messages through the way they perceive, remember, and reason, as well as through their culture. Moreover, your relationship to receivers and the context in which the communication occurs also affect the meaning. The various kinds of interference that messages encounter from the sender, the receiver, or the outside world are referred to as noise.

A great deal of thought goes into sending and receiving messages. Yet messages have many obstacles to overcome.

adaptors—gestures that satisfy a personal need.

affect display—body language that communicates emotion.

channels—sensory media of sound, sight, smell, or touch through which communication travels.

connotative meaning—emotional associations that accompany words.

decode—interpret meaning.

denotative meaning—dictionary definition.

diaphragm—muscle beneath the lungs, used for breathing.

emblems—gestures that stand for words.

encode—put meaning into messages and words.

feedback—response to a message.

haptics—communicating via touch.

illustrators—gestures that reinforce verbal language.

kinesics—communicating via bodily movements.

larynx—top of trachea, contains vocal cords.

noise—physical or psychological barrier to a message.

paralanguage—everything that a voice does besides speaking words.

perception—sensory input of information.

pitch—highness or lowness of a sound.

proxemics—communicating via spatial distances.

rate—speed.

receiver—audience, listener.

regulators—gestures that moderate someone else's speech.

resonators—cavities, or spaces, in the skull where sound rebounds.

sender—one who delivers a message.

symbols—signs, signals.

trachea—windpipe.

vocal cords—vibrating skin flaps that make the sound of a voice.

volume—loudness or softness of a sound.

CHAPTER 3

Listening

In this chapter, you will consider:

- Are you listening as effectively as you can?
- What prevents you from listening effectively?
- How do others know when you're listening to them?
- How do you listen for emotion, information, or attempts to persuade you?
- Can you identify types of faulty reasoning and propaganda?

You've been learning to listen since you were an infant. In this chapter, you'll discover that listening well involves more than hearing. It means making sense out of what you hear. Learning to listen well can improve your relationships, your social skills, your schoolwork, and your performance on the job. You also will learn about the process of listening, the barriers to good listening, and some important techniques that will help you to listen for information and for meanings, ideas, and emotions. Finally, you'll examine methods of faulty reasoning and propaganda.

Reasons for Listening

Most people listen more than they speak. Listening also is a more leisurely activity. The average person can speak 125 words per minute. However, people have the capacity to hear and comprehend 300 words per minute. That means that a speaker can occupy only about one-third of your attention. What should you think about?

Think about improving your listening. Good listening techniques can sharpen your thinking and bring improvements in your family relationships, your social skills, your school performance, and your job proficiency. Good listening helps you to build better personal connections with other people. It helps you to accurately interpret information, thoughts, ideas, and opinions. It helps you to identify people's goals, attitudes, and connotative meanings. It helps you to recognize persuasive techniques and hidden agendas.

In American businesses, listening is one of the most important skills for success. David P. Reynolds, chairman of Reynolds Aluminum, says, "The ability to communicate and listen effectively is probably the most important skill at a manager's command because all other management skills depend on it."

Communication in Careers

Designing Gardens

Kay Hunter is a garden designer. If people see a garden that she has designed and want a similar garden, they call for an appointment. But they don't always know what Kay will do for them.

Kay spends an hour listening to what a new client wants his or her garden to look like, as well as the problems that the garden should solve. She also explains the service she provides. "If I don't get across exactly what I do," she says, "people don't understand what my product is."

Kay's product is a garden design. This design shows exactly what shrubs, trees, and flowers the client should use and where to plant them. As Kay explains it, "People usually have some practical need. They'll want privacy, or they don't want to mow the lawn anymore and want to plant flowers instead. They just don't know what to plant."

Kay shows her clients pictures of various plants and pays attention to what they say. She's expert at knowing the type of soil, the amounts of sun and moisture, and the space that a particular plant needs.

"People have definite likes and dislikes. A lot of people will say they don't like red flowers or yellow flowers, things like that." Kay always asks a lot of questions so that she's sure what her clients want her to do for them.

What Is Listening?

Have you ever sat staring out the window in class? You heard your teacher talking and even heard your name called, but you had no idea what was said. You probably weren't focusing on the teacher's words or their meaning.

When you direct your gaze toward an object, someone might presume you see it. But it's harder for someone to know whether you're listening. If you're listening effectively, you are accurately perceiving a communication. There is a two-way exchange between speaker and listener.

Some cultures are very attuned to listening. The Oglala Sioux prized listening more than seeing. They listened for approaching buffalo, on which the tribe depended for survival. They detected changes in the weather by listening to animals and drawing inferences about their behavior.

How to Listen

Listening begins with a decision. Hearing comes naturally, but listening is a learned social skill. You have to decide to do it.

The process of listening can be broken down into **five** steps: hearing, interpreting, evaluating, remembering, and responding. Here is a description of what occurs in each step.

❶ Hearing

You select sounds. As you focus on some sounds, you tune out others. Barriers to hearing include noise, hearing impairment, fatigue, distraction, and sender deficiency.

❷ Interpreting

When **interpreting**, you decode the signals and understand the sensory input. You relate what you hear to what you already know. Because you process almost three times more words per minute than people can speak, you sometimes let your mind wander.

❸ Evaluating

You distinguish facts from opinions and identify possible biases when **evaluating**. You figure out the speaker's intent after you fully understand his or her point of view.

❹ Remembering

You remember what you understand of what was said. Remembering is not objective; you reconstruct events in your memory according to the way that you perceived them. You consciously commit some things to memory because you need the information or because the experience is important to you.

❺ Responding

You react to the speaker by sending cues. For example, you may nod and say, "I see." After the speaker speaks, you send feedback to clarify what you heard or take your turn at conversation.

What to Listen For

You are probably aware that you listen to people state their thoughts, ideas, and opinions. However, you may not be as aware of listening to their attitudes and emotions. It is extremely important to be receptive and to focus on these elements as well as on the content of the message.

Here are some things to listen for:

* **Information.** People often think this is the only reason to listen. It's what you do most of the time you are in school.
* **Emotion.** The speaker sets out to establish a relationship. Sometimes people talk because of insecurity or nervousness.

* **Attitude.** Distinguish fact from opinion. Speakers may talk about something they've observed but how they say it will convey how they feel about it.
* **Goals and Hidden Agendas.** Sometimes you pick up on a strong theme that may not be expressed directly.
* **Thoughts, Ideas, and Opinions.** Pay attention to what the speaker leaves out. People talk about things that interest them and omit things that don't. The way speakers phrase their sentences and their nonverbal language tells you the emotion attached to the message, which can indicate an opinion.

Talk Show Guests

GOAL

The goal of this activity is to categorize different meanings in spoken messages.

TASKS

1. Watch a television talk show or public affairs program on which the host interviews guests.
2. Listen to one or two guests. Take notes on how the guests respond to questions and what they voluntarily reveal about themselves.
3. Classify their messages as information, opinions, emotions, attitudes, or hidden agendas. What verbal and nonverbal behaviors do the guests use to communicate each of these internal states?
4. As a class, compare and discuss your findings.

OUTCOMES

What categories of messages were the largest? Why do you think this is so?

Barriers to Listening

As a listener, your job is to duplicate in your mind the speaker's exact message and intent. You should become nothing more than a channel that passes along distortion-free messages, with the information flowing only one way.

However, a variety of barriers can hinder listeners and prevent them from accurately understanding a message. An effective listener attempts to understand the barriers and to do what he or she can to avoid them.

There are **four** types of barriers to listening: external barriers, listener barriers, speaker barriers, and cultural barriers.

❶ External Barriers

<u>External barriers</u> begin outside the speaker and the listener, usually in the surrounding environment. Listening requires focused hearing, but you can't close your ears and block out sounds. External barriers can include:

* *Noises.* Some noises can distract you or overpower the message.
* *Other Stimuli.* Other sensory stimuli may grab your attention, like someone waving a hand at you behind the speaker's back.
* *Information Overload.* When there's an overwhelming amount of sensory information, people sometimes tune out to avoid an information overload.

❷ Listener Barriers

<u>Listener barriers</u> are internal or psychological. They begin in the listener. Some listener barriers are:

* *Boredom.* Daydreaming and worrying hinder listening. Sometimes people tune out when the topic doesn't interest them.

* **Laziness.** When people are not familiar with a topic or when the speaker repeats something they've heard before, they tune out. People also pay less attention to a routine situation, sometimes called a script. When you enter a restaurant, for example, you know that the hostess will greet you, take you to your table, hand you your menu, say that the server will be there soon, and to enjoy your meal. You usually don't tune into precise variations in this script.

* **Waiting to Speak.** Rather than listen, people often plan what they'll say when it's their turn to speak. They want to be heard but not to hear.

* **Opinionatedness.** Sometimes, people hear only what they want to hear. Strong attitudes, or **opinionatedness**, hinder listening. In a close personal relationship, people can respond angrily to particular phrases, rather than listening. Verbal conflicts, like scripts, frequently follow a predictable progression.

* **Prejudice.** People whose minds are closed to new ideas often aren't willing to listen. They may be critical of the speaker's manner or appearance. They may block out things that don't match their beliefs so as not to get frightened or angry. They also may distort what they hear.

* **Lack of Interest.** When people are not interested in the speaker, they may not even make eye contact while listening. Overlooking the speaker's feelings and paying attention to words may prevent people from getting the message.

Listener Barriers

GOAL

The goal of this activity is to identify listener barriers in oneself.

TASKS

1. List five to ten specific examples of situations in which you are affected by listener barriers. Find examples from home, school, work, and social situations.

2. Classify each situation as one or more of the six listener barriers listed above.

3. Share and discuss the lists in class.

OUTCOMES

Did you find the most barriers at home, in school, at work, or in social situations? What types of barriers were most common? Why?

How to Improve Listening Habits

Because your brain has spare time while you're listening, use the time to:

✔ Note how you're interpreting, evaluating, and remembering what's being said.

✔ Figure out whether your word meanings are the same as those of the speaker.

✔ Take stock of any listener barriers you may be experiencing.

✔ Note whether the speaker's presentation presents a barrier to you.

✔ Become aware of your biases and attitudes and look for any in the speaker.

✔ Assess whether the speaker is presenting enough evidence.

✔ Evaluate the speaker's opinions.

✔ Take note of whether the speaker's biases interfere with the message.

✔ Watch for nonverbal clues to the speaker's emotions.

✔ Absorb what the speaker says before making judgments.

❸ Speaker Barriers

Sometimes barriers originate with the speaker. Examples of **speaker barriers** are:

* *Appearance.* The overall appearance of the speaker—including clothes, age, color, and sex—can be a barrier.
* *Manner.* The speaker's manner and how he or she behaves, moves, or talks can attract or repel a listener.
* *Power.* The speaker's power or lack of power can influence whether a listener pays attention. You may listen to an expert describe something that interests you but tune out your little brother when he says the same thing.

* *Credibility.* Credibility is the degree to which people can believe the speaker. A speaker's credibility or lack of it may determine whether or not a listener pays attention. People accept information from a believable source. Ask yourself, "Is this speaker open and honest? Is he or she familiar with the subject?"
* *Message.* The message itself may leave your mouth open—either in awe or in a yawn.

❹ Cultural Barriers

Another type of barrier to listening is cultural. Examples of **cultural barriers** are:

* *Prejudice.* Some prejudice has a cultural basis. People tend to think that their way

of being and doing is the logical, natural way. They measure strange or unfamiliar information against what they already know. Their prejudgments, or **prejudices**, can be huge barriers to listening.

* ***Speaking Styles.*** Different cultures have different speaking styles. In western Europe and the United States, the speaking style is direct. People usually say what they mean and mean what they say. In many Asian countries, politeness is more important. In Japan and Korea, being positive often is more important than being truthful.

* ***Source Credibility.*** In some cultures, again like the United States, people want evidence to support what you say to lend you credibility. In other cultures, people tend to believe a message if it comes from a respected source.

* ***Nonverbal Communication.*** Americans usually indicate their interest in and connection with a speaker by looking him or her in the eye. In other cultures, looking someone in the eye is disrespectful.

* ***Accents.*** Non-native English speakers sometimes understand words differently than do native speakers. Their accents and vocal intonations also may be different.

Everyday COMMUNICATION

Listening to Non-Native Speakers

Fanny Wyman grew up in Israel and has lived in Baltimore for 20 years. Though her English is very good, she has an accent. She says, "In cities where Americans aren't used to foreigners, they hear my accent and talk to me real loud and very slowly. They figure that if they get closer and talk louder, I'll understand them better!"

Types of Listening

You can use several different techniques for good listening. Which one you choose depends upon the situation, the speaker's purpose, and your purpose as a listener. The **three** main types of listening are active listening, informational listening, and critical listening.

❶ Active Listening

Passive listeners simply receive information. They may not fully understand what's being said. They don't respect the uniqueness of other individuals and may hear only what they want to hear or what attracts their attention. Passive listeners usually are accused of being self-centered or of having bad social skills.

In **active listening**, you engage your mind and listen for the speaker's meaning. Active listening expresses respect for the other person and for his or her ideas and opinions. Active listening is used mainly in one-to-one conversations or in small groups.

In active listening, you start with the assumption that the speaker is different from you and has something to say that is unique and important. You make an emotional and intellectual commitment to understand what he or she is trying to say through words, attitudes, and nonverbal expression. You repeat your understanding of the speaker's meanings and ask questions to clarify what's being said.

How to Be an Active Listener

There are **five** steps in the active listening process:

1. Find and organize the speaker's main ideas. The ideas may be jumbled, rambling, or disorganized, but try to make logical sense of what the speaker is saying. This is harder to do in a conversation than in an organized talk. It's also harder to do when your emotions are involved or when the subject is controversial.

2. Mentally summarize what the speaker is saying. Mentally put the speaker's words into your own words. Repeat to yourself the key points he or she is making. You're more likely to remember when you paraphrase.

3. Echo the speaker's meaning. Repeat to the speaker what you believe he or she has said to you. Say to the speaker, "What I hear you saying is . . . ." This feedback will enable the speaker to elaborate or to correct you. Feedback is important in interpersonal communication and group discussions.

4. Echo the speaker's expressed or implied feelings. Explain the speaker's feelings as you interpret them. Be as accurate as possible without overstating. This allows you to know whether or not you perceived accurately. It also allows the speaker to see his or her feelings objectively.

5. Ask questions to elicit further clarification. Your questions show your interest and support. Be careful not to stray too far or pry too much.

Active listening assures good communication. It demonstrates to a speaker that you clearly and objectively understand his or her point of view. Whether you agree or disagree, the speaker will appreciate your respect and attention.

Active Listening in Difficult Conversations

GOAL

The goal of this activity is to practice handling a difficult conversation through active listening.

TASKS

1. Form groups of four, then pairs. Pairs will take turns acting and observing.

2. Pairs take turns choosing a situation to role-play: a shoe salesperson and a difficult customer; a hysterical patient describing symptoms to a doctor and the doctor giving instructions for care; someone complaining in a restaurant about bad service; a teen couple breaking up; a woman refusing a date; a friend having a problem.

3. In each situation, one person chooses to be the "difficult" person, the other to be the listener. The speaker chooses an emotion and will express it without naming it. The listener will attempt to actively listen and to empathize.

4. One pair role-plays the situation while the other pair watches and analyzes the speaking and listening behavior.

5. Discuss the speaking and listening behavior of the first pair and the emotions and ideas that were being expressed.

6. Repeat steps 2 through 5, with pairs taking turns acting and observing.

7. In class, discuss ways in which active listeners succeeded and failed.

OUTCOMES

How accurate were listeners in cueing in on emotions? How accurate were speakers in expressing them?

Empathetic Listening

Empathetic listening is a type of active listening. In **empathetic listening**, you use the steps of active listening to seek emotional rather than intellectual understanding of the speaker. You'll use empathetic listening when someone is explaining an emotional event or problem. Through empathy, you attempt to feel the speaker's feelings and to share his or her mood. By empathizing, you can communicate on a deeper level and give needed support.

Salespeople and those who work in customer relations learn to listen to the emotional message of the customer. They focus on the issue rather than the personality of the person who is complaining. They usually sympathize with the customer, calm him or her down, and offer to help.

Achieving empathy can be difficult because of ingrained habits. Sometimes you can't solve someone else's problems. But listening and recognizing the problem can help.

Creative Listening

In **creative listening**, another type of active listening, you listen and use your imagination simultaneously. You listen to stories, drama, standup comics, or even music, receiving others' ideas but using your imagination to conjure up new images. Creative listening is useful in generating ideas in a brainstorming session. Participants build on each other's ideas and attempt to find a solution.

Types of Listening				
Type	**Purpose**	**When to Use**	**What to Listen for**	**Listener Goals**
1. Active	Clarification	In disagreements	Meaning	Understanding
Empathetic	Showing understanding	When someone's feeling troubled	Emotion	Support
Creative	Brainstorming	For problem solving	Ideas	Solutions
2. Informational	Learning	In formal situations	Content	Knowledge
3. Critical	Evaluating	For making judgments	Assumptions and reasoning	Evaluations

❷ Informational Listening

In **informational listening**, you listen mainly for content, attempting to identify the speaker's purpose, main ideas, and supporting details. Informational listening is appropriate in formal situations, such as classroom lectures or work training sessions.

The first step in informational listening is finding the main ideas. Once you locate the main ideas, you can figure out the speaker's purpose in telling them to you. How do the main ideas relate to each other? Are they in a logical order? What facts and details support the main ideas? Are they relevant and timely?

You spend a great deal of time in classes listening to teachers lecture and taking notes that will help you recall what your teachers said. Taking good notes can help improve your listening skills. It also can help you learn to listen for the main ideas and the reasons supporting them.

Checklist

How to Take Good Notes

✓ **Get organized.** Develop a note-taking system. Loose-leaf notebooks allow you to add papers and rearrange them as you go.

✓ **Develop a scheme.** Use abbreviations and color coding. If you can, learn to take notes in outline form, with main points listed as I, II, III; secondary points as A, B, C; and details as 1, 2, 3.

✓ **Use graphic organizers.** Web diagrams, flow charts, timelines, and the like can help you retain what you hear.

✓ **Mentally summarize the speaker's key points.** Record the main ideas. Write more than you think you need to write.

✓ **Get the whole picture.** Pay attention to what the teacher or speaker emphasizes or repeats. One clue is to notice what the teacher writes on the board. Follow the teacher's outline format. For example, "There are three rules" signals that you will be writing down three things.

✓ **Jot down your own comments as you go.** Leave a margin blank so that later you can add facts, clarification, reactions, and other alternatives.

✓ **Ask for clarification.** Get more information about parts you don't understand.

✓ **Review the notes later.** If needed, organize them while the subject is fresh in your mind.

❸ Critical Listening

In **critical listening**, you analyze, evaluate, and draw conclusions about the speaker's ideas. Critical listening also is used in formal situations, especially when listening to persuasive messages. Use critical listening whenever evaluation and judgments are called for.

First, listen to understand. Keep an open mind and avoid prejudging. Listen to the entire message without blocking, filtering, or distorting it by eliminating details or simplifying complexities. Even listen to the unpleasant messages. Recognize that your own biases can interfere with accurate understanding. Is there anything in the environment or the situation that affects your ability to listen objectively? Try not to evaluate until you understand what's being said.

Then separate fact from opinion. Fact can be proved or disproved. An opinion is a judgment. You need to keep an open mind. It's not easy to listen to arguments that go against your beliefs.

Listening Critically

When listening critically, pay attention to these areas:

* **Source Credibility.** Who is the source? How believable is he or she?
* **Attitude.** What is the speaker's attitude toward the listener? Is he or she respectful or condescending?
* **Speaker's Goal.** What is the speaker's goal? Why is he or she trying to persuade me? What does he or she keep repeating?
* **Content.** What is the speaker's main idea? What is being emphasized? Are the ideas well structured? How are they arranged? What evidence is being cited? Does the conclusion follow logically from the evidence?
* **Reasoning.** How well-supported are the ideas being stated? Do facts or ideas contradict? What are the reasons for the speaker's conclusion or opinion? Is sufficient evidence provided? Is there enough evidence to make you change your mind?

Identifying Faulty Reasoning

Watching for faulty reasoning is an important critical-listening skill. In the United States, speakers usually follow the method of **inductive reasoning**, that is, they identify facts and link them together to support a specific conclusion. Thus, when people begin to speak, you may assume that they will follow a logical progression, but this isn't always the case.

Pay attention to the flow of an argument and watch for faulty reasoning. False methods of reasoning are called **logical fallacies**. Fallacies are far removed from facts or are conclusions based on too few facts. Sometimes they occur because an argument wasn't well thought out. At other times, their intent is to persuade. Listen to speakers to be sure that they aren't reaching premature conclusions or conclusions based on flimsy evidence.

Here are **seven** common logical fallacies.

1. When **begging the question**, speakers assume the truth or falsity of a statement without supplying proof. They simply state their ideas, taking for granted that you'll agree. Politicians and advertisers use this technique. "Vote for me because I served this district better than any other Congressman," or "Beef is good for you because it's meat from the cow" are examples of begging the question.

2. In **card stacking**, speakers select only the evidence and arguments for the side that they support. The term refers to a deck of cards used by someone doing card tricks. The evidence is arranged so skillfully and with such sleight of hand that it looks like the speaker has performed magic, and he or she has— on you!

3. When speaking on **false premises**, speakers begin with false assumptions that you assume are true. Listen for a speaker's premises. If the premises are false, everything that follows will be shaky. For example, since volleyball is the most important school sport, then it should receive the largest share of the school athletic budget.

4. When speakers use vague or general words or phrases that express an attitude or idea that has popular support, they are using **glittering generalities**. By doing so, they try to make you accept something by associating it with things you value. For instance, it's popular in politics to say that one upholds "family values." But speakers usually don't define what they mean or provide examples.

5. When speakers don't have enough evidence to support a broad conclusion, or when they selectively leave out details and come to a quick conclusion, they are making **false generalizations**. This type of faulty reasoning is common. Say that you saw a baseball player play in two games, and he didn't get a hit. Your hasty generalization might be to say that he can't hit. Words such as *everyone*, *always*, *never*, and *nobody* may indicate that a generalization is lurking nearby.

6. In a **non sequitur**, speakers assert something that doesn't follow logically or that deals with a totally different subject. The term *non sequitur* means "doesn't follow" in Latin. A recent sales pitch claims, "I'm 41, I'm in great shape, and I can tell you this exercise equipment really works." Being in great shape at age 41 is not necessarily connected to the weight machine.

7. For a **testimonial**, speakers use an authority or a well-known person to endorse a particular subject or position to gain the listener's approval. Nike hired basketball star Michael Jordan to appear in its commercials so that people would associate Nike footgear with Michael Jordan and his athletic ability. If Michael Jordan endorses a product, people believe that it is good.

Identifying Propaganda

Watching for propaganda is another important critical-listening skill. **Propaganda** is a form of persuasion that discourages listeners from making an independent choice. Propagandists state their positions or opinions as though these are accepted truths, without evidence to back their claims. Propaganda tries to create an emotional response that will make people believe and act rather than think.

Propagandists use techniques for spreading information to either advance or destroy a cause. **Six** common propaganda techniques are:

1. **Transfer** makes an illogical connection between unrelated things. Advertisers use this technique so that viewers will associate their products with positive, appealing, or desirable things.

2. Jumping on a **bandwagon** means joining a group in favor of some person, product, or idea. Since "everyone else" is doing it, it's the correct thing to do. The assumption is that a listener will follow the crowd.

3. When speakers use a negative term to refer to a group or an idea—like calling someone a liar or a cheat without giving any evidence or proof—they're guilty of **name calling**. Attacking an opponent rather than an idea or position changes a discussion to one of personalities rather than issues.

4. Language that evokes strong feelings and attitudes in the listener can sway an argument. **Loaded words** have a particular slant and rely on the connotative meanings the listener shares. **Emotional appeals** assume that you share the emotional responses of the speaker.

5. **Stereotypes** are preconceived notions about a person based on his or her membership in a group. These are shortcut ways of thinking about an individual. They often involve a prejudice.

6. Posing arguments as **either/or** choices fails to take into account third or fourth possibilities. This creates drama but doesn't always explain the whole picture.

Faulty Reasoning in Advertisements

GOAL

The goal of this activity is to identify logical fallacies and propaganda in commercial advertisements.

TASKS

1. Tape-record 60 to 120 minutes of prime time network television.

2. In class, fast-forward to a segment of advertisements.

3. Watch a few minutes of advertisements. Look for examples of each of the types of faulty reasoning.

4. Name other familiar TV ads in which you find faulty reasoning.

OUTCOMES

Are some types of faulty reasoning used more often than others? How effective are they? How difficult is it to detect them?

Everyday

A Message She Doesn't Want to Hear

People may pick up on your nonverbal feedback, but they may interpret it differently than you intended. When you clarify your meaning, they sometimes aren't willing to hear it. An example is this conversation between two friends.

"You don't like my brother, do you?"

"Yeah, I do. It's just that . . ."

"That what?"

"That he doesn't get that he's not funny. I mean, at dinner at your house last week, he said, 'Have some more food, Shorty.'"

"That was a joke. You're just too sensitive."

"It's sarcastic. It's a dumb joke and I'm happy about my height. He just has no clue that he offends people."

"You don't have to take it so seriously."

"Don't you two get that I don't think it's funny?"

All you can do is to state your message clearly and plainly. Listeners have to be receptive to the message that speakers are sending.

Learning to listen well can improve your family relationships, your social skills, your school performance, and your job proficiency. The trick is to focus on listening and to actively involve yourself in it. Real listening goes beyond passive hearing. It includes interpreting, evaluating, remembering, and responding. You listen not only to the speaker's words and information but also to his or her emotions, goals and hidden agendas, attitudes, and opinions.

Four types of barriers can prevent effective listening. These listening barriers can be external, in the listener, in the speaker, or cultural. Barriers to listening can get in the way of hearing what's being said.

Skillful listeners use different listening techniques in different situations. For personal relationships and in small groups and discussions, they use active and empathetic listening, which help them accurately uncover a speaker's meanings and emotions. When listening to drama and comedy and in brainstorming sessions, they use creative listening, which helps them to generate new ideas. When a speaker offers information, as in classrooms and training sessions, they use informational listening, which helps them to organize and analyze content. When a speaker or sponsor is attempting to persuade them, they use critical listening, which helps them to analyze the argument and to uncover faulty reasoning and propaganda techniques.

Speech

active listening—listening for meaning.

bandwagon—propaganda technique that encourages listeners to join a group that favors a particular person, product, or idea because it's popular.

begging the question—type of false reasoning in which speakers assume the truth or falsity of a statement without supplying proof.

card stacking—type of false reasoning in which speakers select only the evidence and arguments for the side that they support.

creative listening—receiving another's ideas but using them to generate one's own creative ideas.

credibility—believability.

critical listening—examining informative or persuasive messages and drawing conclusions.

cultural barriers—learned responses that predispose one to see things a particular way.

either/or—propaganda technique that poses arguments between two opposite choices, failing to take into account other possibilities.

emotional appeals—propaganda technique that assumes that the listener shares the emotional responses of the speaker.

empathetic listening—listening to discern another person's feelings and emotions.

evaluating—judging the worth or importance of something.

external barriers—environmental hindrances to listening.

false generalization—type of false reasoning in which speakers don't have enough evidence to support a broad conclusion, or they selectively leave out details and come to a quick conclusion.

false premise—type of false reasoning in which speakers begin with false assumptions that are assumed to be true.

glittering generalities—type of false reasoning in which speakers use vague or general words or phrases that express an attitude or idea that has popular support.

inductive reasoning—identifying facts and linking them together to support a specific conclusion.

informational listening—listening for content and attempting to identify the speaker's purpose, main ideas, and supporting details.

interpreting—understanding.

listener barriers—psychological blocks to effective listening.

loaded words—propaganda technique that uses language that evokes strong feelings and attitudes in the listener to sway an argument.

logical fallacies—false methods of reasoning.

name calling—propaganda technique that uses a negative term to refer to a group or an idea without providing evidence or proof.

non sequitur—type of false reasoning in which speakers assert something that doesn't follow logically or that deals with a totally different subject (from the Latin for "doesn't follow").

opinionatedness—adhering to one's preconceived notions.

prejudice—judgment made before all facts are known.

propaganda—form of persuasion that discourages listeners from making an independent choice by stating opinions as though they are accepted truths.

speaker barriers—obstacles to listening that originate with the speaker.

stereotypes—propaganda technique that applies preconceived notions to a person based on his or her membership in a group.

testimonial—type of false reasoning in which speakers use an authority or a well-known person to endorse a particular subject or position to gain the listener's approval.

transfer—propaganda technique that makes an illogical connection between unrelated things.

CHAPTER 4

Communication Confidence

In this chapter, you will consider:

- How well do you know yourself?
- How have people in your life contributed to your self-concept?
- How can you improve your self-concept?
- What makes you nervous when speaking to groups of people?
- In what kind of situations do you feel confident?
- In what kind of situations do you not feel confident?

In this chapter, you'll find ways to develop confidence as a communicator. Your confidence as a communicator begins with what you think and how you feel about yourself. You can think of yourself in physical, intellectual, emotional, and social terms, which all combine to define who you are. The way you perceive yourself—your self-concept—and your self-esteem influence the way you speak and interact with others. You can change the way you think of yourself. This chapter helps you to consider these issues, then presents a number of techniques for helping you to build confidence and to become comfortable speaking in different situations.

Self-Awareness

Self-awareness is the first step in understanding yourself. It means having a sense of your individuality.

You were born with innate ways of behaving. Others' responses to you also have affected your behavior and led you to think of yourself in specific ways. People's reactions to you are like a mirror, allowing you to become aware of how you appear.

Sides of the Self

The self has several aspects. The 19th-century philosopher William James called the parts of the self the material me, the social me, and the spiritual me.

The material or **physical self** is how you look—your hair and skin and eye color; your height, weight, and body type; and your face. It also includes the socioeconomic status of your family and has much to do with where you were born.

The **social self** is how you appear to others, or your **personality**. It includes such factors as how you behave among people, whether you're an outgoing **extrovert** or a quiet **introvert**, bubbly or subdued, easygoing or stubborn.

The **spiritual self** comprises your beliefs, attitudes, and intellectual abilities and talents. Some of this side of you remains hidden to others and maybe even to yourself. This is who you really are; or, perhaps it's more accurate to say that this is who you potentially could become.

SOCIAL   SPIRITUAL

Self-Concept

The way you perceive yourself is your **self-concept**. It represents the total of the beliefs and attitudes you have about yourself.

When you were very young, you learned how to communicate with those persons closest to you. You learned what to do to get a response from them. When you began talking about your feelings and ideas, others' reactions to you further developed your self-concept. Gradually you developed an idea of who you were, based to a large degree on how people treated, reacted to, and spoke to you.

Cultural Influences

As you matured, you began to identify with groups outside your family, such as others of the same sex, religion, ethnicity, language group, and nation. Your self-concept became more refined as you saw yourself, for example, as an athlete, scientist, or musician.

The **culture** around you and your parents, teachers, peers, and the media still teach you values, attitudes, and beliefs. Most people compare themselves with these cultural standards. For example, in the United States, certain professions are highly regarded, and others are not. How comfortable do you think most people are in choosing a profession that carries no prestige?

In the United States, cultural standards also include notions about how you should look, dress, speak, and structure your life. Pressures to conform can be very powerful.

For example, surveys show that a very high percentage of Americans are unhappy with the way they look, mostly because their looks don't match images of male and female beauty presented by the media. Yet many Americans also reject such unrealistic cultural standards and evaluate themselves by their own subjective, personal standards.

You form impressions of yourself when you look in the mirror or listen to yourself talk. You make judgments about your clothes and about what you think looks good on you. Your experiences teach you what you're good at and not so good at. The more positive experiences you have in doing things, the more positive will be your self-concept.

Factors That Can Distort Self-Concept

Your self-concept—the way you perceive yourself—may be different from the concept that others have of you. Your parents, for example, may see you as an excellent pianist or think that you're a born teacher. You may disagree, having seen others whose talent exceeded yours. Or perhaps your parents think that you are not gifted academically, but you have learned from teachers, peers, and your own observation that you actually are quite capable.

Some of your beliefs about yourself may be accurate, but others probably are not. They may have to do with the way you want to be or the way you believe yourself to be.

Exploring Self-Concept

GOAL

The goal of this activity is to analyze your self-concept.

TASKS

1. List ten words or phrases that describe how you perceive yourself.

2. Rank them in order, starting with the one that describes you best.

3. Evaluate your list. How many of your listed attributes are physical? How many are intellectual? How many are emotional? Are there things on your list you'd like to remove? Are there things missing that you'd like to be able to include?

OUTCOMES

What do you think are the sources of your values and your attitudes toward yourself? How much control do you think you have over these sources?

Maintaining Self-Concept

People resist changing their self-concept. If you believe that you're a poor artist, you probably disbelieve someone who compliments your work. However, it's possible that you're not seeing yourself accurately. Pay attention to the origins of your negative self-concept. Evaluate the positive responses you get. Try to work toward adopting a more positive view.

Maintaining self-concept is a continuing process. People respond to your behavior by approving or disapproving it. You often decide whether to maintain or to change how you perceive yourself. As you go through your day, you can ignore other people's responses to you and disregard some messages. You may listen only to messages that reinforce your self-concept. But sometimes messages can change your self-concept.

Some people try so hard to maintain their self-concept that they lie or act in ways that seem phony. For example, take Liz, who all of her life was praised for being cheerful and bubbly. Her friends always expect her to entertain them. As a result, she doesn't feel that she can have a bad day. When she's feeling depressed, she still tries to be the entertainer.

Others maintain their self-concept by ritualizing their behavior. For example, José sees himself as tough. He always acts and talks tough. This behavior enables him to keep others at a distance. It also buffers him from criticism because no one knows who he really is. Though he also has a gentler, more sensitive side, he doesn't feel comfortable sharing that with anyone.

Improving Self-Concept

When you do something that violates your standards or your self-concept, it is a strong motivator to change. For example, if you think lying is wrong, but you catch yourself lying, you'll compare your behavior with your belief. You'll either change the behavior or change the belief. Or perhaps you may have hurt someone's feelings by being sarcastic. You may decide to avoid sarcasm and develop your humor in another direction.

The anxiety of holding beliefs that don't fit your behaviors, or of behaving in ways that go against your beliefs, is known as **cognitive dissonance**. This anxiety often leads you to change either the belief or the behavior.

Self-Esteem

At some point, you begin to see all your good and bad qualities and to accept yourself as you are. You may decide to work on improving your good qualities and changing the ones you don't like. **Self-esteem** is the amount of satisfaction you have with yourself. People with high self-esteem perceive themselves as approaching their vision of an ideal self. People with low self-esteem perceive themselves as being far from their ideal selves.

Self-esteem is your own self-judgment. It doesn't necessarily reflect your real qualities but rather who you *think* you are. For example, a thief may have high self-esteem because he may value qualities that he thinks he has, such as skill, loyalty, and cheerfulness.

Self-esteem is revealed by the words you choose, your tone of voice, and what you say about yourself. Using self-critical, pessimistic language may reveal low self-esteem. Blaming and criticizing the accomplishments of others may be a sign of low self-esteem. Whining and saying, "Why should I try?" also suggests low self-esteem.

Self-Awareness and Communication

Positive communications from others help you to become more self-aware and to create a good self-concept and high self-esteem. Negative communications contribute to a poor self-concept and low self-esteem. Someone with high self-esteem seems confident and unafraid to approach new situations. Someone with low self-esteem may say negative things about himself or herself and others.

People with a strong self-concept focus on their positive experiences. If you think about only the good things and excuse yourself for the bad ones, you reinforce your positive self-concept.

Being an effective communicator means working on yourself. As you take a look at your self-concept and self-esteem, think about the following:

* Be honest in evaluating yourself. Recognize your limits and take credit for your strengths.
* Be realistic in setting goals.
* Be supportive of your own efforts.
* Be supportive of the efforts of others.
* Be forgiving of your own faults—and those of others.

Areas That Affect Perception of Others

Three areas affect your perception of others:

1. *Accuracy of your self-concept.* The more accurate your self-concept is, the more accurately you'll perceive others. If you can't assess your own strengths and weaknesses, you're unlikely to accurately assess those of others.
2. *Acceptance of yourself.* The more you accept yourself, the more likely you are to see others favorably. If you don't like yourself, you'll be less apt to like other people.
3. *Your personality.* Your personal qualities influence how you see other people. For example, if you're a trustworthy person, you're more likely to see others as trustworthy.

Perceiving Messages

Self-concept affects how you receive messages. People with poor self-concepts tend to perceive information as negative and nonsupportive. This distortion creates inaccurate, negative, and weak communication. Communication based on poor information relies on hunches, feelings, and impulses, without regard for facts.

You communicate with others according to what you believe they are like. Of course, you can and often do misjudge other people's motives. For example, Janeen perceives herself as dumb. When her classmate told her he liked her report, Janeen thought he was teasing her. Rather than respond to his genuine friendliness, she thought he was mean and avoided him.

Self-Disclosure

Self-disclosure can help you to correct others' impressions of you that are based on inadequate information. Sharing thoughts, feelings, and biographical information that are unknown to another person is called **self-disclosure**. Self-disclosure is influenced by gender, culture, personality, the listeners, and the topics at hand. It is an important ingredient in developing relationships.

Here are some examples of self-disclosure:

* ***Biographical information:*** "I was cross-eyed and had to wear corrective lenses when I was little."
* ***Thoughts:*** "I don't think that high school students should have jobs."
* ***Feelings:*** "I'm terrified when I have to give an oral book report."

Should You Self-Disclose?

Disclosure can lead to better communication. But each type of disclosure carries a risk. It may have a positive result and lead to a better understanding. Or the person to whom you're revealing may disclose this information to others. He or she also may reject you or use the information in hurtful ways.

There are benefits to self-disclosing. You need to weigh them against the risks when wondering whether or not to share personal or intimate information about yourself.

Self-Disclosure

GOAL

The goal of this activity is to help you rate types of information that you may or may not want to disclose about yourself.

TASKS

1. On a sheet of paper, rate each of the following areas according to the scale below.

   Areas to rate:

   Hobbies, taste in music, political views, religious beliefs, personal characteristics that you're proud of or that you want to change, things you've done that you regret, guilty secrets, dreams and wishes, aspects of your body,

   unhappiest times, happiest times, the person you most resent.

   Rating scale:

   Low risk—You could discuss this topic with anyone.

   Moderate risk—You could discuss this with people you know pretty well.

   High risk—You could discuss this only with intimate and trusted friends.

2. Form groups of three to five.

3. Discuss your ratings. You don't have to disclose the exact nature of any of them, but discuss circumstances under which you'd reveal different information.

OUTCOMES

How are your ratings alike? different?

The Johari Window

The Johari Window is a device to help you visualize what you want to share and what you should keep private. Each of the window's **four** quadrants symbolizes one type of information about you.

1. The Open quadrant includes information that you and others know about yourself. This includes your obvious physical appearance, the language you speak, and things you've said and done in public.	**3.** The Hidden quadrant contains your tastes, preferences, thoughts, beliefs, fears, and anything that others won't know unless you tell them.
2. The Blind quadrant includes things about you that are known to others but not to you. These include the way your voice actually sounds, how you look when you walk, how you look from behind, the intensity of your gaze, your nervous tics, and other behaviors that you're not aware of.	**4.** The Unknown quadrant comprises things about you that neither you nor others are aware of. These could include your motivations, undiscovered talents, and psychological complexities.

Trusting Others

Trust is reliance on the character, ability, strength, or truth of someone or something else. Building trust is essential in sharing information about yourself and receiving it from others.

It's best to reveal your deepest feelings and fears only in established friendships, after you've developed mutual trust. Some disclosures are not appropriate in casual situations. You might also want to make sure that your friend is ready to hear your disclosures. Some people object to hearing very personal information too soon in a relationship. They feel that you are getting too close too fast.

When a person shares personal information with you, you should show respect and understanding. Never make fun of someone who's sharing feelings with you. Communicate an accurate understanding of what he or she tells you. However, if someone tells you something you don't want to hear, you can tell her or him that you think it's too personal.

Sharing Feelings

An important part of knowing yourself is knowing and identifying your **feelings** or emotions. Sometimes finding words for feelings helps you to clarify them. Clarifying feelings also helps you to manage them.

People often distance themselves from their feelings. Rather than saying, "I liked the movie," they say, "I think that the movie was good." At other times people use the word *feel* when they mean *think*. "I feel that we need more time" really means "I think that we need more time." It's an **opinion** and an intellectualizing of the feeling, not the feeling itself.

Are You Sharing Feelings or Opinions?

GOAL

The goal of this activity is to distinguish between expressing feelings and opinions.

TASKS

Examine each pair of statements below.
On a separate piece of paper, rate each statement as F (directly expressing a feeling) or O (expressing a thought or opinion).

1. **a.** I was really moved by the lyrics.
   b. I feel that this is worth an Emmy.
2. **a.** I feel you're a good artist.
   b. Your artwork makes me happy.
3. **a.** Can you imagine working in that place?
   b. I get depressed every time I walk in there.
4. **a.** I am no good as a team captain.
   b. I'm sad that I can't get it right.

Answers:

1. **a.** Feeling; **b.** Opinion disguised as a feeling. The word *feel* doesn't necessarily describe feelings. "This is worth an Emmy" is an evaluation, not a feeling.
2. **a.** Opinion (the word *feel* may confuse you); **b.** Feeling
3. **a.** Opinion in form of a question; **b.** Feeling
4. **a.** Opinion; **b.** Feeling

OUTCOMES

With your classmates, discuss how you say things with feelings, describe feelings, or express feelings. How good were you at distinguishing between feelings and opinions?

Communication Competence

Competence means having the ability to do something. A successful communicator knows what to say and when to say it.

Because communication is about conveying who you are to others, knowing who you are is basic to **communication competence**. A competent person is able to understand others, understand a situation, figure out his or her place in the situation, and choose behavior appropriate to the situation and the other person. Competent communicators also try out different behavior if they feel that the communication is not going well.

Some of the most useful skills of a competent communicator are:

* Ability to modify to fit the situation **(adaptability)**.
* Ability to express oneself clearly and effectively **(articulation)**.
* Ability to find something funny in a situation (humor). Humor is helpful for easing tension and alleviating embarrassment.

Managing Nerves

One sign of competence in a speaker is self-awareness of what is happening and knowledge of how to manage the situation. When you have to deliver a speech, for example, you wrestle with all kinds of different feelings and opinions. You especially tend to worry about your abilities. When speaking in public, most people are afraid of ridicule. They fear looking foolish or stupid by forgetting what they want to say or by saying something unacceptable.

The nervousness starts before giving a speech, peaks right as you stand in front of an audience, then drops.

Being nervous isn't necessarily a bad thing. It indicates that you're taking the task seriously. You can think of it as excitement rather than nerves, but your body doesn't know the difference.

Many people are apprehensive about talking to anyone, let alone to a large audience.

Communication in Careers

A Shy Guy on TV

Beginning speakers often look to professionals who are in the public eye for their role models. The truth is, professional or not, many people have to deal with confidence issues and stage fright. Famous performers such as Barbra Streisand, Carly Simon, and John Lennon all suffered from severe stage fright.

Alan Davis is an on-camera news reporter for a local TV station. Alan says, "I started out with an internship at a radio station. They gave me a microphone and told me to ask the question of the day to people on the street. It was hard for me to approach total strangers and ask questions. I'm a shy person. I almost didn't graduate because I couldn't get out of speech class."

Alan eventually got a job as an on-camera reporter for television news. "On television, I'm only talking to a photographer who's usually bored. I'm not really talking to a person, but a piece of glass. If I thought about how many people were going to be watching, I wouldn't be able to do it."

Alan has to deal with another aspect of communication confidence—interviewing people and getting them to let him tape them for stories. "People get hostile and upset. They go wild. You have to use common sense. Experience and street smarts help. You have to have your antennae up. If I make eye contact with someone, I go right for them."

Alan has been reporting on-camera television news for 24 years and he still gets nervous.

Stage Fright

The thought of standing on a stage in front of hundreds or even dozens of people scares many people stiff. In fact, probably most people who go on stage actually experience fright at some point. **Stage fright** is the nervousness felt at standing in front of an audience. The good news is that it usually gets easier as time goes on.

Symptoms of Stage Fright

The symptoms of stage fright are similar to those for fright of any kind—dry mouth, tense voice, fast breathing, sweaty palms, shaky legs, pounding heart, and churning stomach. As bad as it feels to you, stage fright often goes undetected by the audience.

Like other fears, stage fright is often exaggerated and irrational. Moreover, it requires mental energy that could be better used for something else. Turning negative thoughts into positive ones can reduce your anxiety level.

Experiencing stage fright can be an advantage when you learn how to control it.

Controlling Stage Fright

Knowing that you'll probably be scared is a good beginning. At least you'll be prepared. The next step in controlling stage fright is to evaluate what you're feeling. Most beginners fear they'll forget their speech. Fear produces a mental disorganization that results in freezing. Heightened feeling prepares your body for emergency action, caused by increased adrenaline in your blood. Athletes experience this before a competition, just as speakers do in front of an audience. This heightened feeling can become pure fear if you don't keep it in check.

Being very well prepared and rehearsed is the best antidote for stage fright. If you go before an audience without a plan, you'll have a rough time. However, if you're well prepared and if you've set up your notes properly, you needn't worry. You can fall back upon the lines you have practiced. Once your presentation is underway you will become more relaxed and your nerves will settle down.

Evaluate the feelings causing your fear. Make a list that describes your fear and the behavior that accompanies it, the effect the behavior and fear have on you, and what you can do to change the behavior.

What Do You Fear?	
The Fear	**What to Do**
Topic of speech won't be interesting.	Do the best possible research and know more about the topic than your audience does.
Looking foolish or forgetting your speech.	Structure the content of the speech so that it's easier to remember.
Sensing the audience won't like you.	Construct a memorable introduction for your speech to capture the audience in the first 30 seconds.
Looking at the audience.	Talk with audience rather than at them. Think of them as friends.
Fearing you might stutter.	Slow down.

Relaxation Techniques

Tension is a cause of stage fright. It comes from wanting to make a good impression and fearing that you'll fail. This mental tension moves into your body and into your muscles. To ease it, you'll need to relax your mind and your body. Here are techniques for relaxing the mind and body.

Mental Relaxation Techniques

1. *Relax your mind.* Despite your fears, you won't actually die from giving a public talk. Close your eyes and think of a pleasant memory.

2. *Remember your goal.* In public speaking, you're not there to perform but to communicate an idea.

3. *Concentrate on your message.* Think about the ideas you want to express.

4. *Study your topic.* Research it thoroughly. Know your facts.

5. *Prepare your introduction and conclusion.* These are the critical moments. The introduction establishes the connection with your audience. Start with a few strong sentences and memorize them. After a strong start, you'll be able to concentrate on the major points.

6. *Control your anxiety.* With any anxiety, the key to control is realizing why you're anxious. Remind yourself that this anxiety is very normal. Make a decision not to let fear spiral into panic. Why should it? You'll probably feel differently once the speech starts. As vividly as you can, picture yourself walking out and having a great success.

7. *Listen to music.* Choose music that relaxes you and puts you into a good mood.

8. *Think of your audience as friendly.* Pretend that you're explaining your topic to your best friend.

Physical Relaxation Techniques

9. *Make yourself yawn.*

10. *Breathe by inhaling deeply.* Breathe through your nose, counting to five as you fill your lungs with air. Hold your breath and count to two. Then exhale slowly, counting to five. Do this during the day and right before you are about to speak.

11. *Do slow head rolls.* Let your head drop forward. Then rotate it slowly clockwise, then counterclockwise.

12. *Sit in a chair and go limp.* Let your muscles relax.

Building Confidence

People experience varying degrees of apprehension in communicating. Some have **self-confidence** and believe that what they say is important and will be well received. Others lack confidence and think that no one wants to hear their thoughts. Confidence isn't necessarily connected with reality.

You've probably been in classrooms where someone constantly raises his or her hand to give the wrong answer, while you sit on your hand, afraid to give the answer that you know is right. One study showed that more people fear public speaking than death—perhaps because people seldom speak in public. The more you speak in public the less you fear it.

Extemporaneous Speaking

GOAL

The goal of this activity is to provide experience in speaking.

TASKS

1. As a class, brainstorm for simple topics that any person in the class could speak on, such as why I like T-shirts, the best school colors, or my favorite musical groups. Write possible topics on a piece of paper and put them in a hat.

2. Take turns drawing topics out of the hat.

3. When you get your topic, give a one-minute speech.

4. Critique one another's speeches. Pay attention to the nonverbals and the expressiveness and coherence of the speeches.

OUTCOMES

How comfortable or uncomfortable were you in speaking? Why? What can you do to increase your confidence for the next speech?

How to Look Confident

Looking confident communicates power. A confident person:

- ✅ Maintains eye contact.
- ✅ Controls emotions and doesn't let them take control.
- ✅ Admits mistakes.
- ✅ Manages interpersonal interactions.
- ✅ Draws others into a conversation.
- ✅ Avoids tag questions ("Don't you think?" "Isn't it?").
- ✅ Doesn't fidget.
- ✅ Uses appropriate facial expressions.
- ✅ Avoids vocalized pauses ("um," "ah").
- ✅ Maintains appropriate distance.

Confidence-Building Exercises

Practice speaking as much as you can. Speak in public as often as you can, to get used to it. Confidence is built on experience. After all, public speaking is only speaking. Take every opportunity to speak in groups of people, even if you just make more of an effort to raise your hand and speak up in class. Begin by asking a question or making a comment.

As you speak informally, practice following these guidelines:

- ✳ Concentrate on other speakers and listeners.
- ✳ Focus on the topic.
- ✳ Use gestures.
- ✳ Make eye contact.
- ✳ Use humor.

Confidence in Public Speaking

When you move into a public speaking situation, these tips can make you feel more confident:

- ✳ As you speak, concentrate on your topic. Don't think too much about yourself and how you look.
- ✳ Feel your energy and direct it away from yourself. Focus your attention on your listeners. Look at their faces. Make eye contact.
- ✳ Release the tension in your body by moving. Use gestures and some simple kind of **platform movement**. Moving around can help you use your energy in an active way. Almost any movement is better than no movement.
- ✳ Use appropriate humor. This will make everyone relax, including yourself.

Communication confidence begins with assessing your strengths and weaknesses and becoming comfortable with who you are. Having a strong self-concept helps you to position yourself in relation to other people. Building on your strengths and focusing on the positive messages you receive from others can help you to develop a positive self-concept and high self-esteem. The way you perceive yourself also affects how you communicate and interact with others. Sharing ideas and feelings with others can be risky, but it can help you communicate who you are. Even people with high self-esteem experience stage fright (fear of speaking in front of people). Learning to relax mentally and physically can help lessen stage fright, as can thorough preparation and confidence in your abilities.

Speech

adaptability—ability to adjust to situations and individuals.

articulation—ability to express oneself readily, clearly, or effectively.

cognitive dissonance—anxiety of having beliefs and behaviors that contradict each other.

communication competence—sum total of abilities to communicate.

culture—totality of socially transmitted behavior patterns, beliefs, customs, and institutions passed through generations.

extrovert—outgoing personality.

feelings—emotions.

introvert—personality turned inward.

opinion—mental view, judgment, or appraisal.

personality—totality of a person's behavioral and emotional characteristics.

physical self—appearance and socioeconomic status.

platform movement—physical movement as you stand at a lectern speaking.

self-awareness—having a sense of your individuality.

self-concept—total of beliefs and attitudes one has about oneself.

self-confidence—being aware of your abilities.

self-disclosure—revealing information about yourself that's not generally known to others.

self-esteem—amount of satisfaction one has with oneself.

social self—personality.

spiritual self—person's beliefs, attitudes, and intellectual abilities.

stage fright—nervousness felt at speaking in front of an audience.

trust—reliance on character, ability, strength, or truth of another.

CHAPTER 5

Interpersonal Communication

In this chapter, you will consider:

- **What types of one-to-one relationships am I a part of?**
- **How well do I communicate and listen in one-to-one relationships?**
- **What prevents me from really understanding someone?**
- **How aware am I of how I appear to others?**
- **How well do I negotiate conflicts?**
- **What are the proper ways to introduce people, handle social and business phone calls, leave voice messages, and write business e-mails?**
- **What is the best way to prepare and conduct an interview?**

In this chapter, you'll examine one-to-one, or interpersonal, communication. You'll discover that all communications have two parts: words and emotions. You'll explore the concepts of self-monitoring and your public and private selves. You'll learn four essential interpersonal skills, as well as eight healthy interpersonal attitudes that can help make all of your relationships work. You'll also come to understand the rules of conversation, of social rituals, and of conducting interviews.

The Basics of Interpersonal Communication

Interpersonal communication, or one-to-one communication, occurs between two people. Relationships are at the heart of, and inseparable from, interpersonal communication.

You have many types of one-to-one relationships. You have casual relationships with acquaintances and with service people such as clerks, cashiers, waitstaff, bus drivers, and so on. You have more formal relationships at school with teachers and principals and at work with supervisors, fellow workers, and subordinates. You also have closer personal relationships with friends, family members, and loved ones.

Interpersonal skills help you to operate comfortably with casual contacts and to build and maintain appropriate one-to-one relationships with school and business contacts and with close friends and loved ones.

How Well Do You Self-Monitor?

The following statements represent different situations. Carefully read each one. Answer T (true) if you think the statement applies to you. Answer F (false) if it doesn't.

1. ___ I find it hard to imitate the behavior of other people.

2. ___ I guess I do put on a show to impress or entertain people.

3. ___ I would probably make a good actor or actress.

4. ___ I sometimes appear to others to be experiencing deeper emotions than I actually am.

5. ___ In a group of people, I rarely am the center of attention.

6. ___ In different situations and with different people, I often act very differently.

7. ___ I can argue only for ideas I already believe.

8. ___ To get along and be liked, I tend to be what people expect me to be rather than who I really am.

9. ___ I may deceive people by being friendly when I really dislike them.

10. ___ I am always the person I appear to be.

Scoring: For questions 1, 5, and 7 give yourself 1 point if you answered F. For the rest of the questions, give yourself 1 point if you answered T.

Add up your points. 7 and above—high self-monitoring; 3 or below—low self-monitoring.

Self-Monitoring

Interpersonal communication begins with you. **Self-monitoring** is observing and regulating one's own behavior. People vary in their awareness of how they appear to others. Some people—like models, politicians, and actors—are very aware of the effects of their appearance and behavior. Because they monitor or regulate their appearance to an extreme degree, they sometimes are called high self-monitors.

Other people seem to have no sense at all of how they appear to other people or what effects their behavior has. Because they have little or no skill at monitoring themselves, they are low on the self-monitor scale. Most people are somewhere in the middle. Some self-monitoring ability is definitely preferable to none.

Self-monitoring is healthy and shows that you recognize the importance of other people.

Your Public and Private Selves

You show different sides of your personality in different areas of your life. One side is your **public self**, the personality that you display to the world. If you're a high self-monitor, this side may be very well controlled.

People usually project the kind of personality that they think will win approval. Whether they present themselves as jolly and cheerful, as studious and quiet, or as warm and empathetic, they hope to please others.

Your other self is your **private self**, your real personality, your deeper feelings and thoughts. This private self may exactly correspond to your public self or be very different from it. You usually reveal your private self only to your close friends and loved ones.

As you move through a great variety of casual, business, and personal relationships, it's important to judge the situation and behave appropriately. When chatting with the grocery checkout clerk, it's appropriate to laugh and joke around. But that behavior won't work in most business situations.

Interpersonal Messages

When two people communicate, they send and receive messages. Interpersonal messages have meaning in two dimensions: the content of the message and the relationship between the two communicators. Interpersonal communications not only contain information; they also help to define the relationship.

The **content dimension** of the message consists of information conveyed through words. The **relationship dimension** of the communication consists of emotion conveyed through nonverbal symbols and paralanguage (such as tone of voice). The relationship dimension tells you how to react and respond to the message.

For example, Barry tells his mother that he'll wash the dog today. That's the message's content. But his mother sees him slouched in the chair and hears his reluctant tone of voice. That's the relationship part of the message. This tells her that Barry really doesn't want to wash the dog. She concludes that he just might "forget" to do it.

The way you speak to another person shows how you perceive the relationship. When you're talking to your car mechanic, you're probably fairly strong and assertive. Being the customer you're in charge, and you need to give the mechanic directions. You'll probably speak more gently and carefully to your grandmother.

Communication Problems

Most communication problems occur in the relationship dimension rather than in the content dimension. This shows that communicators are not as adept as they should be in interpreting another person's feelings.

For example, James misunderstood the relationship dimension in his communications with Gwen, the cashier at the corner store. She was friendly with all customers, though never too familiar. Gwen joked with James, and he interpreted her friendliness as something more than she intended. One day, when he didn't have enough money for a soft drink, he was surprised that Gwen wouldn't let him take the soda and pay later.

Relationships require different amounts of effort. Close personal relationships require the most work. They call for mental, emotional, and physical effort and commitment. Once your feelings are committed, you need mental effort to understand the relationship, emotional effort to make and deepen the connection, and physical effort actually to dial the phone, write the letter or e-mail, speak, or just be together.

Interpersonal Skills

Four of the most important interpersonal skills are:

1. Exchanging information.
2. Explaining points of view.
3. Listening, sympathizing, and empathizing.
4. Making and taking constructive criticism.

❶ Exchanging Information

Information exchange is basic to communication. Events and relationships are ever-changing and continuous. Every message you send reveals, in some way, how you have developed right up to that point. Your verbal and nonverbal behavior communicates how you define yourself. Both communicators constantly change, adjusting your thinking as you interact, concerned not only with how your initial message affects the other person but also with how his or her response affects you.

To fully understand any single communication, you need to know all that has come before. Each encounter with someone builds upon your previous encounters with that person and affects future encounters.

For example, you may discover that a friend has a prejudice of which you were previously unaware. This new information will change the way you communicate with that person.

Whenever you speak to someone, you reveal something about how you see the relationship between yourself and that person. But your ideas don't necessarily reflect the other person's attitude. That's why, for example, it's so difficult to ask someone for a first date. You see a closer relationship as a possibility. But you just can't be sure that the other person is attracted to you, too.

Everyday COMMUNICATION

Nicholas Takes a Risk

Nicholas is a tenth-grade boy in a school where the unspoken rule is that tenth-grade boys don't go out with twelfth-grade girls. In fact, it's unheard of.

But Nicholas likes Jessica, a girl in the twelfth grade. Nicholas and Jessica met in art class and have become friends because they both like to draw. Nicholas believes that Jessica will see him as an individual rather than as a tenth grader. So he plans to ask Jessica to go to a dance with him.

Jessica can accept or reject the invitation. She may or may not like Nicholas, and she may or may not care about the unspoken rule. If she accepts, she confirms Nicholas's beliefs. If she rejects or ignores him, she challenges his beliefs.

If Jessica rejects him, Nicholas has some choices. He may decide to adjust his view of himself, or he may pay more attention to the unspoken rule. Or, he may change his view of Jessica, deciding that perhaps she wasn't as she appeared to be after all.

Communication is not always deliberate. You may pick up on things that an acquaintance didn't intend to communicate, such as how nervous she feels. Or perhaps she senses that you don't like her because of something she said. Perhaps you didn't like the person that she communicated herself to be.

As you communicate, be aware of both the content and the relationship dimensions. Before jumping to conclusions, ask questions or give feedback. This type of "reality check" can help you to communicate accurately and effectively.

❷ Explaining Points of View

Another interpersonal skill has to do with explaining points of view. All people filter perceptions in their own unique ways. Rather than take in all sensory information that surrounds them, people perceive selectively. They limit the number of stimuli to which they attach meaning.

For example, if you're a big hockey fan at a championship game, your attention is riveted on the action, and the crowd seems virtually to disappear. But here and there in the crowd are the non-hockey fans. Most of them are ignoring the game and concentrating on crowd watching.

Because people have different interests, experiences, perceptual categories, and knowledge, they have different perspectives and **points of view**. Each person's culture, parents, religion, education, and peers influence how he or she sees the world. People change as they grow, dropping old categories and forming new ones.

People usually focus on messages with which they agree. Information that they dislike or disagree with gets filtered out. They don't let it through, or they adjust to it.

As a result, you need to be aware that others do not think the same way you do. You can respect their unique views even if you can't agree with them. When you voice your point of view, be aware of your listeners and respectful of their right to disagree. Be willing to hear them out, too. Try to keep an open attitude. You might learn something new.

Points of View

GOAL

The goal of this activity is to recognize how point of view affects communication.

TASKS

1. As a class, watch speakers on a television talk show such as *Good Morning America.* (If necessary, prerecord the show.)

2. Record your impressions of two or three speakers on the show. What were their points of view? How did they indicate them verbally and nonverbally? Which speakers were the most and least successful communicators? Why?

3. Compare notes with your classmates.

4. Create a list of desirable verbal and nonverbal ways to communicate one's point of view.

OUTCOMES

How often did you make assumptions about a person's point of view before he or she explained it? How often did you and your fellow students agree about a speaker's point of view? Did all of you pick up on the same cues?

❸ Listening, Sympathizing, and Empathizing

Listening, sympathizing, and empathizing are important interpersonal skills. Listening is discussed in detail in Chapter 3. **Sympathy** is feeling sorry for another and wanting to help him or her. **Empathy** is the ability to show another that you understand his or her situation and feel similar emotional reactions to it. Empathy may not lead to a desire to help. Instead it enables you to adopt another person's perspective and feel the same emotion. Sometimes a person wants you to help find solutions. Sometimes he or she simply wants someone to listen.

Deborah Tannen, a professor who has researched the different communication styles of men and women, concludes that a gap exists between the way men and women communicate. She notes that women often express their feelings and seek the sort of emotional support that comes from empathy. On the other hand, men tend to offer solutions, which is more like sympathy than empathy. These two different approaches can clash and frequently cause communication problems.

❹ Making and Taking Constructive Criticism

A fourth interpersonal skill has to do with criticism. Since nobody's perfect, criticism is a part of everyone's lives. It's difficult getting negative feedback from other people. Criticism can be very hurtful. When you realize how it feels to get criticism, you'll be more sensitive to the other person's feeling when you feel compelled to criticize. **Constructive criticism** refers to personal comments that are designed to be helpful.

Before criticizing, consider that there is more than one way to speak. People grow up in households with very different expectations and habits. What seems normal within one household may be quite strange in another. When you come together to communicate with others, be open-minded and keep this diversity in mind.

If you want the other person to listen to your criticism, avoid angry attacks and blaming language. An angry attack usually triggers an angry defense in response. Blaming language usually hurts the other person and compels him or her to launch a hostile defense. Then the interchange turns into a power struggle.

If you must criticize or challenge another person and you want him or her to consider seriously what you say, phrase your remark in a positive way and in a way that is centered on yourself. For instance, rather than say, "You talk like your mouth is full of potatoes," you might use what's called an **I-message**: "I wasn't able to hear you when you mumbled."

Taking criticism is easier if the other person doesn't use blaming language or approach you angrily. You can feel more comfortable admitting—as people sometimes must—that you made a mistake or could use some improvement.

If someone's message is unclear to you, try to figure out what's missing and then give the feedback, such as, "Can you be more specific?" or "Can you define that word? I don't know what you mean."

Constructive Criticism Through I-Messages	
Instead of This	**Say This**
You use too many hand gestures when you speak.	I got distracted because I keep watching your hands.
Do you have to whine all the time?	It depresses me to listen to so much negativity.
You're such a terrible gossip!	I don't feel comfortable talking about other people's business.
Why can't you speak clearly?	I didn't understand what you said.

Interpersonal Attitudes

For greater success in interpersonal relationships, practice using these **eight** interpersonal attitudes:

1. Other-orientation
2. Positiveness
3. Openness
4. Effectiveness
5. Expressiveness
6. Interaction management
7. Closeness
8. Appropriateness

❶ Other-Orientation

<u>Other-orientation</u> is one of the most important interpersonal skills. When you're talking to someone, where is your attention? Are you thinking about an upcoming basketball game, a scheduled haircut, or your math assignment? Or are you able to be truly attentive to and interested in the other person?

Other-orientation communicates focus, consideration, and respect. If you are other-oriented, you ask questions about the other person and encourage him or her to express feelings, thoughts, and opinions.

❷ Positiveness

Perceiving and expressing things in a negative way can be draining to a relationship. <u>Positiveness</u> is an upbeat attitude that makes a relationship pleasant and fun. Watch the way you phrase things and the slant that you take. It's OK to express disappointments and share feelings when you're depressed. But if your negative feelings are constant, they leave little room to build a positive relationship.

❸ Openness

<u>Openness</u>, or self-disclosure, is a willingness to reveal personal information and to admit how you feel about something. It indicates a willingness to get close to someone. Therefore, it is most appropriate in close personal relationships.

Openness also means taking responsibility for your own feelings by using
I-messages. Instead of saying, "You're
always criticizing my clothes," say, "It
hurts my feelings when you say that you
don't like my clothes."

❹ Effectiveness

How effective are your communications?
Do people often misunderstand you?
Effectiveness means learning to express
your thoughts clearly and accurately. Get
to the point quickly, without droning or
rambling. Be sincere, so that the listener
knows that you mean what you say.

❺ Expressiveness

Expressiveness means sharing thoughts
and feelings freely. An expressive person is
involved in the interaction, not just a spec-
tator. People don't know what you think or
how you feel unless you tell them. The
degree to which you express your thoughts
and feelings shows the person how much
you want to be involved. But pay attention to
cues you're getting, too. Expressiveness is not
appropriate in all situations. Has the person
asked you about your thoughts or feelings?

❻ Interaction Management

Interaction management is the ability to
keep a conversation flowing. If you do it
well, you maintain your role as a speaker
or listener, passing back and forth the
opportunity to speak. Don't interrupt the
other person. Managing the interaction
shows your competence and your respect
for him or her. Watch the verbal and
nonverbal cues that signal when to stop
speaking or to take your turn. Pay attention
to cues that the other may be attempting
to end the conversation.

❼ Closeness

Closeness expresses the degree of connection between two people, varying from
extreme closeness to extreme distance.
How attentive and responsive you are
communicates your connection to the
other person. In some situations, you want
to communicate closeness. At other times,
you need to maintain a distance.

Nonverbal ways to communicate
closeness are:

* Keeping physical proximity.
* Making frequent eye contact.
* Limiting looking around at others.
* Facing the person squarely.
* Using the person's name.
* Asking questions for clarification.
* Smiling and complimenting.

If you don't want to communicate
closeness, avoid using these behaviors.

❽ Appropriateness

Appropriateness means choosing forms of
communication suited to the context or
occasion. Be careful not to behave inappropriately in casual and business situations.
In closer relationships, pay attention to cues
from others.

In general, treat people with respect and
courtesy. Don't surprise your friends by
bringing up sensitive topics in public.

Negotiation

In North America, many people feel that the purpose of communication is persuasion. If a conflict arises, they think that the way to reach agreement is to change the other person's mind. How often do we all attempt to persuade, convince, educate, straighten out, cure of delusions, or make someone see things our way?

Commercial advertising, sales phone calls, debate teams, adversarial law, and the two-party political system all provide examples of this emphasis in North American communication.

__Negotiation__ takes another approach. Instead of a goal such as "I win, he or she loses," negotiation tries to find a "win-win" solution, one that works for both parties. Rather than trying to convince each other, the two parties listen to each other. Together they work to find a goal that satisfies them both.

Situations That Call for Negotiation

Though individuals may be compatible and agree most of the time, everyone has to negotiate sometimes. Conflicts arise from people's differing preferences and sometimes from their conflicting needs.

Negotiating is a form of compromise. It expresses respect for the other person's right to disagree with you. Even seemingly small things may call for negotiation—

Negotiation Role-Play

GOAL

The goal of this activity is to explore some simple negotiations.

TASKS

1. Choose a partner and team up with another pair of students. One pair will negotiate, and the other will observe; then you'll switch roles.

2. The first pair chooses a topic on which to negotiate. Here are some possibilities: one person wants to see an action movie, the other a comedy; one person wants pizza, the other Chinese food. You also can create your own topics.

3. Members of the negotiating pair take opposing positions on their topic and, within five minutes, try to negotiate a solution that makes both feel good. The observers judge whether the outcome seems balanced.

4. When the negotiation is over, the observers analyze the negotiation process and the solution.

5. Pairs switch roles and repeat the activity.

OUTCOMES

Were the pairs able to negotiate solutions that both could enjoy? What were some common trouble spots?

agreeing to do a job for a fee, going to a restaurant or movie, or bartering chores for a chance to drive the family car.

Getting to "Yes"

Negotiation tries to produce a wise agreement, one that meets the interests of both sides. It should be efficient and should improve the relationship, not damage it.

Sometimes people get locked into their positions. They decide on a limit or a position, and they're determined to stick to it no matter what. This can abort a negotiation. For example, if you say, "This is my final price," the negotiations may end, and you won't make a sale. The more that people clarify and defend their positions, the more committed they are. Negotiating then becomes a contest of wills.

If you and a friend are going out for lunch and you say, "I refuse to set foot in a diner," and your friend says, "Everything else is closed today," what do you do next? If your friend is hungry enough, she may decide to go without you. If your goal was to spend time together and you take a hard-line position, you may not find a way to agree.

In a successful negotiation, participants focus on mutual interests, not on their stated positions. If their mutual interests are to sell and buy, they concentrate on that. If their mutual goal is to eat together, they focus on that. Both should try to solve the problem rather than to win. This opens them up to a new range of possibilities. For more information about negotiating and conflict resolution, see Chapter 8.

Conversation

When you think about **conversations**, you probably think of the verbal aspect or the words that are said. But you shouldn't overlook the role that the nonverbal aspect plays.

Verbal Aspects of Conversation

By speaking together, people learn about each other. People usually look for similarities in those that they meet and often are attracted to people who are similar to themselves. Similarities lead to agreement, which is something else that people look for in others.

When you agree with a person, you feel more secure with him or her. You feel that you have some control. You can predict future encounters with this person. If you have an agreeable conversation with him or her the first time you meet, you expect future conversations to be stable, predictable, and controllable.

Light, casual conversation is called **small talk**. Small talk is a mode of conversation that has evolved to help people get to know each other and find common areas of agreement. Small talk provides a way to raise safe, neutral topics—such as the weather, sports, or whatever is in the immediate surroundings. Small talk is almost entirely about the relationship and seldom about the content.

Small Talk about Cats

Are Heather and Vicky learning more than just how each other's cats behave? What is the value of their small talk?

Vicky: "My cat's overweight. I have to give him diet cat food."

Heather: "I've never had an overweight cat."

Vicky: "Mine's like 20 pounds. I know it's as bad for cats as it is for humans to be overweight."

Heather: "You probably feed him table food. I don't feed my cat people food."

Vicky: "I don't either, anymore. But whenever people come over and there's food on the table, she goes over to the table and sneaks up on the food by stretching out her legs. I let her do it because everyone has fun watching her."

Heather: "My cat always runs away when other people are around."

Vicky: "Not mine. She jumps in their laps. She's even been sat on a few times because she jumps on chairs when they get up."

Heather: "I know why mine runs away. People would pet him if he stayed."

What can you learn about Vicky from this small talk? about Heather?

Nonverbal Aspects of Conversation

Body language and paralanguage play a big role in conversation. Maintaining eye contact, facing the other person directly, and varying the musicality of your sentences all indicate your involvement or lack of involvement with your partner. Be aware of the conversation's content and context and your relationship with the other person. This will help you choose appropriate nonverbal signals, such as how close or how far away to stand, and whether a touch on the shoulder would be appropriate and acceptable.

Parts of a Conversation

Like other forms of communication, including speeches and letter writing, conversation can be thought of as consisting of **three** parts—the opening, the business, and the close. How you converse depends upon the relationship, whether it's casual, businesslike, or more intimate.

❶ Opening a Conversation

Verbal and nonverbal greetings indicate that communication channels are open and that one is ready to talk. Because your tone can be warm and friendly or cool, formal, and distant, your greeting carries information about the relationship. If the conversation never progresses beyond a greeting, the greeting itself helps to maintain the relationship. A friendly, sympathetic greeting can make bad news less painful. It also can soften someone up before you ask for or discuss business matters.

· Like many people, you may find it difficult to open conversations. In the beginning, you're uncertain about the mood of the person to whom you're talking. You don't know what to expect.

❷ The Business of the Conversation

The business of a conversation is the main reason you're talking together. In this part of the conversation, people exchange information but tend to stay on one topic. Listener and speaker exchange roles frequently. The listener should ask questions to clarify the speaker's meaning and to show attentiveness.

An effective conversationalist doesn't dominate the interaction. He or she tries to maintain balance between speaker and listener roles. He or she avoids interrupting and tries to draw the other out by asking for opinions.

❸ Closing a Conversation

Have you ever talked with someone and found it difficult to get out of the conversation? Changing the subject and moving to close the conversation, or **transitioning**, can help. "Well, let's think about it and be in touch," is a transition you can use before you say, "Goodbye" or "See you later."

The close itself can perform functions similar to the opening, such as helping to maintain the relationship. If you say something like, "Give me a call," or "Stay in touch," the other person feels that you're interested in maintaining the relationship.

HISTORY OF SPEECH

The Science of Conversation

Almost 2,000 years ago, the famed Roman orator and statesman Cicero discussed what he called the science of conversation. Some points he made can be helpful today.

Cicero said that, above all, one shouldn't monopolize a conversation but allow everyone to have a turn. Word choice should be appropriate to the subject. Conversation should focus on family affairs, politics, and

arts and sciences, but be sensitive to the tastes of the present company. One should avoid criticizing anyone not present or boasting about oneself.

Cicero encouraged the use of humor and a lively and clear vocal pattern. He noted that one should know how to end the conversation with tact when the subject becomes boring.

Conversation Rules	
This Behavior	**Communicates**
Taking turns talking and listening	Equality in the relationship
Being polite	Respect for the other
Keeping eye contact	Equality, respect
Staying on the subject	Ability to connect
Normal tone of voice	Emotional control

Sending and Receiving Messages Accurately

When people speak, they won't know whether you heard or understood unless they get some sort of feedback from you. It's frustrating to speak and to be met with stony silence.

At the very least, say something non-committal, such as, "I see," or "I hear you." If you intend to maintain this particular relationship, you may want to engage yourself a bit more. Try giving and getting frequent feedback and rephrasing what the person said.

Accuracy is particularly important during times of emotion or conflict. To be sure that you are hearing someone correctly, repeat or rephrase what the other person says. For example, say, "What I hear you say is. . . ." The other person will either affirm or deny that you got the message.

To communicate your meaning well, take care to use exact language, send clear nonverbal cues, and use appropriate behavior for the situation and the context. To receive a message accurately, practice good listening skills, pick up nonverbal cues, and pay attention to feedback.

Unspoken Rules and Courtesy

Conversation rules are culturally accepted ways for individuals to interact verbally. You start learning conversation rules when you learn to talk, although you probably never read a book about them. How familiar do the following rules sound?

* Don't interrupt.
* Say "please" and "thank you."
* Look at me when I'm talking to you!
* Tell me what you're thinking.
* Stop whining!
* Don't nag.

Learning to converse is part of becoming socialized. Conversation behaviors convey cultural values. For example, taking turns and looking your partner in the eye signal that both participants are on equal ground and have equal opportunity to speak. Not interrupting and saying "please" are ways of showing respect to each other. It's not socially acceptable to be pushy. Whining and nagging are considered annoying and negative.

You may not be aware of nonverbal behavior that signals a shift in communication. For example, in a smooth **turn-taking** transition, the speaker signals a readiness to give up the floor and switch roles by breaking eye contact, looking at the floor, lowering his or her voice, then resuming eye contact.

In Asian cultures, like China and Japan, conversation rules tend to emphasize preventing your partner from feeling embarrassed, a practice known as **saving face**. Americans sometimes have been confused in business dealings with Japanese who prefer to say, "We will carefully consider your offer," rather than "No, thanks."

Cross-Cultural Conversation Rules	
Culture	**Frequent Emphases in Conversation**
All cultures	Politeness
United States	Truthfulness Relevance (connected topics)
China	Self-denigration
Japan	Peaceful relations

Enjoying Conversation

There are many ways to sharpen your conversational skills. If you need things to talk about, try to broaden your interests, read more, and pay attention to the world. Anyone can learn to speak with enthusiasm and vigor. Think about your listeners and try to choose subjects that will interest all of them. Find out what is special or unique about people to whom you are talking. They might even turn out to be interesting.

Conversation can be one of life's great pleasures. When you relax with another person and put aside critical and evaluative listening, then conversation can be like play. Telling and commenting on each other's stories, for example, not only helps you to get to know each other better but can be pleasurable and entertaining. As you work to become more interesting for others to listen to, you'll find that you are able to listen to them better as well.

Social Rituals

Following **social rituals**—established forms of social behavior—tends to create order and prevent feelings from being hurt. Social rituals allow a speaker and listener to keep their interpersonal relationship stable, predictable, and controllable. Social rituals also solve the problem of what to do or say in particular situations. For example:

* In greeting each other, one person says, "Hello. How are you?" and the other responds, "Fine, thanks. And you?" This isn't meant to be a health inventory but a way of opening the lines of communication.
* People take turns in conversations so that one person isn't always dominating the conversation and the other always listening.
* After one person says something, the other gives feedback rather than sitting mute.
* If a topic is introduced, the next person's response deals first with that topic before moving on to something else.
* People speak to each other in a normal tone of voice, neither shouting nor whispering.

Because American culture prefers informality, many people are unfamiliar with social rituals of communication. However, many of those rituals can still be used to ease and facilitate the difficult task of sending and receiving messages.

Let's look at the social rituals that exist in American culture for introducing people, social phone calls, business phone calls, leaving voice-mail messages, and writing business e-mails.

Protocol in the Mongolian Embassy

Jared Critchfield of Lewiston, Idaho, is a political section intern at the U.S. embassy in Mongolia. This year, Critchfield performed all the tasks of the political officer who was on leave for the summer. Jared's responsibilities included dealing with local Mongolians and with U.S. visitors and handling meetings with government officials.

Embassy officials must be sensitive to the customs of the host country. Observing protocol—codes of strict etiquette and precedence—is necessary so as not to offend local customs or hierarchy. Like a good guest, Jared always checked with a local Mongolian about correct protocol. "There are many 'Miss Manners' things to be concerned with," Jared says. "In Mongolia, a person's history in office can determine how he or she is seated at a table."

Status is extremely important. All invitations must be properly addressed. Jared notes, "We know each person's title because of his or her office or family, but we still hired a protocol officer to continually confirm who was who." At the NATO summit, the embassy handled Mongolian guests according to who had been in the office the longest. The longest-standing member had the highest status.

Jared recalls a reception at the embassy when the highest-ranking member of Parliament was in the hospital. Another member of Parliament became the center of attention. Then the hospitalized member showed up late, "and suddenly all the attention was on her, and everyone forgot about the other guy. Then she left, and the attention was back on him again."

Everyone knew how to handle this situation so as not to offend the higher ranking member of Parliament.

Introducing People

If you are introducing two people who don't know each other, the rule is to begin by first naming the person who is older or who has the higher status. For example, you would present your parents or your boss to your friend by saying, "Mom, this is Matt," or "Mr. Baxter, this is my brother."

If the people are the same age or status, you would present the more familiar person first. "Mom, this is my boss, Mr. Baxter."

If someone presents him or herself to you and says, "Hi, I'm . . . ," you would respond by saying, "I'm. . . . Pleased to meet you."

When you're being introduced and the other people are standing up, you should stand up, too.

Telephone Etiquette

Etiquette refers to socially accepted practices that guide people's behavior in different situations. Books written on etiquette explain such things as how to perform introductions and how to write wedding announcements. Telephone etiquette includes rules about proper ways to make social and business phone calls and how to leave voice messages.

Social Phone Calls

The important first lesson in making phone calls is to call at appropriate times. You certainly want to avoid waking someone early in the morning or late at night. It's also best not to call at dinner time, though today it is difficult to know exactly when people are eating dinner.

When you call, let the phone ring about six times. Six rings allows a person 18 seconds to answer the phone. When someone answers, identify yourself and politely ask for the appropriate person. Keep the call to a reasonable length.

When you receive a call, say, "Hello?" and wait for a response. When you hear who it is and what he or she wants, be honest but courteous. Since you can't see the speaker's nonverbal behavior, pay attention to his or her emphases, inflections, mood, and emotional content. Use questions and feedback to be sure you've understood the speaker accurately.

Business Phone Calls

Because business phone calls have a specific purpose, they're usually briefer and more efficient than social calls. Your paralanguage—your tone of voice and rate of speech—are conveyed over the phone just as in face-to-face conversations and may carry more weight because the other person can't see your nonverbal behavior.

If you're not sure with whom you should speak, ask the company receptionist or operator for help. Be polite and act professional. State your name, company, and the purpose of your call, and make sure that this person understands you.

You may get transferred several times before you're connected with the person who can help you, so be patient. If you become frustrated or angry, don't let your voice show it. Hang up and call tomorrow. People will be more willing to help you achieve your goals if you're friendly and courteous.

Voice-Mail Messages

Busy people have answering machines and voice mail so that they won't miss any calls. They really do want you to leave your name, number, time that you called, and a brief message. Unless the greeting asks you to leave a detailed message, keep your message short and professional. Most business people answer their voice-mail messages within 24 hours.

E-mail Etiquette for Business

The practice of electronic mail, or e-mail, hasn't been around very long, but it already has acquired certain rules. If you're being paid to work in an office, your correspondence, whether hard copy or e-mail, belongs to the business and may be stored on a company server. Your supervisor or boss can read it at any time. Therefore, make sure that your messages all have something to do with your job.

When you're writing business e-mails, here are some points to remember:

* Though a salutation and signature aren't required, they add a human touch.
* Send copies only to those who really want or need a copy. Many business people receive hundreds of e-mails every day. Reduce the clutter whenever you can.
* Define your subject in the Subject heading so your recipients can preview the e-mail's content and easily find it again.
* Keep your e-mail short and to the point.
* Don't use italics, boldface, underlines, and so on, since many receiving e-mail programs will remove the formatting.
* On a first business contact, sign the e-mail with your name, title, company, address, phone, fax, e-mail address, and Web site address.
* Always proofread your e-mail before sending.

Interviewing

For business, government, and news media, **interviewing** is a way to gather information. Believe it or not, interviewing had a definite beginning and hasn't been around for very long. The first interview took place in the mid 1800s. Interviewing people, or asking them questions, was not an acknowledged activity even in American journalism until after the Civil War.

Even after Americans began the practice of interviewing, Europeans scoffed at it, finding it rude. Yet interviewing now is so commonplace that it's hard to imagine a world without it. **Four** rules follow for conducting a successful interview. For more information about interviewing, see Chapter 12.

❶ Be Prepared

Before you interview anyone, you need to know something about the person and the subject so your questions will be well informed. Decide on the purpose of your interview. What do you want to learn from this particular person? Can he or she provide a unique perspective? When you arrange the interview, communicate your goals to the interviewee.

❷ Structure the Interview

Plan your questions, putting them in order in the direction you hope the interview will go. Keep the questions short. Start with basics: the biographical (name, address, age) and demographic (job, education), then lead into more personal information. Explore areas that you are curious about. Chances are that others will be interested in this, too.

Interviewing follows some norms and expectations. The reporter may either ask a question to gather information or ask what is called a "known information" question. This is like elementary school, when the teacher knows the answer, but asks the question anyway.

Remember that an interview often has a third party—the reader or audience.

Sidebar

Types of Interview Questions

The way that you formulate questions controls the answers that you get. Following are pairs of interview questions for you to compare.

1. An initial question introduces a topic. A follow-up question asks for elaboration. Of the two questions below, which is which?

   * "What part did you have in the play?"
   * "Talk about your favorite scene. Why was it your favorite?"

2. Open-ended questions allow free and undirected responses. Close-ended questions can only be answered in limited ways. Of the two questions below, which is which?

   * "Tell me about being the lead in the play."
   * "Did you like being the lead in the play?"

3. Direct questions are pointed. Indirect questions allow "wiggle room." Of the two questions below, which is which?

   * "Why did you have a fight with the co-star?"
   * "Can you tell me about your relationship with your co-star?"

4. Questions can be posed in a neutral way, without providing any value-laden words, or they can show a bias. Of the two questions below, which is which?

   * "Do you consider your acting a bit melodramatic?"
   * "How did you prepare for the part?"

❸ Be a Good Listener

After you ask your question, let the subject talk. Be quiet and give him or her time to answer. Summarize what you understood.

Though you'll have a plan, remain flexible. Your subject may reveal surprising or unexpected information. If a topic comes up that you hadn't anticipated, be prepared to follow up with it, even if it means leaving your outline.

Listen creatively and critically. Ask yourself, what is this person really telling me about himself or herself?

❹ Build Trust and Respect

Tell your subject why you want the interview. When he or she answers your questions, express interest, sympathy, and understanding. Remain neutral if he or she brings up a topic with which you disagree. The interview is about your subject, not about you.

After you've asked all your questions, review a bit about some central idea and ask whether there's anything you didn't ask that the subject wishes to address.

Interview Role-Play

GOAL

The goal of this activity is to do a warm-up interview and become familiar with interviewing.

TASKS

1. Form pairs. Choose someone in class that you don't know very well.

2. Each person formulates five or six questions to ask the other person. Make sure that your questions are appropriate and not too personal.

3. Take turns interviewing and being interviewed. Each turn should take no more than 10 minutes. Neither interviewee should volunteer information unless he or she is specifically asked for it.

4. Introduce your partner to the whole class, using information you gained through your interview.

OUTCOMES

Compare the amounts of information gathered. Did some questions work better than others? Why?

How to Improve Interpersonal Communications

✓ Consider ways to improve your casual, business, and close personal relationships through better communication.

✓ Pay attention to the differences between relationship messages and content messages.

✓ Become aware of your communication strengths and weaknesses so that you can improve your interpersonal skills.

✓ Think about communication skills and attitudes that you can improve.

✓ Observe communication norms and social norms.

✓ Be willing to negotiate solutions to problems rather than insisting on "winning."

✓ Notice areas of agreement you find with others when communicating.

✓ Listen creatively to people to hear what they are really saying about themselves.

Wrap-up

Since interpersonal communication is the complete interaction between two people, who you are and what you do matter as much as the words you say. Verbal and nonverbal messages describe and define your relationship with the other person, as well as whatever information you wish to exchange. Interpersonal communication is an ongoing process.

You can improve your interpersonal communication skills. People respond well to others who speak effectively and appropriately, are open to various points of view, pay attention to others' feelings, make and take criticism appropriately, and follow conversational rules. Healthy interpersonal attitudes—such as other-orientation, positiveness, openness, effectiveness, and expressiveness—tell other people that you're interested in them and that you're interesting as well. The ability to negotiate to a fair solution smoothes interpersonal conflicts.

Knowledge of social rituals—such as introductions, telephone etiquette, and appropriate forms for e-mail—helps you to communicate appropriately.

appropriateness—choosing forms of communication suited to the context.

closeness—degree of connection between communicators.

constructive criticism—personal comments designed to be helpful.

content dimension—the aspect of interpersonal communication that consists of information conveyed through words.

conversation—verbal exchange.

conversation rules—culturally accepted ways for individuals to interact verbally.

effectiveness—ability to put thoughts into precise words and get to the point.

empathy—ability to adopt another's perspective and feel what he or she feels.

etiquette—socially accepted practices that guide people's behavior in different situations.

expressiveness—sharing thoughts and feelings freely.

I-messages—communication deriving from oneself and communicating one's own feelings.

interaction management—ability to keep a conversation flowing.

interpersonal communication—interchange between two people.

interpersonal skills—learned capabilities of relating effectively to other people.

interviewing—asking questions to draw information out of another person.

negotiation—process of reaching a compromise.

openness—not being secretive.

other-orientation—being considerate of your partner in communication.

point of view—personal perspective.

positiveness—having an upbeat attitude.

private self—your real personality, including your deeper feelings and thoughts.

public self—the personality that you display to the world.

relationship dimension—the aspect of interpersonal communication that pertains to the human connection, consisting of emotion as conveyed through nonverbal symbols and paralanguage.

saving face—protecting another person from embarrassment or shame.

self-monitoring—observing and regulating one's own behavior.

small talk—light, casual conversation.

social rituals—established forms of social behavior.

sympathy—feeling sorry for and wanting to help another person.

transitioning—smoothly changing a subject to lead into the next stage of conversation.

turn-taking—speaking and letting the other person speak.

Group Dynamics and Characteristics

Communication in groups is one-to-one communication multiplied many times. Groups meet to reach decisions, solve problems, and share information. In this chapter, you'll learn about the purposes, structures, and norms of groups; about group roles and subgroups; and about group behavior and dynamics. You'll also find out about the various tasks and maintenance roles that group members perform to help the group function well and reach its goals.

Group Purposes, Structures, and Norms

Groups may be formed to make decisions, solve problems, or share information. But groups are as different as their reasons for existence and the individuals who are in them.

Group Purposes

Groups are more than crowds of people who happen to be together. Groups are formed by individuals who share a common purpose. When you take part in a group, you're part of a team. Your participation is valuable as long as the group works toward a common goal. If your group is working well, its members feel a connection to each other and communicate regularly with each other.

The old saying "two heads are better than one" applies to group decision making. When several people combine their creative thinking to solving a problem, they can generate more solutions than can one person alone. For this reason, members should attend group meetings with their minds open to the suggestions of others.

Group Structures

Groups follow certain organizing rules. Some groups need more structure than others to carry out their goals. Groups can be formal or informal.

Formal groups are highly organized. They have set rules for communicating during meetings. Group members clearly state who is responsible for tasks. The order of business during meetings is clear and often detailed in an agenda. Each meeting follows a similar order. Examples of **formal groups** include student council, city government, and business board meetings.

Informal groups have fewer rules. Such groups may come together quickly to solve a specific problem or to inform themselves. They don't want to take the time to define themselves precisely. Examples of **informal groups** include clubs, small organizations, and neighborhood groups.

Group Norms

Group members develop ways of interacting among themselves. Sometimes their standards are rigid, as when they follow specific procedures. Sometimes standards are loosely defined, as in a social group. These expected behaviors are called **group norms.**

Groups can have norms for behaving and norms for communicating. Behavior norms include such things as who can be a member, how to dress, whether you should be punctual or can arrive late to meetings, or whether there will be a break.

A group's communication norms include what topics can be raised during discussions, how to express disagreement, and how much disagreement is acceptable.

Group Decisions for Survival

GOAL

The goal of this activity is to compare the effectiveness of individual decision making with that of group decision making.

TASKS

1. Form groups of five to seven.

2. Each group reviews a list of items that it may need on a deserted island. The items are a magnetic compass, dehydrated food, 15 yards of nylon cord, 3 gallons of water, flares, first aid kit, solar-powered radio, inflatable life raft, a box of matches, a wool blanket, and an army knife.

3. Each member ranks these items in order of importance. Some of the items may need to be left behind.

4. Then the group discusses and determines the final rankings together.

OUTCOMES

How do the rankings compare? What problems did the group have in arriving at a final list?

Group Roles and Subgroups

As an individual, you play many roles. You can be a student, son or daughter, brother or sister, friend, employee, and volunteer. As a group member, you also play many roles.

Group Roles

In a group, you can be a leader, group member, speaker, listener, fact finder, questioner, and opinion seeker. **Group roles** are the patterns of communication that define one's place in a group. The role of each person helps to define the contribution he or she makes to the group.

Subgroups

Groups don't always function as single units. Often smaller units, or **subgroups,** form. For example, the student council forms committees to carry out particular jobs. Sometimes members feel more attached to their subgroup than to the main group. They may be more involved with the subgroup and feel more at home with the subgroup's other members. They may even lose sight of the larger goals of the group.

Cliques

Sometimes a few group members form a particular kind of subgroup called a **clique.** Members of cliques exclude outsiders and associate primarily with one another. The members of cliques have a strong affinity for, or bond with, one another. They can be disruptive to groups because clique members are cohesive and usually back up each other's personal goals.

If members of a clique are more active than other group members, their influence can be strong. To counteract a clique, all other group members need to voice their opinions. The discussion leader also can manage the discussion so that the clique can't dominate.

Behavior and Dynamics

You may have been on committees, in clubs, or in discussion groups in which information flowed easily and the group accomplished its tasks. You also may have been in groups where nothing got done except arguing. You may have thought these groups were a waste of time.

If groups are to function at all, their members must cooperate. As a group member, you're a member of a team that must agree on a common goal. If you and the other members help advance this common goal, your group will succeed in what it sets out to do.

Personal Goals

Although each group member joins to achieve the common goal of the group, each also has a personal agenda. When individual agendas of group members conflict, the group's common purpose can be harmed. For example, when Damien and Loreen joined the School Spirit Committee, both tried to control the group. Both were running for class president and wanted to use the group's accomplishments to help them get elected.

Group discussions can be damaged by cliques and by members' personal goals. Suppose Clarence joined the Homecoming Committee because Ethel was on it. Clarence wanted to go out with Ethel and supported all of her suggestions uncritically, which annoyed the other group members.

This situation represents a clear case of personal goals taking precedence over group goals. Handling problem behavior in groups is discussed in more detail in Chapter 7.

Cohesiveness

The degree to which members share a common goal is a group's **cohesiveness**. When a group has cohesiveness, its members are committed to group unity. Groups can be cohesive if members realize that they should be operating not as individuals but as group members.

Communication in Careers

Solving Problems in a Group

Lindsey Bramwell participated in a work group at the Health Care Financing Administration's (HCFA) central office. HCFA oversees the Medicare program, which provides health care to the elderly around the country.

Lindsey's work group wanted to develop a procedure for improving the quality of care for a specific group of patients. These patients need surgery on blocked arteries. At first, Lindsey's group members didn't understand each other at all. Eventually they realized that one of

their problems was that different doctors use different types of charts when dealing with this surgery.

"We all were familiar with our own charts, but not with the other guy's charts," Lindsey said. The group analyzed the charts to see whether there was any similarity among them. They finally reached a consensus that it wouldn't be possible to substitute information from chart to chart. Without choosing a specific chart, they developed a list of common information. The group maintained cohesiveness even though they disagreed as to which chart is preferable.

Physical Factors Affecting Group Dynamics

Physical factors affect peoples' moods and emotions and exert an impact upon a group's effectiveness. **Four** environmental factors affect group dynamics.

❶ Setting

The physical environment where the group meets for discussion affects the quality of meetings. A small group meeting in a living room full of sofas, stuffed chairs, and soft lighting will be more relaxed and comfortable than the same meeting in a school cafeteria or auditorium. How do you think that the mood of a group would be affected by meeting in a restaurant? a rundown basement room? a corporate boardroom?

❷ Seating

The seating arrangement in a room also affects the nature of the discussion. Seating determines who makes eye contact with whom. When people in a group sit in a circle, they can make eye contact with one another. When the group sits in rows of chairs facing forward, they mainly make eye contact with and listen to the person in the front of the room, who clearly is in a leadership position.

Seating also determines proxemics (the closeness or distance between people). If people are physically close to one another, they are likely to share more intimate information than they might in a large hall. However, people shouldn't be seated too closely together or they may feel that their personal space has been invaded.

❸ Time of Meetings

The timing of meetings also has an effect on the group's functioning. Groups should decide on an optimal time of day to meet. Some people function better in the morning, others later in the day. Meeting right after a heavy meal is not a good idea, since many people may begin to feel sleepy.

The time that you set for a meeting often determines who can and cannot attend. In today's busy world, scheduling a time when several people are available often takes real effort.

Try to be as flexible as you can. People will appreciate the fact that you chose a time and date when they could participate.

❹ Group Size

It takes three to form a group, but five to seven members is a good number for small group discussions, such as book clubs and the like. Small groups can get by with fewer formal rules.

A large group with a complex task needs more rules to keep the discussion on track and to maintain order among members. A large group may adopt a more formal procedure than a smaller group, such as someone to take notes and even to moderate (or lead) the meeting.

Whose Role?

GOAL

The goal of this activity is to recognize problem behaviors in groups.

TASKS

1. Form groups of five or six.
2. One person from each group leaves the room.
3. Each group remaining chooses a group discussion situation to role-play. The group can be leaderless, with no one wanting to take control. It can be a group with many leaders, with no one wanting to give up control. Group members can be confused as to their activity. The group can be totally uninterested in the activity.
4. When the group has chosen a role to act out, the other member returns.
5. The absent member observes the group in action and tries to figure out what the group's problem is.

OUTCOMES

How did it feel being in a group that was leaderless? in a group with too many leaders? in a group that was confused? in a group that wasn't interested in the activity?

Task and Maintenance Roles

Groups have two roles: task roles and maintenance roles. **Task roles** are actions that concern a group's stated business and help the group to complete its tasks or to reach its goals. **Maintenance roles** help to maintain the relationships among group members.

Whether a group succeeds or fails depends upon how well its members accomplish task and maintenance roles. Groups function best when all members are willing to take part in the task and maintenance functions.

Group members—especially the discussion leader and the secretary—perform many of the task roles but may lock into specific ones. Locking into specific roles may not be best for the group. Everyone should have an overview of the whole group's functions and be ready to pitch in where needed.

Task Roles

Task roles help the group focus on reaching its goal. These major roles facilitate getting the group's work done. Though the **five** roles are listed separately below, they all are functions that typically occur during group discussions.

❶ Moderating

Moderating means leading a discussion and making sure that everyone has a chance to contribute. This task involves asking those who have been quiet to share, putting more aggressive group members on hold, and helping other members stick to the agenda rather than going off on tangents.

❷ Analyzing

Analyzing means observing the discussion and keeping track of its order. This role involves recognizing that the group has skipped a task or wandered off course.

❸ Summarizing

Summarizing means pulling together the ideas shared up to that point as well as restating problems, suggestions, and conclusions. The person in this role has a list of questions for the group to address that should encourage them to contribute ideas, facts, and opinions.

❹ Consensus-taking

Consensus-taking means testing to see whether the group has reached agreement on an issue. Sometimes members continue to talk unnecessarily, not realizing that they've all been saying the same things for some time.

❺ Public Relating

Someone needs to deal with others outside the group, informing them of the group's activities and plans. Be prepared to be the one to report the group's findings or even carry out the solution in the end.

In many ways, groups function better if all of their members have leadership skills. To be effective group members, participants need to prepare for meetings, take an active role, listen critically and carefully, respect the opinions and feelings of others, and use appropriate tones of voice.

The best group members commit themselves to furthering the goals of the group. Outside of meetings, they spend time thinking about issues and gathering information that might help the group. In group meetings, they share what they know, ask questions about anything that isn't clear, and listen carefully to others, showing respect for their contributions.

Task Messages

People in groups constantly exchange messages. Typically, group discussions are a mix of task messages and maintenance messages. **Task messages** are those that help the group reach a decision or a goal. The **six** task messages are initiating, idea generating, information seeking, information giving, clarifying, and evaluating.

❶ Initiating

Initiating messages suggest a group task or goal, a direction for the discussion, or ideas for the group to work on.

❷ Idea Generating

Idea generating messages contribute ideas to the discussion. Idea generating requires keeping an open mind and an open imagination. Looking at a problem from a variety of angles can help free up the creativity of the group.

❸ Information Seeking

Information seeking messages ask fellow group members for information, ideas, and suggestions. Some ask questions to clarify facts that have been presented. Though everyone should play a role in seeking information, often only a few group members really do their homework.

❹ Information Giving

Information giving messages offer facts, opinions, beliefs, and suggestions, whether or not anyone asks for them. An effective communicator offers information at an appropriate time and is careful not to stray from the subject.

❺ Clarifying

Clarifying messages reword something under discussion. Some people are good at asking questions to clear up or define terms that seem confusing. They clarify the way someone has worded a suggestion or how new information fits with the stated goal.

❻ Evaluating

Evaluating messages judge the group's decisions, question its logic or practicality, and provide feedback, both negative and positive.

Practicing Task Messages

GOAL

The goal of this activity is to practice using task messages.

TASKS

1. Form groups of three to five.

2. Choose a problem to solve as a group. Topics might include organizing a fundraiser, doing volunteer work in the community or around the school, or having a class party.

3. Work on solving the problem, but systematically use task messages listed in this chapter.

   * Initiate the direction.
   * Generate ideas.
   * Ask questions.
   * Give facts or information.
   * Clarify statements or suggestions.
   * Judge or evaluate suggestions.

4. List examples of task messages used during your discussion.

OUTCOMES

Were some of the task messages more crucial than others? If so, which ones? Why do you think this was so?

Community Activist

In Bert Greenwood's suburban neighborhood, Wiltondale, a community association meets monthly to discuss ways to fight commercialization on York Road, one of two increasingly busy streets bordering Wiltondale. The group also plans holiday events, operates a neighborhood swimming pool, and oversees maintenance of community property. It opposes commercialization because it brings more traffic, noise, unattractive structures, and potential crime targets to the area.

Bert believes that if there were no problems to solve, attendance at his community association meeting would drop off. "Crises really attract people to meetings," he observes.

Recently, Wiltondale joined with other communities to oppose the plan of the hospital that's a block off York Road. The hospital wanted to replace a 6-foot-high sign with a 20-foot-high sign. The neighborhood groups set a meeting with the hospital. Bert represented Wiltondale, and two neighboring communities also sent representatives. But Bert said that there was no cohesion in their group; each representative seemed to have a separate agenda. "The group wasn't united. We lost," Bert says. He feels that they should have conferred before the hospital meeting, to form a united front.

Bert has been active in a variety of groups and has been the moderator of several of them. He has this advice about handling groups. "You've always got to define the issues. They can become fogged and cloudy. Also, if you're going to make a point, you need to listen to what's been said. When there's repetition, the leader has to say, 'Let's not continue to beat that horse.'"

Maintenance Roles

Maintenance roles deal with the interpersonal relationships within the group that help to build the group. Although the group has business to attend to, it is made up of people whose personalities and feelings often conflict. Sensitivity to individuals' needs helps to keep the group together and keep participants interested in coming.

Maintenance Messages

Maintenance messages are those that help keep harmony in the group. **Seven** maintenance messages include:

❶ Active Listening

Active listening messages offer feedback and support to fellow group members. These messages praise members when they contribute a great idea or when they've really done their homework.

❷ Nurturing

Nurturing messages offer encouragement and comfort to group members when needed. Be aware of times when group members need a break, a snack, a stretch, or even a joke. Nurturing can't be studied or approached consciously, since it comes from being sensitive to people around you.

❸ Harmonizing

Harmonizing messages attempt to reduce tension and reconcile any misunderstandings that come up. Harmonizers encourage fellow group members to be objective and not take things personally. Disagreeing with someone's opinion is not necessarily rejecting the person, only expressing another point of view.

❹ Gatekeeping

Gatekeeping messages keep the channels of communication open among all the members. Notice when someone wants to speak but can't seem to interrupt, or when someone hasn't yet contributed anything.

❺ Compromising

Compromising messages are those in which members modify their positions to find a solution that works for all. When conflicts arise, there often are ways to bring together two seemingly opposite positions.

❻ Participating

Participating messages encourage group members to be actively involved. Some members will go along with others and passively accept their ideas. Such behavior is more appropriate to an audience than to group members.

❼ Standard Setting and Testing

Standard-setting and testing messages remind the group of its existing procedures and suggest norms that the group may want to adopt. These kinds of messages remind the group of its purpose and help keep the group on task.

Checklist

How to Promote Healthy Group Dynamics

✓ Select a site appropriate to the group's purpose.

✓ Arrange seating to encourage a particular mood.

✓ Be prepared to incorporate discussion rules in a large group.

✓ Be aware of the roles that facilitate smooth group functioning.

✓ Help the group by communicating task messages when needed.

✓ Avoid individual agendas that harm a group's common purpose.

✓ Watch out for the negative influence of cliques.

Wrap-up

For whatever reason a group forms, its members always share a common purpose. Group structures vary depending on the group's purpose, size, and membership. Some groups have a formal structure whereas others are relaxed. Group members carry out certain roles that help the group stay together and achieve its goals. When members are aware of what helps keep a group functioning smoothly, they can perform the necessary tasks. Group members who allow their individual goals to preside over collective goals can hinder their groups. Effective interpersonal skills are also vital skills for group members.

Speech

clique—exclusive subgroup whose members are cohesive.

cohesiveness—sharing a common goal.

compromising—modifying one's position.

consensus-taking—checking to see whether members are in agreement.

formal group—highly organized group with set procedural rules.

gatekeeping—encouraging participation of all members, promoting sharing.

group norms—standards of interacting in a group.

group roles—patterns of communication that define one's place in a group.

harmonizing—reducing group tension, reconciling disagreements, exploring differences.

idea generating—task message that contributes ideas to the discussion.

informal group—casual, unstructured group.

initiating—getting the discussion started.

maintenance roles—functions that help maintain relationships among group members.

moderating—leading a discussion and keeping participants on the subject.

nurturing—task message that encourages and comforts.

participating—task message that encourages involvement.

standard setting and testing—determining whether the group is satisfied with the procedure and reminding the group of the rules.

subgroup—smaller unit within a group.

task messages—messages that help a group reach a decision or goal.

task roles—functions that concern the group's stated business and help the group to complete its tasks or to reach its goals.

CHAPTER 7

Group Discussions

In this chapter, you will consider:

- **What kinds of group discussions do you engage in?**
- **What are the purposes of these various groups?**
- **How effectively do the groups you know achieve their goals?**
- **How well do you speak or listen in the groups you're in and how can you make improvements?**
- **What are some of the common problems in group discussions?**

When three or more people gather to discuss ways to solve a problem or answer a question, they engage in group discussion. All of the interpersonal communication skills of speaking and listening are necessary for effective group discussions. In this chapter, you'll discover the purposes and types of group discussions, the work life cycle of groups, and a five-step model of problem solving that can make groups more efficient. You'll also learn a set of guidelines for effective speaking and listening in groups. You'll then find out about various outcomes of group discussions, discussion formats, and alternative decision-making techniques, such as brainstorming and parliamentary procedure.

Types of Group Discussions

People gather in groups for a variety of reasons—to plan events, to solve neighborhood or city problems, to learn from each other. Individuals in groups don't always see problems in the same way. But, by joining a group, they indicate their willingness to reach a group solution rather than an individual one. This point should always be kept in mind as groups work through their business.

Group Purposes

Group discussions occur for a variety of reasons. Groups form for **two** major purposes: decision making and enlightenment.

❶ Decision Making

Most of the time, groups form to make decisions. When the French social critic Alexis de Tocqueville visited the young United States in the 18th century, he noted that Americans readily formed groups to solve problems. This still is characteristic of the United States. Groups spring up all over the country to solve community problems.

Decision making is a dynamic process. Groups approach the task in a number of ways, depending on the type of group, its size, and the nature of the problem.

❷ Enlightenment

Another reason that groups form is to gain information. Examples of **enlightenment** groups are the League of Women Voters, who come together to learn about political issues; and book discussion groups, where all members read a book and discuss it.

Nature of the Group

Groups can be closed to outsiders, as when students from the same class gather to study for a test. Or they can be public, as when a town meeting is convened to discuss an important social issue.

Closed Groups

When members of a group are communicating among themselves, they're engaged in a **closed group** discussion. Clubs—such as fraternities and sororities—and civic organizations—such as the Lions Club and Rotary Club—are examples of closed groups. Sometimes closed groups employ a selection process in which members are interviewed and, if accepted, are initiated into the ways of the group.

Public Discussion Groups

Public **forums** are discussion groups open to anyone interested in attending. Government bodies often organize them, but so can groups of concerned citizens or individual citizens who are looking for a solution to a common problem. For example, discussions about a new traffic pattern, pollution of a local stream, or neighborhood crime watch committees are open to anyone. Their goals are to find ways to address specific problems.

Problem-Solving Groups

A group is a dynamic entity that has an existence of its own apart from each individual member. When a group forms to discuss a specific problem, it journeys through a life cycle, from infancy to maturity, like a living organism.

1. FORMING

2. STORMING

3. NORMING

4. PERFORMING

Group Work Life Cycle

Groups typically go through a **four-stage** life cycle. The stages are called forming, storming, norming, and performing.

❶ Forming Stage

<u>Forming</u> is the beginning stage, when members come together. Members all listen to each other as they introduce themselves, tell why they have joined the group, and share what they think that the group will accomplish.

At this forming stage, all members focus on what they have in common. If group members recognize that they have common goals, things run smoothly. If there's little compatibility, the group can become tense.

Group members also meet each other as individuals. They determine which members want to take on leadership roles to guide the group along. If there's no leader in the beginning, the group will designate one. Members also try to figure out what one another's roles will be.

❷ Storming Stage

When the group has found enough similarity among goals and personalities, it can then move into the adolescent **storming** stage. At this stage, members assert their individuality. Some try to influence the rest of the group, persuade others, or take control. Others may wonder whether they belong in the group at all. Sometimes the leadership is challenged as various members vie for control over the group.

The group tries to stay focused, decide on rules for decision making, and achieve some sense of order.

❸ Norming Stage

As the group starts to resolve internal conflicts and settle on the procedures it will use to reach goals, it calms down and normalizes. In this **norming** stage, the group becomes cohesive and achieves a certain identity. Its rules or standards for appropriate behavior—its **group norms**—become established. Members know the limits and rules. Members learn to work together and trust one another. They share leadership functions.

Group norms can give groups distinctive characteristics that collectively are known as the **group culture.** Norms apply to the individuals in the group and the group as a whole. Group norms are easier for members to accept when the group itself and the views of its other members are important to them.

❹ Performing Stage

At this final stage, group members feel as if they are part of a team. They begin to focus on the task. They know each other well enough that they can predict each other's responses. They feel united and are able to work together effectively. Their energy is focused on solving the problem. Trust and sometimes even affection develop among members as the group works out details during the **performing** stage.

Ineffective Groups

Sometimes strong cohesiveness in a group and interpersonal attraction among members can lead the group too far. The group can develop a sense of solidarity that demands absolute agreement from all its members and prevents any kind of dissension.

In such groups, the members fail to think critically. They insulate themselves from outside reality. They become complacent and rationalize their behavior, convinced of their rightness. They stereotype outsiders and react to them without reflecting. They share the illusion that all are unanimously agreed. Some fringe cults, secret societies, and radical political movements take on these characteristics.

A Five-Step Model of Problem Solving

Because problem solving is such a common group task and the focus of many group discussions, various problem-solving methods have been identified as effective for groups to follow. When group members are aware of the steps involved in problem solving, they can move smoothly through each step and recognize when each has been accomplished.

Groups that are problem solving naturally follow these steps. However, when they follow a **five-step model of problem solving** or another conscious method, their discus-

sions can run more smoothly. Knowing the proper sequence for solving a problem or reaching a decision can help to keep group members on track and focused.

This model suggests **five** steps for solving problems.

❶ Identify the Problem

The first step in having a successful discussion is to define the problem and limit its focus. A topic should interest several group members and should be significant to the task. Group discussions usually take time, so the topic should be manageable in the time allotted.

The group should state the problem in clear and concise language. Some members may prefer to phrase the topic as a question. Since discussions can easily get off track or get hazy, a clear statement of the problem at the beginning can prevent group members from talking about entirely different issues.

❷ Analyze the Problem

Members of decision-making groups should come prepared. They should do their homework and bring along with them as many facts as possible. The group needs to uncover the facts and understand the history, causes, and state of the current situation. Is the problem a question of fact, value, or policy?

* *Questions of fact* involve analysis of a situation. For example, is the river actually polluted? Members decide whether they need to find a solution.
* *Questions of value* deal with the worth of a situation, whether something is desirable or not, and issues of right or wrong. For example, should there be a dress code in the high school? To find a solution, members depend on facts as well as opinions.
* *Questions of policy* examine change related to the course of action and what role the group should take. For example, should the government sell a 5,000-acre parcel of national forest land to a logging company?

❸ Set Criteria for a Solution

The group next decides what would make a solution workable. What standards will the group set? What does the group consider to be an effective, valuable, or useful solution?

❹ Develop Solutions

Solutions can be generated in a number of ways. Members may suggest ideas and discuss them one by one. Or members can **brainstorm**—generate many ideas in a free-form format, without making any value judgments. Once generated, the ideas can be tackled individually or discussed afterward.

❺ Select a Solution

In selecting a solution, there is no single "right" answer. Group members evaluate ideas and solutions based on how appropriate or adequate each is for the problem. They seek the solution that fits the best, analyzing possibilities to determine their strengths and weaknesses as well as their adherence to the committee's criteria.

Some solutions won't work, aren't practical, or aren't fair. Some don't meet the criteria that the group has set out. For example, a solution may be too costly. Members choose the best solution, not the "right" one. Consensus is the best way to choose.

Once it has selected the solution, the group must find a way to accomplish what's been decided. It must also decide who will carry out the solution, which sometimes determines what the solution will be.

Club Meeting

Notice how the **moderator** in this group conversation tries to keep things coherent. She summarizes some of the random statements that are tossed out.

Moderator: How many topics do you want to include in our discussion?

Taniya: The three that were in the e-mail you sent.

Moderator: Any more?

Percy: Yes. I'm glad that I see these same faces at our meeting, but what about those who aren't here? How can we get them to participate?

Moderator: OK, participation. That's four topics. Maria, then Ruben.

Maria: How many are interested in building a center?

Ruben: Outreach within our community—why do people leave and how to bring them back?

Moderator: That's two more topics. Which do you want to start with?

Taniya: One more. If the committee is planning an activity for several months, why do we wait until three or four days before the event to get the word out? And if the rest of you do get the notice in time, why don't you go and support the activity?

Moderator: If I can paraphrase, you're urging better participation in the organization. OK. Where should we start?

ACTIVITY

Practice Problem Solving

GOAL

The goal of this activity is to provide experience in following the five-step model of problem solving.

TASKS

1. Form groups of five.

2. Within each group, select a topic to discuss. As a result of this discussion, the group should plan to take some action. Sample topics: What community services can we perform? How can we educate students about drunk driving? How can we solve the parking problem at school?

3. Follow the five-step model of problem solving.

4. When finished, meet as a class and discuss the process. Did the process help the groups to find a solution? What were common difficulties, if any?

OUTCOMES

Were there ways in which the five-step model hindered the groups? Do you think that the same process would work for two people trying to solve a problem?

Member Communication

Not everything in a group discussion pertains to the subject at hand; some of what occurs simply keeps the group and the discussion alive and well. Group members take on behaviors they choose or that are designated for them.

Speaker and Listener Responsibilities

The interpersonal communication responsibilities of speakers and listeners don't change in a group. In fact, they are even more important. All interpersonal skills are useful in group discussions.

Member Skills

Some people are apprehensive when speaking in groups. How comfortable you feel will be influenced by how familiar you are with other members and how much you feel a part of the group.

When you're speaking in a group, use these speaking skills:

* *Be prepared.* Problem solving slows down when members don't know the background facts.
* *Be objective.* Keep your emotions in check.
* *Know the points you wish to make.* Those who ramble waste their time and that of others.
* *Manage conflict.* Offer positive feedback and look for areas of agreement.
* *Share your ideas thoughtfully.* Take time and contribute as much as you can.
* *Remember, this is a group effort,* not an individual one.
* *Speak respectfully to everyone.*
* *Don't dominate the discussion.*

When you're listening in a group, your responsibilities are to:

* *Be an active listener.* Ask questions to clarify what someone else is saying.
* *Support others.* Encourage them to contribute.
* *Avoid barriers.*
* *Think about what you're hearing.* How are ideas connected?
* *Give nonverbal feedback.*

A Semester at Sea

Julie Badiee taught art history during a Semester at Sea program. About 650 American college students spent a semester on a ship, traveling to Japan, Hong Kong, China, Vietnam, Malaysia, India, Israel, Turkey, Italy, Morocco, and back to Florida. Teachers with expertise in particular areas introduced the students to each country as they approached it.

Julie relates that, as the ship approached the port of Haifa, Israel, a conflict emerged among the teachers. In Israel, Arab Palestinians and Jews have been fighting for years. Teachers in the group sympathized with different sides. The specialists in Judaic studies and in Islamic studies had opposite points of view. They finally reached a compromise and decided to grant equal time to the Islamic and Judaic studies.

However, the students experienced the same conflicts, and they didn't know about the equal time plan. As Julie tells it, "The first teacher started teaching about Judaism, and then discussed the Holocaust, showing a harrowing part of the movie *Schindler's List.* As he explained how the Jews were killed in Germany and why they needed a nation of their own, an Arab girl stood up and started screaming, 'Why aren't you talking about what the Israelis are doing to the Palestinians?'" Julie says that the teacher then explained the agenda, which calmed the students.

Julie continues, "When I taught about art and architecture in Israel, I dealt with the three major religions and their major monuments and significance. Then I asked that we pray that some solution be found and at the end say Amen, Amin, and Ameen." These words are the Christian, Jewish, and Moslem way of ending prayers, respectively.

The teachers met again and agreed to hold extra meetings so that students could speak more about the issues.

Outcomes of Group Discussions

Groups reach their decisions in a few different ways. When a group meets to solve a problem, it succeeds when a decision is reached. Groups that gather for enlightenment on a topic succeed when everyone learns new information from one another, and when they find fresh ways of viewing a situation because of the exchange of ideas.

Group discussions can result in **four** types of outcomes.

❶ Decisions by Decree

Sometimes a group leader dictates the decision, thereby making a **decision by decree.** The leader listens to the discussion and then reaches his or her own decision. This approach to decision making lowers the morale of the group. If members have no say in the final outcome, they'll tend not to work very hard for the committee.

❷ Decisions by Consensus

The ideal outcome is a **decision by consensus,** which occurs when all members agree unanimously. It's possible to help this type of decision along by carefully wording the problem question so that all members agree on a solution.

False consensus occurs when people reach an agreement, but they may not all be agreeing to the same thing. This can happen when a question is worded so ambiguously or vaguely that not everyone interprets it the same way.

❸ Decisions by Compromise

When members contribute something to the solution, but give up other things, they reach a **decision by compromise.** Group members need to focus on the goal of problem solving rather than thinking about who wins and who loses.

❹ Decisions by Majority Vote

When groups don't seem to agree, they take a vote. Before voting, someone should clearly state what the members are voting on. Because voting means that some people feel that their side has lost, voting isn't always the preferred way to reach a decision.

When more than half of the members favor a decision and vote for it, a **decision by majority vote** becomes the solution of the group.

Common Discussion Formats

There are **five** commonly used discussion formats, appropriate to different goals, tasks, and topics.

❶ Committees

A <u>committee</u> is usually a subgroup of a larger group and is formed to study a specific task. Sometimes committee members report on a specific area of the task. Other times, they do general business or talk about proposals. Sometimes the entire group discusses some committee responsibilities.

❷ Roundtable Discussions

A <u>roundtable discussion</u> is informal. Group members sit in a circle. They share information or solve problems informally, without a formal pattern determining who speaks when. There may be a moderator.

❸ Panel Discussions

In a <u>panel discussion,</u> a subject is explored by four to eight group members in front of an audience. Speakers are seated so that the audience can see them all. The panel makes statements, asks questions, and comments on what others have said.

Usually a chairperson moderates the discussion by introducing the speakers, leading the discussion, calling on speakers during the discussion, and summarizing main ideas. The panel tries to reach some agreement on its ideas before the end. Panel members need to be prepared and must be well informed about their subject areas.

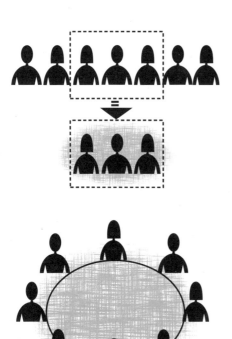

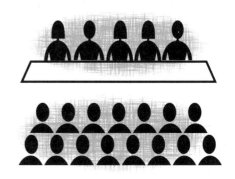

❹ Symposiums

A **symposium** is a discussion during which members give short speeches to the audience. It is similar to a panel discussion but is more formal. A symposium is a good format when you wish several experts to present views to an audience. Each presenter gives a speech with a different point of view on the subject under discussion.

In a symposium, speakers normally don't talk with each other unless there's a question-and-answer period after each speech. As in a panel, the leader introduces the symposium members and the topic. He or she also closes the symposium by summarizing the speeches.

❺ Forums

During **panel forums** or **symposium forums,** audience members interact with members in panel discussions or symposiums. In these formats, the audience can ask questions of people on the panel or symposium. Sometimes, after speakers are finished, the audience forms discussion, or buzz, groups. These continue to discuss the ideas presented by the speakers and try to decide on some solution to the problem.

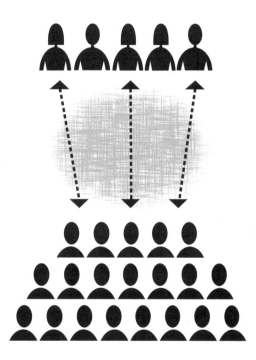

Alternative Group Decision-Making Techniques

Alternative group decision-making techniques include brainstorming, parliamentary procedure, the nominal group technique, and consultation.

Brainstorming

Brainstorming is often used in business as a technique to generate a large number of ideas in a brief time. It involves three or more people who come together to create a list of ideas on a specific topic. In a brainstorming session, people are told to be creative and to propose anything that comes to mind. People rapidly throw out ideas, without stopping to question or evaluate each one. One group member records the ideas. After the session, the group can go back and consider the ideas one by one.

Brainstorming

GOAL

The goal of this activity is to explore the alternative group decision-making technique of brainstorming.

TASKS

1. Form groups of five.

2. Each group selects a topic, a problem for which the group must find a solution. Possible topics: How can we help students in this school get jobs? What going-away gift shall we get for our popular gym teacher? How can we publicize the health risks of smoking? Or groups can choose their own topics.

3. Each group brainstorms about the chosen topic, with one student writing down all of the ideas. Note that no one should judge another person's ideas. The objective is to produce as many original and creative ideas as possible.

4. Meet as a class and discuss the process. Was this an effective technique for generating ideas? What were some of the common drawbacks? What helped to make brainstorming successful?

OUTCOMES

Did anyone give negative feedback? Did anyone hesitate to contribute ideas? How did your ability to find a solution compare with your more methodical problem-solving method?

Parliamentary Procedure

Parliamentary procedure is a set of procedures for conducting fair and orderly meetings. These rules originated in England's Parliament, which was founded in the 13th century. Now used by groups ranging from student governments to the U.S. Congress, parliamentary procedure helps leaders to run meetings in a way that is orderly, fair, democratic, and efficient.

Since there are several published sources on parliamentary procedure, any group using this system should adopt a standard text to use as a reference. One of the best known sources is *Robert's Rules of Order,* originally written in 1876 by Henry M. Robert, a U.S. Army general, and now updated as *Robert's Rules of Order, Newly Revised.*

Here are some of the basic principles of parliamentary procedure:

* A fair and impartial president or Chair runs the meetings.
* A **quorum,** or a certain percentage of the membership, must be present for a group to make valid decisions. This helps prevent minority rule.
* No member can speak unless the Chair recognizes him or her. A member can speak only once on a question if others haven't yet spoken.
* The body addresses only one issue at a time.
* The group holds open discussions, in which every member's opinion is respected and treated equally.

* Each member has a single vote and all votes have equal value.
* The majority rules.

Parliamentary procedure provides an efficient and democratic way for a group to consider issues and take action. The process includes **four** steps: a motion, a second to the motion, the discussion, and the vote.

1. **The motion.** Anyone wishing to propose an action to the group may make a statement called a **motion** at an appropriate point in the agenda. After being recognized by the Chair, a member says, "I make a motion that...." The motion should be short and its wording should be specific.

2. **The second.** In many groups, a second is needed ("I second the motion") before the motion can be discussed by the group. This ensures that at least two people are interested in a discussion of this motion. Once a motion is made, secondary motions may be made.

3. **Discussion.** After a motion has been seconded, members discuss the issue, respectfully taking turns as recognized by the Chair. When discussion is finished and there are no secondary motions or requests to speak, the Chair repeats the motion, and then asks for the final time, "Is there any further discussion?"

4. **The vote.** If not, the Chair calls for a vote, then announces the result.

Robert's Rules of Order

Robert's Rules of Order is an official and respected handbook for parliamentary procedure. *Robert's Rules of Order* lists the following order of business:

* Agenda
* Reading of minutes
* Reports of officers
* Committee reports
* Old business
* New business

Nominal Group Technique

Nominal group technique is meant to reduce problems of group dynamics that can arise. Among these problems are long-winded discussions and the efforts of various members to dominate the proceedings. The nominal group technique avoids these problems by using minimal discussion.

The technique begins as the problem is clarified. Each member writes down a personal list of possible solutions to a stated problem. Then each person selects only one idea from his or her list and contributes this to the group. The ideas that are contributed are written so that all may see them.

All members rank the ideas in order of preference. The rankings are combined in a group ranking. The solution that gets the highest ranking becomes the group's solution.

The drawback of this technique is that it doesn't allow for in-depth discussion of any of the ideas. It also doesn't spend any time defining the problem.

Consultation

Consultation is a technique in which group members try to achieve unity in the process of reaching a decision. One of the principles is that there can be no ownership of ideas. Any idea that anyone generates immediately becomes property of the group.

As soon as ownership of ideas is eliminated, group members don't feel attached to their own ideas. If someone else dislikes the idea, the person who gave it doesn't feel criticized or minimized in any way. This approach to ideas keeps people from promoting a personal agenda.

Although each person should speak his or her mind on a subject, he or she must refrain from personal criticism and attack. The goal is that all be allowed to say freely what they think to find the best solution and reach a consensus.

A chairperson is designated to lead the discussion but has no other authority. If consultation is done correctly, group members will not allow anyone to dominate the discussion or push a personal agenda.

A Personal Group Checklist

✓ Understand the purpose of your group.

✓ Understand the norms of your group.

✓ Learn the five-step model of problem solving.

✓ Practice interpersonal communication skills as a speaker and listener in group discussions.

✓ Use alternative problem-solving methods when appropriate.

Evaluation

GOAL

The goal of this activity is to observe the amount of cooperation in your group.

TASKS

1. Form groups of five.

2. Each group chooses a topic and discusses it, following the problem-solving steps listed on pages 112-113. Possible topics include a theme for a float in the Homecoming Parade; how to publicize a disaster relief food drive; how to eliminate cliques at this school.

3. As your group goes through its problem-solving steps, take note of the group dynamics. What behavior helps the discussion? What behavior hurts or hinders the discussion?

4. When the discussion is over, members of the group write lists to evaluate the group and themselves:

   * Include strengths, weaknesses, and constructive criticism for each group member.

   * In analyzing the quality of the group's discussion, answer these questions: Was the goal clearly stated as question of fact, value, or policy? Was there an outline for the discussion? Were conclusions drawn that were based on the information in the discussion? Was the decision defensible?

   * In analyzing your own participation, ask yourself: Am I prepared? Am I objective? Do I ask questions? Do I stay on track? Do I evaluate the information presented? Am I respectful? Do I cooperate? Do I enunciate? Can I help manage conflict?

5. Compare lists with those of others in the group. Did group members agree about most points?

OUTCOMES

What were the common pitfalls for the groups? For individual members? How honest do you feel the members' criticisms were?

Evaluation

To improve discussion skills, members should take advantage of objective evaluation and criticism. One way to evaluate how a group is working is to observe what each individual group member is doing. Another way is to analyze the discussion process. You can keep a record of who does the talking.

Keep track of your discussion by making a diagram of it, as in the picture below. In your diagram, draw boxes to represent each of the members involved in the discussion. Put their initials in the appropriate boxes. Each time one speaks to another, mark the lines that connects the boxes with their initials.

Wrap-up

Groups form for different purposes, such as decision making or enlightenment. Groups can be closed to outsiders or open to anyone. All groups follow a natural life cycle and can become efficient and methodical at problem solving. Whether you're a speaker or a listener, it's important to practice communication skills that will help the group to run well and meet its goals. Regardless of the decisions your group reaches and its formats or methods, the group will be only as effective as its individual members allow it to be.

Knowing that groups follow predictable patterns of forming and maturing can keep you from feeling anxious as the group goes through its processes. Use of the orderly procedures suggested in this chapter can help your group stay on task and accomplish its goals.

brainstorm—generate large numbers of problem-solving ideas in a brief time period.

closed group—group in which members communicate only among themselves.

committee—subgroup formed to study a specific task.

consultation—problem-solving technique that seeks unity and consensus by eliminating ownership of ideas.

decision by compromise—decision that settles a discussion by making mutual concessions.

decision by consensus—decision made when group members agree on a solution without taking a vote.

decision by decree—decision dictated by the group leader.

decision by majority vote—decision in which more than half of group members agree.

enlightenment—type of group that gathers to gain information.

false consensus—situation in which group members agree on a poorly worded solution and may not have the same thing in mind.

five-step model of problem solving—identify the problem, analyze the problem, set criteria for a solution, develop solutions, and select a solution.

forming—beginning stage of a group's life cycle during which members first meet each other.

forums—form of discussion during which audience members interact with speakers.

group culture—behavioral and attitudinal characteristics that distinguish the group.

group norms—rules or standards for appropriate behaviors acceptable to a group.

moderator—person who keeps the discussion moving in an orderly way.

motion—formal recommendation for a proposed action.

nominal group technique—problem-solving technique that involves minimal discussion and secret voting.

norming—stage in a group's life cycle when the group becomes cohesive and achieves a certain identity.

panel discussion—form of discussion during which a subject is explored by four to eight group members before an audience.

panel forum—form of discussion in which audience members interact with speakers in a panel.

parliamentary procedure—formal set of rules for conducting a meeting.

performing—final stage in a group's life cycle in which members feel that they are a team and focus on a task.

quorum—number of group members needed for a meeting to count as valid.

roundtable discussion—informal discussion that doesn't follow a procedure.

storming—early stage of a group's life cycle during which members sort out each other's tasks.

symposium—form of discussion during which several experts present information to an audience.

symposium forum—form of discussion in which audience members interact with speakers in a symposium.

CHAPTER 8

Leadership and Conflict

In this chapter, you will consider:

- **What do you think are the qualities of a leader?**
- **Whom do you consider a leader in your school, among your friends, and in your community?**
- **What skills do you expect a good leader to have?**
- **What are the qualities of a good team member?**
- **What do you think are the main ways to resolve conflicts?**

In this chapter, you'll find what it takes to be an effective leader and team member. Knowing these skills will help you in any profession. It is easy to be a team leader or a team member when everyone is in agreement. But, in the world of work, as well as in your family or community, knowing how to resolve conflicts will make you a true leader and a valued member of a group. You can practice leadership and team skills in many ways—at home, at school, in your community, and in any part-time job you may have.

How Leaders Are Made

The great American business leader Henry Ford once quipped, "The question 'Who ought to be boss?' is like asking 'Who ought to be the tenor in the quartet?' Obviously the man who can sing tenor."

In his play *Twelfth Night*, William Shakespeare observed, "Some are born great, some achieve greatness, and some have greatness thrust upon them."

Every group effort—whether at home, at school, or at work—needs an effective leader and strong team support. Where do leaders come from? Henry Ford seemed to think that all leaders are born. We all can think of many "born leaders." Examples might be Dr. Martin Luther King, Jr., Mahatma Gandhi, and Mother Teresa of Calcutta.

Shakespeare took a wider view. He saw that not all leaders are born leaders. Some simply have learned the skills of leadership. Some have been forced into leadership roles. You see examples of this every day. Your volunteer soccer coach may have a knack for getting the best out of every player. Your mother or your uncle may have taken over in a crisis, then successfully rebuilt your family's business. Leadership skills can be acquired.

Leaders and Team Members

We often hear the terms *leader* and *follower,* but these words can create problems. To many people, the leader is the "boss," and all followers are weak and unoriginal.

To avoid these unfair judgments, some businesses call their leaders *coordinators, facilitators, team captains,* and *guides.* Followers are referred to as *the team, group, colleagues,* and *associates.* The Disney Stores use the unique name of "cast members" for their employees. What might be achieved by this choice of words?

Families, schools, businesses, and communities need both leaders and team members. In the 1990s, the Chicago Bulls basketball team won six national titles. If you asked them why, they'd point to powerful leaders such as Michael Jordan and Scottie Pippin but also to the strong roster of team players who backed them up.

Think about the groups to which you now belong. What is your role in each group? What do you think that leaders and team members can accomplish for the group?

Leader or Team Member?

GOAL

The goal of this activity is to help you identify your roles in various groups.

TASKS

1. Look at the list below. What are your roles in each of these groups? Are you primarily a leader or a member of the team? Note your answers on a piece of paper.

   * Math class
   * English class
   * Other class of your choice
   * School club or organization
   * Sports team
   * Church, community, or other group (Scouts, YMCA, Girls or Boys Club)
   * Close friends

   * Family
   * Neighborhood
   * Part-time job

2. Think about your findings. Did your roles in some groups surprise you? If so, how?

3. Choose your three favorite groups. Consider each group separately.

4. What role would you like to play in each group? If you'd like to lead, think about ways that you could begin to exercise leadership. If you'd like to remain a team member, consider how you might contribute more effectively to the group.

OUTCOMES

Did you find ways to improve your contribution to these groups?

Leaders—Appointed, Elected, or Emerged

There are **three** main ways to become the leader of a group, whether in your class or in the world of work. Leaders usually are appointed, elected, or emerged.

1. **Appointed leader.** A person or group of people in charge chooses the leader. In business, managers are hired or promoted by their superiors. At organizations like the Symphony Guild, committee heads are appointed. In history class, your teacher chooses students to lead group discussions or projects.

2. **Elected leader.** A group or team votes for a leader. At your school, students elect class representatives. Union members elect their shop representatives. In the United States, citizens elect local, state, and national officials.

3. **Emerged leader.** A leader forms the group or steps out of the group. In some business firms, the person who suggests the best idea for a project leads the team that carries out the plan. In sports teams and social groups, one person often becomes everybody's choice as leader. Emerged leaders may not have any "real" authority. Even so, others look to them for guidance because of their knowledge, skill, or personality. In business, such leaders may later receive promotions with more responsibility and a pay raise.

Different Types of Leaders

Pros

Appointed Leader
The process is fast.
Supposedly, the best person is chosen.
It satisfies the chooser.
It pleases the chosen person.

Elected Leader
The majority of the group gives its support.
Selection fits the group's personality.
Term of office is limited.
Elected leader wants to be leader.

Emerged Leader
Others recognize "natural" leadership.
Leader is motivated.

Cons

Appointed Leader
The choosing may be unfair.
The team may not like the leader.

Elected Leader
The process may be slow.
Elections can be expensive.
The election may split the group.
Election may not be won on the basis of the issues and candidate's qualifications.

Emerged Leader
Group wants this leader to be in charge.
Leader may just want control.
Leader may be the loudest, rather than the best.

Leadership Qualities and Skills

In the May 1999 issue of *Management Today*, advertising executive Winston Fletcher identified these important leadership skills or traits:

* Initiative
* Consistency
* Consideration
* Vision and the ability to communicate it
* Ability to persuade other people that your vision is the right one
* Ability to take risks
* Ability to take personal responsibility for the outcome

A Leader's Personal Qualities

Initiative, consistency, vision, and ability to take risks and assume responsibility all are personal qualities. It isn't easy to develop these traits. People with well-developed leadership qualities usually also have self-confidence, high self-esteem, and a strong set of personal values.

Leadership qualities cannot be developed without personal introspection. Leaders need to be able to think for themselves and to stand alone. Introspection means thinking about who you are, about what is most important to you, and about the type of person you want to be. It also means analyzing what is going on around you and how you feel about it. This type of thinking helps you to build individuality and a set of unshakable core beliefs, goals, and values to guide your daily behavior.

Many leaders have endured long periods of struggle and introspection. Dr. Martin Luther King, Jr., had to resolve his own questions about anger and violence before he could embrace the philosophy of nonviolence. John F. Kennedy and Franklin Delano Roosevelt both were forced into long periods of isolation because of painful medical problems—Kennedy's broken back and Roosevelt's polio. Both used their time alone to think long and hard about their beliefs and goals.

Can you identify some core values and beliefs that you have right now? Think of a time when making a decision was easier because you had these beliefs or values to guide you.

Sidebar

Leadership in Business

In his book *Seven Miracles of Management*, Alan Downs tells the story of David Packard, founder of Hewlett-Packard. Packard used forgiveness to handle a very costly multimillion dollar mistake made by one of his general managers. When asked whether he planned to fire the manager, Packard replied, "Why should I? I just paid dearly for him to learn a lesson."

Source: Alan Downs, *Seven Miracles of Management*.

Ten Values by Which to Live—and Work

1. Honesty
2. Forgiveness
3. Trust
4. Respect
5. Intelligence
6. Imagination
7. Dedication
8. Responsibility
9. Caring
10. Inspiration

GOAL

The goal of this activity is to identify ways to practice leadership values in various work settings.

TASKS

1. Form groups of two to three students.
2. Within each group, create a list of four places you know of that employ teens.
3. Brainstorm ways that you could solve problems in these workplaces by practicing the leadership values listed above.
4. List the workplaces that you chose and the best ideas that your group generated.
5. Share your conclusions with the class.

OUTCOMES

Reflect on the conclusions of this activity. What kinds of workplace problems did you try to solve? Do you feel that it is possible to solve these problems?

Leaders and Their Team Members

Effective leaders realize that they need the efforts and loyalty of other people to achieve their goals. They listen to their team members, meet their needs, make them feel important and valued, and make sure that their talents are well used.

President Hugo Chávez of Venezuela realized that his constituents wanted personal contact. Every Sunday, President Chávez hosted a two-hour radio program called "Hello, President," inviting phone calls from any Venezuelan who had a problem. Afterward, Chávez met citizens at his palace. After he started these programs, Chávez's approval rating in Venezuela soared to 75 percent.

Other leaders have created great team loyalty by enduring every difficulty that their followers endure. Mother Teresa of Calcutta (1910–1997), the Albanian-born founder of the Missionaries of Charity, lived in poverty and wore a simple sari as she and her nuns cared for the blind, lepers, aged, the disabled, and the dying of India. Alexander the Great (356–323 B.C.), Macedonian conqueror of Asia, slept on the ground with his troops, refused to eat if they lacked food and water, and personally led his army into every battle.

You don't have to be conqueror of the world to exercise good leadership. Another example is Kim Lee. In her new position as an investment counselor, Kim realized that many of her clients would depend upon getting her services over the holidays. As a result, she decided to reschedule her December vacation for a less busy time.

Expectations of Leaders

Typically people want **four** things from their leaders:

1. *Direction.* People want leaders to have a plan and to take initiative. As one country-western song puts it, "If you don't stand for something, you'll fall for anything."

2. *Trust.* To gain trust, a leader must be truthful. People are more likely to trust competent people who behave consistently and can be counted on.

3. *Hope.* People may believe those who are negative and pessimistic, but they want leaders who make them feel optimistic and who bring hope for the future.

4. *Results.* The most eloquent, inspiring words soon lose their appeal if results don't follow. As one CEO said, "You can't go zero for ten in your decisions and expect people to respect and follow you. Short-term successes keep morale up and keep us focused on the long-term goal."

Which of these qualities do you think is most important? Can you think of a person who models these qualities?

Communication in Careers

Hoping for a Promotion

At 35, Davis Johnson managed a food service chain at the Los Angeles International Airport. Davis was well liked and a hard worker. He had a college degree in business and many years of food service experience. Now he was being considered for promotion to a top executive position.

Working at this large international airport, Davis encountered challenging communication problems each day. Many restaurant employees and patrons spoke little or no English. Many diners were stressed from long hours of travel. Davis treated each customer and employee courteously. He remained calm, learned not to take comments personally, and trained his staff to do the same.

Davis Johnson sounds like the ideal manager, but he didn't get the promotion. What happened? As Davis explained, "The letter of regret said it was my communication skills. I made lots of mistakes, both in speaking and writing. I was moving into a top executive position, and I couldn't communicate my ideas well enough in writing or in a meeting."

Davis Johnson didn't give up. He hired a tutor and worked hard to improve his skills. Davis sums up the experience by saying, "Speaking and writing didn't seem that important when I was in school. I just didn't look ahead. As a result, I had to go back and learn the fundamentals. That was a hard lesson, but I'm proud to say I met the challenge."

Leadership and Communication

Leaders must master many communication skills. They need to stay in touch with their team members and persuade other people to support them. In a group situation, if a discussion gets sidetracked, they need to help the group focus on the task. They also need to summarize ideas that have been stated and put them all into perspective. Leaders must be able to communicate their vision and ideas clearly.

Initiative in Action

"Sometimes I wake up in the morning and there's nothing doing, so I decide to make something happen by lunch."
— Hollywood agent Irving Lazar

Leadership at Work

Employers often complain that students are not prepared for the work world when they leave high school. Often they refer not so much to academic skills as to job skills—qualities that students must have to succeed in the working world. Among these are dependability, a good attitude, and leadership.

Consider this example. Margot got a part-time job at the public library. She hated the early morning hours and sometimes showed up late. "Why is 10 or 15 minutes such a big deal?" she once asked her manager. "There's not much to do at that time of day anyhow." Margot was pleasant to the patrons, but she never quite followed the procedure for collecting fine money and would often put it in her pocket to pay

back later. "The library won't miss a little change for a couple days," she explained. "I needed money for lunch." After three weeks of training, a friend told her about a job at a restaurant. Margot just stopped going to her old job at the library.

If you were Margot's job counselor, what specific changes in attitude and behavior would you recommend to her?

Sidebar

www.achievement.org

Imagine sitting in on a conversation with Donna Shirley of the Mars Exploration Program, entertainment executive George Lucas, civil rights pioneer Rosa Parks, and Nobel Prize recipient Linus Pauling. You can do just that when you visit the American Academy of Achievement's Web site on the Internet.

Here you will find inspiration and insight on leadership through the firsthand accounts of many leaders of the last half of the 20th century. You can learn how achievers in the fields of the arts, sports, public service, business, and science managed to achieve their goals. You will also discover the role that qualities such as passion, vision, preparation, courage, perseverance, and integrity played in their work.

Leadership Duties and Roles

A key element of a leader's role is to provide motivation and inspiration. If you're in charge of a group or project, define your ideas, goals, and action plan. How can you present these in an inspiring way? Think about what group members want and need from you and from the project. Start by showing an interest in the members. Get to know them individually. Find out what their talents are, and then get them involved in doing the committee's work. Show your appreciation for their contributions.

Encouraging Cohesiveness

Groups are made up of many diverse individuals. Some may participate eagerly, some may sit in silence, and some may be disruptive. Your job as leader is to mold them into a team. You can accomplish this in many ways. Be equally friendly to and interested in everyone. Handle unruly participants with humor. Encourage quiet people to join the discussions and to work with others. Find ways to encourage friendly relations among team members. For example, try staging a group social event to help everyone bond together.

Leadership in Group Meetings

Along with these general roles, leaders often have to run meetings. Say, for example, that you've just been put in charge of raising funds for the senior trip. You will get all interested students together for a noon meeting. What are your duties and roles as a leader? **Four** of the primary responsibilities are:

❶ Call the Meeting

Meeting date, room, publicity. Set a date, reserve a room, and notify people of the meeting well in advance. The publicity should include the five Ws—Who, What, When, Where, and Why.

Materials and equipment. Find a volunteer to gather all needed materials and equipment: paper, name tags, felt pens, chart paper, an overhead projector, and a handout for all attendees. Gather a few volunteers and think through the meeting in detail.

Agenda. Make an agenda, or written plan, of the meeting. The list of topics to be covered will help move the meeting along. Hand out copies of the agenda to all who come.

❷ Open the Meeting

Get it started. Begin the meeting on time. Welcome those who come, introduce committee members, and make any general announcements. Mention the time limit for this meeting.

Meeting notes. Ask someone to take notes during the meeting, including all suggestions, decision items, and recommendations.

Focus the meeting. Define the purpose of the meeting and why the senior trip is important. Summarize any background information or ask another committee member to do it. Explain any limits on your budget, mileage, or dates and times for the event.

❸ Regulate the Discussion

Ground rules. Review ground rules for the discussion. Ask people to listen politely, to refrain from interrupting others, and to stay on the subject.

Get started. To start the discussion, summarize senior trips for the past five years, how they went, and how students liked them.

Keep it moving. To keep the discussion moving forward, consider your goals. Do you want to hear people's ideas at this meeting or to reach a final decision? If brainstorming ideas is today's goal, allow plenty of time to hear suggestions. The goal in brainstorming is to come up with as many ideas as possible without discussing or debating them. Record all ideas on a whiteboard or chalkboard.

Control the group. In any group, personalities emerge. Someone hogs the conversation. Someone else tends to argue or crack jokes. As the leader, it is up to you to make sure everyone has a chance to speak and to be heard in a fair manner. Stop and review the rules for brainstorming if necessary.

❹ End the Meeting

Vote or summarize. If the meeting's goal is to make a decision, ask for a vote on the ideas presented. If not, summarize the ideas presented in a fair and impartial manner.

Set a date. Establish a time for the next meeting.

Outline the next steps. Ask people to follow up on ideas that require research.

Clean up. Have a group of people ready to help clean up the room and return all equipment.

Leaders Wanted!

Here is a list of situations that call for
leadership. Some situations may call for
good organizational skills, others for inspiration or creativity, and still others for
problem solving or the ability to mobilize
people quickly.

* It's time to plan the annual Outdoor
  Adventure.
* A group of students and teachers from
  France will visit your school as part
  of a Sister City event. You need to plan
  something special to welcome them.
* An oil spill has polluted a stream near
  your school. Birds and other wildlife are
  struggling. Something needs to be done
  quickly to help the wildlife.
* Your favorite spot for dancing is being
  closed because the owner is tired of
  cleaning up graffiti and trash. You and
  your friends do not want this to happen.

GOAL

The goal of this activity is to help you
identify the leadership qualities and actions
needed to help to solve these problems.

TASKS

1. Form groups of three to four students.
2. In each group, choose one of the situations listed above.
3. Discuss and then list actions that could
   be taken and leadership qualities that
   would be required to solve that problem.
4. List potential problems that might arise
   in meeting the goal. How would a good
   leader meet these challenges?
5. Outline an action plan that the leader
   could use to lead a group to a successful
   outcome.
6. Report your results to the class.

OUTCOMES

Did you find that the problem was easy
or difficult to solve? Do you feel more
confident about leading a group project as
a result of doing this exercise?

Being a Team Member

The world needs both leaders and followers. Our social structure depends upon it. Schools, workplaces, and families all have leaders and team members who help work toward common goals. Democracies have elected leaders and citizens who both follow and question them. A nation filled with millions of leaders would not function well.

In the world of work, corporations seek out employees who possess strong team skills. It is easy to train a new employee to use specific software programs or company procedures. It is much more difficult to teach people to work effectively as part of a group. This skill is vital in corporate structures and in many other office situations.

Team Members' Roles and Duties

Home-run kings Mark McGwire and Sammy Sosa can't win games alone. If their teammates don't pitch, hit, run, and field well, the team will lose. In the end, it's the team that wins or loses.

Team members can help their organization or group by:

* Focusing on the goal. They listen carefully and understand their part in achieving the group goal.
* Following through on important activities related to the goal. The group can count on them to complete their part of a project well and on time.
* Taking the initiative to increase their value to the organization. If they see things that can help the organization or group, they do them without being asked.
* Sharing their ideas and information. This increases the group's pool of ideas.
* Encouraging the group or team with a positive attitude.
* Giving credit where credit is due.
* Admitting their own mistakes.

Problem Team Members

You have probably been in groups or meetings that included at least one very unhelpful member. Beware! Do you recognize these profiles?

* *Whiner.* Instead of contributing, whiners seek sympathy. They always have an excuse for not doing their part and whine when they are asked to do something.
* *Glory hog.* Glory hogs talk too much, interrupt others, talk over others, and want to be in the spotlight all the time.
* *Grouch.* Grouches disagree with everyone and argue for the sake of argument. Grouches sap energy from a group in record time.
* *Bully.* Bullies criticize, intimidate, ridicule, blame, and insult others.
* *Clam.* Clams don't talk. Instead, they appear to sulk, daydream, doodle, or act bored. In short, clams offer nothing to the group.

* *Clown.* Clowns make jokes out of every-thing. They goof around, distract the group by changing the subject, and go for a laugh instead of a solution to the problem.
* *Sidetracker.* Sidetrackers hinder the group by bringing up irrelevant issues, by leading the group down unimportant side paths, and by making a big deal out of small points.

Self-Evaluation

Nobody is perfect. Anyone can become a better leader and a better team member. During your life, you will sometimes be a team member and sometimes a team leader. You need to know and learn both roles. Practice looking honestly at yourself. Take responsibility for changing behavior in yourself that you don't like. This ability to admit your mistakes and make mid-course corrections will be helpful all your life.

What Roles Do You Play?

GOAL

The goal of this activity is to help you determine which positive and negative team member roles you play in groups.

TASKS

1. List groups in which you act as a team member. These include your family, friends, and groups at school, church, or work.

2. For each group, evaluate yourself as a team member. Do you usually con-tribute to the group by focusing on the goal, following through, taking the initiative, sharing ideas and information, encouraging the group, giving appro-priate credit, and admitting mistakes? Or are you sometimes a whiner, glory hog, grouch, bully, clam, clown, or sidetracker?

3. Rate yourself for each group on a scale of 1 to 10.

4. Identify at least one change that you intend to make as a result of this quick review.

OUTCOMES

How will you know when you have met your goal? Put it in writing and review it on a regular basis to assess your progress.

Never Too Late

Marta was always late for everything. Her friends thought it impossible, but one day she devised a way to get herself to school, to meetings, and to her part-time job on time. She decided to set her watch and every clock in her house 20 minutes fast. Even though she knew the real time, the change made a big difference. Her boss was impressed with her improvement and gave her a small raise. Her friends gave her plenty of positive feedback.

Armed with her success, Marta set another goal for herself: to work on her listening skills. She plans to try to stop interrupting other people and finishing their sentences—both in meetings and in social situations with her friends.

How do you think Marta could remind herself to change this annoying habit?

Conflict Resolution

Defining Conflicts

What is <u>**conflict**</u>? The dictionary calls it "a state of disharmony between incompatible or antithetical persons, ideas, or interests; a clash." A conflict is more than a simple disagreement. In a conflict, opposing parties hold strong views, opinions, and positions.

Within any group of people there are bound to be conflicts. You have experienced conflicts in your family, in your friendships, in school, and perhaps in your neighborhood or community. Some of these conflicts involve deep feelings and convictions. They are not always easy to resolve. Part of resolving conflicts begins by recognizing that people hold different views than you do.

A Process for Resolving Conflicts

Conflicts are a normal part of life, but everyone has a choice about how to deal with them. We live and work with many different kinds of people. It is important to get along. When people cannot agree, they can become increasingly angry or even violent—unless someone involved knows about **conflict resolution,** a peaceful process for solving problems.

Many businesses hire conflict resolution specialists, or mediators, to help them resolve disagreements among departments or individuals. Helping employees to learn how to talk to one another and solve their disputes helps any business function better. People can concentrate on their jobs instead of focusing on ongoing disagreements. Many cities also use mediators to help citizens resolve neighborhood disputes over such things as animals, noise, cars, and trash.

Communication in Careers

Solving Conflicts in the Community

Paul Masanto is a mediator. He was hired by the local police department to help people solve their problems before they require police intervention.

Paul went through a training course that was similar to the training received by peer mediators in schools. Paul finds his job challenging, but very satisfying. He is a community peacemaker. Paul just finished mediating this conflict between the Browns and the college students next door.

The Brown family was ready to scream, but they knew that no one could hear them. The music next door was too loud. The booming from the neighbors' band practices lasted late into the night.

Everyone in the Brown household was grumpy and bleary-eyed from lack of sleep. Yet after many attempts, they couldn't reach an agreement with the college students living next door. Finally, the Browns asked Paul Masanto to help.

Both parties sat down with Paul. They signed an agreement to abide by any decision they reached in the sessions. Then the work began. They listened and brainstormed. They talked about their frustrations and needs. Finally, after three meetings, they came up with a workable compromise. The process of mediation surprised all of them. The Browns grew to like the kids next door and to appreciate their talent and persistence. The students realized that the Browns were willing to be reasonable. They reached an agreement that met everyone's needs and made their lives more pleasant.

Can you think of some possible solution to this conflict that would satisfy both parties?

Possible Solutions to Conflicts

Three possible solutions exist to any conflict:

1. *I win, you lose.*
2. *You win, I lose.*
3. *I win, you win* (also called a win-win solution).

In the first two solutions, there are a winner and a loser. These solutions aren't completely satisfactory. The winner may be happy at first, but he or she cannot prevail all of the time. The loser is bound to be resentful or angry about the group, the decision, or the people involved. His or her resentments may lead to further conflicts and undermine future working or personal relationships.

Win-Win Solutions

The conflict resolution process tries to reach win-win solutions that turn conflict into cooperation. Does this sound like wishful thinking? Well, it does require people to work together on a mutually satisfactory solution. But, in real life, many people already are trying to reach win-win solutions.

Consider the example of Ross and Angela. He wants to catch the latest action-adventure film on Saturday. Angela does, too, but she knows they need to study for a big history test on Monday. Finally, Ross and Angela agree to study together for the test early on Saturday afternoon. If they make good progress, they will see the movie on Saturday night. Otherwise, they will wait until Sunday. In this solution, both people's needs and desires are met without either person losing. This is a win-win solution.

A Conflict Resolution Session
1. Open the session.
2. Gather information.
3. Find common interests.
4. Brainstorm options.
5. Choose a solution.
6. Write an agreement.
Conflict resolved!

First Steps of Conflict Resolution

In this conflict resolution process, the mediator opens the session and asks participants to sign an agreement to abide by the decision reached during the process. Then the mediator gathers information from both parties to discover the sources of the conflict.

To gather this information, the mediator uses a method called active listening. To find a peaceful resolution for personal conflicts with others, you can use the same method.

In active listening you:

1. *Encourage* the other person to state his or her views and to keep talking.
2. *Clarify* what he or she said to you. Ask questions to get more information so you can better understand his or her point of view.
3. *Restate* his or her basic facts and feelings in your own words.
4. *Summarize* the important ideas stated by this person.

Active listening helps resolve conflicts by restoring respect and fairness to the conflict. When you listen actively, you honor the other person's individuality and respect his or her point of view. You listen with an open mind. The other person feels that he or she has been fairly heard. And in the end, even if you do not agree, the other person is likely to return your respect.

Finding Common Interests

To find common interests, both parties need to explain goals, needs, and desires. Then both parties use brainstorming to create a list of as many solutions to a problem as possible. As you know, **three** rules apply when you are brainstorming:

1. *Try to come up with as many ideas as possible.*
2. *Share any ideas that come to mind.*
3. *Agree not to judge any of the ideas.*

Solution and Agreement

At the end of the conflict resolution process, the mediator helps the parties choose possible solutions that meet as many of both parties' needs as possible. The parties agree on a solution and sign an agreement to abide by it.

A Good Resolution to a Conflict
Solves the problem for good.
Can really be accomplished.
Is fair to everyone involved.

Conflicting Needs—
Baseball and Roses

Your younger brother and sister play base-ball with other kids in the neighborhood. There is only one place to play nearby. The neighbors aren't happy about it. They are upset by all the balls and the little feet that follow, making a mess of the beautiful roses in their gardens. The neighbors want these games to stop. The kids are upset and come to you for help.

GOAL

The goal of this activity is to find a solution to this problem that is agreeable to everyone involved.

TASKS

1. Form groups of three to four students.

2. Within each group, follow the six steps of a conflict resolution session to find a solution to this problem that will be agreeable to everyone.

3. When finished, each group reports its solution to the class.

OUTCOMES

Did most groups come up with the same solution(s)? Which solution(s) do you think were best?

Peer Mediation

Many schools have peer mediation programs that use techniques of active listening and conflict resolution. Students go through a training program to become peer mediators. They are trained to listen and to support their fellow students in resolving conflicts that arise in and outside of school. In schools with peer mediation programs, students take responsibility for solving their own problems.

Checklist

How to Fight Fairly

✔ As calmly as possible, explain what happened and how you feel about what happened.

✔ Share your feelings without criticizing the other person.

✔ Listen to the other person quietly and with an open mind. Respect his or her feelings

✔ Take responsibility for your own actions and words. Find out what you can do to help resolve the problem.

✔ Work for a win-win solution.

Problems Teens Experience

Here are some common problems that teens experience in groups, as discussed in Clay Carr's book, *Team Leader's Problem Solver.* How many of these problems have you experienced in cooperative group projects, clubs, or other teams?

* ***Interpersonal problems within the team.*** For example, the team wants to get rid of one of its members or a member wants to leave the team.

* ***Interpersonal problems affecting the whole team.*** For example, team members compete when they should cooperate; team members blame one another for mistakes.

* ***Problems with a team member's behavior.*** For example, one team member tries to take the credit or rejects everyone else's ideas.

* ***Problems with a team member's performance.*** For example, a team member doesn't keep his or her commitments to the team.

* ***Problems with the team's performance.*** For example, team members won't help each other.

* ***Problems with team leadership.*** For example, the team won't support the leader it chooses—or won't accept leadership from anyone.

Nonproductive Criticism in a Group

GOAL

The goal of this activity is to help you practice using conflict resolution methods to solve problems that arise in groups.

TASKS

1. Read the scenario below. Have you ever been in a group with someone like this?

   Jackie won't accept being a leader, but constantly criticizes anyone who puts ideas forward. She also constantly undermines the group leader.

2. Form groups of three to four students.

3. In each group, use conflict resolution methods to figure out how you can get this person to stop criticizing and to become a productive member of the group.

4. Reach agreement on the best strategy to use with this person.

5. Compare solutions with other groups and role-play before and after scenarios.

OUTCOMES

Did most groups arrive at the same solutions? Which solutions presented the best win-win alternative?

Agreeing to Disagree

What happens if you cannot agree? Some conflicts arise from conflicting needs rather than from differing viewpoints. Solutions to a conflict can often be reached in mediation sessions if both parties are willing, although it sometimes takes time. But often resolution cannot be reached—at least not then. A group may get stuck on one point. It may be important to gather more information or to allow time for everyone to cool down.

It is perfectly all right to "agree to disagree," at least for a time. Be sure that everyone knows that the point will be revisited and is not just being forgotten. And when you move ahead later, you may discover that the solution presents itself.

Keep on Trying

Whenever you experience conflicts, whether individually or in a group, remember to keep communicating—especially if you have to "agree to disagree." The more you continue communicating, the better the chances that you will find a solution. Be sure to thank all those involved in the process of resolving the conflict—no matter the outcome.

Participating in win-win conflict resolution gets easier each time you do it. It is a skill that will make you a valuable partner, friend, team leader, and follower in every area of your life.

Wrap-up

Leaders are not all born to assume the role. Sometimes leaders are appointed, elected, or simply emerge from a group. Becoming a leader means spending time building your personal beliefs and values, your skills at working with others, and your communication skills. We expect leaders to motivate and inspire us, to encourage cohesiveness, and to perform well at specific leadership tasks. But hardworking team members are just as vital to the success of any group. Team members can help the group by focusing on the task, following through with their responsibilities, participating actively, and admitting their mistakes. Problem team members—such as whiners, grouches, and clowns—can hold back any group.

Conflicts are a normal part of life, but they can disrupt any activity. Conflict resolution provides a method for resolving disputes and helping both parties to a win-win solution.

Speech WORDS TO KNOW

appointed leader—a leader chosen by someone outside of the group.

conflict—opposition or sharp disagreement.

conflict resolution—the process of reaching agreement.

elected leader—a leader chosen by ballots or voting.

emerged leader—a member of a group who steps into the leadership position on his or her own.

CHAPTER 9

Informative Speaking

In this chapter, you will consider:

- **What are the four main types of informative speeches?**
- **What elements should you consider in planning an informative speech?**
- **How can you capture the audience's attention?**
- **What are the best ways to get your point across?**
- **How can you bring an informative speech to an effective conclusion?**

We live in an age of information. This chapter will help you with essential skills for the future: writing and presenting informative speeches. You'll first learn about the four types of informative speeches and the key steps in speech planning. You'll then examine the three main parts of the informative speech—the beginning, the body, and the conclusion. You'll find out how to begin your speech in a captivating way. You'll study techniques that help you get your point across in the speech's body. Then you'll learn how to write a compelling conclusion and to conduct a question-and-answer session. Knowing how to present an effective informative speech will help you at work, at school, and on special occasions.

Types of Informative Speeches

Casually or formally, people give one another information all the time. You are surrounded by informative speakers. Your football coach shows you how to block. Your father explains how to open a checking account. Your teachers describe historical periods, scientific principles, and math problems. You are an informative speaker, too. You've given friends driving directions to a party. You've explained processes that you understand to others.

Informative speeches present or describe information, ranging from cooking tips to formal business training programs. Informative speakers share what they know with the audience. They may state different opinions, but their main goal is to explain something clearly and logically. They're not trying to sell their opinions. However, most informative speeches include at least a little persuasion.

Long or short, formal or informal, there are **four** basic categories of informative speeches, which are introduced below.

❶ Definition Speeches

Definition speeches tell the audience what something is or what it means. This type of speech might answer the question "What is democracy?" It also could define the Romantic Movement or explain the qualities of a "liberated woman."

Many types of speech start out with some definition. There are several ways to define something:

* Use a dictionary definition, such as "*democracy* means 'government by the people.'"
* Compare something with others in its class. For example, explain how a Bengal tiger is similar to and differs from other large cats.
* Define by using a synonym, a more common word that has the same meaning. For example, tell the audience that *French cinema* simply means "French film."

Discussions of such topics as race relations, gender equality, and censorship may require **extended definitions,** which are longer, more detailed explanations that thoroughly explain the subject and incorporate the speaker's feelings. Sometimes an entire book defines a topic, such as *What Is Education?*

An extended definition uses many strategies to make sure the audience understands the term that is being discussed. How would you define *country-western music* for an audience unfamiliar with it? You might begin by comparing it to other types of music, such as bluegrass. You could describe its history, audience, themes, styles, rhythms, and instruments. You might talk about Nashville and country music's most famous songs and singers. You'd play country-western songs and show videos. Finally, you might say what country-western music means to you personally.

Writing Tips

Here are some writing tips for definition speeches:

* *Narrow your topic.* Be sure you can cover it completely in the time allotted. For example, don't try to define *modern art* in a five-minute speech.
* *Supplement dictionary definitions.* Write descriptions in your own words and add quotes from other people.
* *Be specific.* You have to do better than "a horse is an animal with four legs," because so is a cat.
* *Avoid* <u>circular definitions,</u> which are definitions that use a form of the word itself to define it. "A plumber is a person who fixes the plumbing" doesn't help you understand what a plumber does. A true definition explains the term.

❷ Description Speeches

<u>Description speeches</u> describe a person, place, thing, or event. They concentrate on what something looks like, smells like, tastes like, sounds like, or feels like. They appeal to the senses and the imagination.

If you are describing the Grand Canyon, you'll include details that would help your audience to picture it. If you're describing a flower or a food, you'll appeal to the senses of taste and smell. If you're describing the sky, however, you'll probably use another descriptive aid—similes and metaphors. You might say that the sky is like a huge blue bowl or that the clouds are piled up like marshmallows. Good descriptions add life to any speech.

Definitions and descriptions are tools used to construct a speech. If your speech focuses mostly on definitions, it is considered a definition speech. If your speech contains mostly descriptions, it is considered a description speech. Very seldom are speeches all definition or all description. Most oral presentations use a little of both.

Writing Tips

Here are some tips for writing descriptive speeches:

* *Visualize your subject clearly.*
* *Declare your own geographic position* and describe elements in a logical order.
* *Decide on a main impression* you want to give, and then select the best details to create that impression. Don't try to include everything.
* *Be specific and concrete.* Don't say, "She looked just marvelous." Instead, describe her features, her hair, her clothing, and so on.

❸ Demonstration and Process Speeches

<u>Demonstration and process speeches</u> tell the audience how to do something or how something is done. A **process** is a series of actions that leads to a planned or expected outcome. On a TV cooking program, the chef shows you how to prepare a linzer torte, demonstrating the process step-by-step.

Process speeches can be informational or directional.

Informational Process Speeches

Informational process speeches give information about how something happens or is done, but the listener is not expected to repeat the process. For example, if you explain photosynthesis or how material in a star explodes into a supernova, you know that your listener won't be imitating the process. He or she simply will become better informed.

An informational process speech might explain how the Vietnam War started or how the buffalo were destroyed on the Great Plains. Or, at work, your trainer might explain the entire production process so you can see how your job fits into it.

Directional Process Speeches

Directional process speeches give detailed information about processes so that listeners can repeat them. Directional process speeches might deal with how to take the SATs, how to assemble a bicycle, or how to install a hard drive on a computer.

An actual demonstration of the process helps the audience to remember it. It is easier to demonstrate a directional process than an informational process. You can show someone how to drive a stick shift in a directional process speech. It's harder to demonstrate something like how Caesar gained power in ancient Rome. But a good demonstration can add clarity and life to any speech.

Writing Tips

Here are some tips for writing demonstration and process speeches:

* *Know your process well* before you explain it.
* *Be aware of your listeners.* This is especially important for process speeches. How much do they already know about your topic? Don't insult or bore them by explaining too much or confuse them by explaining too little.
* *Put the steps in order* according to time. But remember that in some processes several steps happen at the same time.
* *Define new or unfamiliar terms.* If you're telling people how to change a tire, you had better tell them what a lug wrench is. Better yet, show them a lug wrench.
* *Show steps visually.* Use a demonstration, graphics, models, or props.
* *Warn your audience* of possible difficulties, dangers, or common mistakes. What are the usual pitfalls of taking the SATs? If a process is dangerous, what precautions can be taken? In designing Web sites, what common mistakes are made?
* *Explain the purpose of a step* when necessary. If your listeners don't understand why a step is needed, they might decide to skip it.
* For a demonstration, *have all equipment ready* and tested. Rehearse your speech under presentation conditions. Have a "Plan B" in mind in case of equipment failure.

❹ Social Ritual Speeches

At some point in your life, you may be asked to speak in a sales or business meeting, at a wedding reception, or during an awards ceremony—places you perhaps can't imagine yourself today! Most of these special occasions will be happy. But you may also be asked to say good-bye to an old friend at a special dinner or to speak at the funeral of a family member or close friend.

Speeches such as these are **social ritual speeches,** or occasional speeches. They are given on special occasions. Some common types of social ritual speeches are introductions, presentations, acceptance speeches, commencement addresses, keynote speeches, commemorative addresses, dedications, speeches to entertain, public relations and sales speeches, and impromptu speeches.

For more information about social ritual speeches, see Chapter 11.

Planning Your Informative Speech

Planning your speech can be simple and efficient. The process includes **four** main steps:

❶ Evaluate the Speaking Situation

Begin by evaluating your speaking situation. You need information about the time, the occasion, and the audience. Then you can determine the goals of your speech.

* **Time.** Find out how long your speech is to be. If you're part of a program, when does your speech occur?
* **Occasion.** Fit your message to the occasion, whether it's serious, happy, sad, formal, or informal. Your message should reinforce the mood. If you're unsure of what's appropriate, ask those in charge.
* **Audience.** Learn about the members of your audience—their ages, genders, occupations, levels of education, and knowledge of your topic. For help in learning about your audience and suiting your speech to them, see Chapter 13.
* **Goals.** What do you want to achieve by giving this speech? Your goals will depend partly on the occasion and your audience.

❷ Choose a Topic

Once you have evaluated the speaking situation, choose your topic. It should be appropriate to your time limit, the occasion, your audience, and your goals.

A little brainstorming—creative and noncritical thinking—will help you to choose a topic. Try some **free writing**— writing without worrying about form or content—to generate new ideas. Do some preliminary library or Internet research to help clarify and fill out your ideas.

For more help in selecting and narrowing your topic, see Chapter 13.

❸ Choose a Type of Speech

Your topic helps dictate the type of speech that you choose. Ask yourself, "Am I primarily trying to inform or to persuade?"

If your main goal is to inform your audience, you'll find detailed guidance in this chapter. If your main goal is to persuade, turn to Chapter 10, which is dedicated to persuasive speeches. But bear in mind that most informative speeches include elements of persuasion and vice versa. If your speech is primarily informative, it is highly likely that you will blend definition, description, and process techniques. If you are giving a social ritual speech, you will want to look at Chapter 11 more closely.

❹ Research the Topic

It is always best to speak on a topic that you personally know and find interesting. But an informative speech may also require research. Research can broaden your information and give you confidence. Depending upon your topic, you may use personal sources such as your own experience, interviews, or surveys. You may do your research in the library or on the Internet.

Chapter 12 offers detailed information on research sources and methods.

Anatomy of an Informative Speech

All speeches, including the informative speech, are anatomically alike. They usually have **three** parts—an introduction, a body, and a conclusion. Many conclude with a question-and-answer-period. This section will help you maximize your speech's effect in each of these areas.

❶ Introduction of an Informative Speech

The first few minutes of a speech are the most important. If you don't catch your listeners' interest, they may tune you out. They might leave mentally, by daydreaming, or even physically, by getting up and walking out.

So when you begin an informative speech, you want quickly to:

* Get the audience's attention.
* Build interest.
* Preview the topic.
* Apply the message to the audience.
* Establish your credibility.

Get the Audience's Attention

Here are some ways to get your audience's attention at the beginning:

* *Make a dramatic statement.* State a problem or a popular misconception. Use an unusual analogy. For example, begin by saying, "You'd be healthier by eating the weeds growing in your front yard than vegetables from the supermarket. Weeds have more vitamins and minerals, and you can grow them without chemicals."
* *Ask a question.* "Where do you want to be five years from now?" Many speakers use **rhetorical questions**. They are not expecting answers and will give the answers themselves.
* *Use a quotation*—someone's exact words—or a reference to a well-known book, movie, or television show. For example, if your speech defines success, you might quote M. H. Alderson: "If at

first you don't succeed, you're running about average."

* **Tell a joke or anecdote,** a brief story that is connected to your topic. If you're addressing incoming high school students, tell them a story about your first year.

* **Use descriptions** to appeal to emotions. Describing some favorite spots on your school campus will get the attention of a nostalgic alumni audience.

* **Present a contrast.** To explain what you are doing now, for example, contrast it with what you did in the past. "Since I'm a guy, I didn't consider aerobics classes 'real' exercise. Then I went to one of those classes. In five minutes, I was a puddle of exhaustion and sweat. I'm now going into my second year of aerobics classes."

Build Interest

Speakers face a lot of competition. The last time you listened to a speech, what did you do? Talk to a friend? Daydream? Doodle on a piece of paper?

How do you captivate an audience's long-term interest? Try some of the tips below:

* **Use meaningful, specific information.** Don't say, "Many people die from smoking-related diseases." We can't feel sorry for or worried about "many." Give the audience concrete data. How many people died last year? Who were they? What were the diseases? Tell a story of a specific person. For long-term interest, people need concrete information, and they must be touched emotionally.

* **Keep your speech simple and well organized.** Shape your speech around a purpose and a **thesis,** or main idea. In your speech plan, make sure that every point supports your purpose and thesis. You can't get the message across if you are confused.

* **Use attention-getting techniques** mentioned above. Support your points with interesting examples that come alive through description. Give relevant examples and quotations from authorities. Back up what you say with statistics. Share your personal experiences.

* **Use catchy slogans,** short and easily remembered key phrases. Television and magazine ads make very effective use of slogans.

* **Introduce a visual aid,** such as a chart, prop, video clip, or recording. Listeners perk up when you involve more than one of their senses.

Sidebar

My Speech Plan

Here is an example of a speech plan.

Purpose: I'm explaining how to apply for a job.

Thesis: You've got to be prepared for a job interview.

1. What to do before the interview.

2. What to say during the interview.

3. How to follow up after the interview.

Keep on Trying

GOAL

The goal of this activity is to adapt commercial slogans for speech use.

TASKS

1. Collect advertising slogans from newspapers and magazines.

2. Work as a class to create a slogan collage. Or write 10 to 15 slogans on the board.

3. Form groups of three or four.

4. Try to fit some of the advertising slogans to speeches that you might give. For instance, what popular ad slogan might you use in a speech on getting a new job? Consider topics that these slogans suggest. Which slogans might be appropriate to a definition, description, process, or social ritual speech?

5. Present your group's best slogan, topic, and suggestion to the class.

OUTCOMES

Which slogans suggested the easiest and best ideas? Which slogans were unusable? What audiences might the most popular slogans appeal to? Why? What type of speech was the easiest to match with a slogan?

Preview the Topic

Once you have the audience's attention and have attracted its interest, give a preview of your speech's content. When you prepared your speech, you determined your audience's interests and level of knowledge. Explain any background or terms that listeners need to know. Then tell them what you're about to tell them.

Your preview is like a road map. Audience members will enjoy the scenery on the way to the destination more if they know where they're going. Your preview will help build interest in your topic.

With longer, more complex presentations, you might use a computer presentation program or an overhead projector to display the main points of your outline. Or you might pass out handouts that outline the entire speech. These aids help the audience follow the presentation more easily.

Apply the Message to the Audience

Move from your road map to the motive. Your listeners know where you want them to go. Now tell them why they should go there.

How does this topic affect their lives? their personal survival? their finances, health, or self-esteem? Perhaps it touches their family, children, friends, or community in some way. It might also connect with their values, such as their sense of responsibility.

Establish Your Credibility

Let your audience know you. This is the secret weapon of getting attention. People will listen to you and respect what you say if they respect *you*. If you have some special knowledge, skill, or experience that enables you to speak with authority on your subject, share it with your audience. If not, give a speech worth listening to. Give the audience a reason to listen to you and believe you.

Don't Go Here!

Don't begin a speech with statements like these:

"I really don't know much about this . . . ."

"I couldn't find much information . . . ."

"This is really hard to understand . . . ."

You're guaranteed to lose your audience.

❷ Body of an Informative Speech

You've completed the first part of your informative speech, the beginning. Now you've reached the second part, the body of the speech. In this section, your goal is to get your message across. To achieve this, you need to follow **four** steps:

1. Organize Information

The first step in getting your message across is to organize the information well. Every speech can use several different types of organization, but certain types of organization are appropriate to certain types of speeches. Most process speeches, for example, should be organized in time-based, chronological order. A description speech often is organized in a spatial pattern.

Common patterns of organization taught in English class also apply to organizing speeches. Think about your topic. What is the most logical way to present it?

* **Time Order.** Describe events or process steps in chronological order. Use this for speeches that tell stories or recount events (my adventure in Yosemite, the Battle of Waterloo, the 1968 Olympics) or when explaining a process (washing a dog, buying a new car, building a garage).
* **Spatial Organization.** Describe an object or a geographical location in a logical sequence, from top to bottom, left to right, up to down, or near to far. Consider what will best help your audience to visualize the subject in speeches about places or objects (a tour

of Gettysburg, a trip down the Mississippi River, features of a renovated theater).

* **Comparison and Contrast.** Describe elements by explaining how they are alike and different. Use this for comparison speeches (why buy a notebook computer rather than a desktop, how New Orleans has changed in the last 100 years).

* **Classification.** Show what makes up a group, and then its parts. Use this for scientific speeches (the newest fossil discovery).

* **Cause and Effect.** Explain events, actions, or problems by beginning with the cause and moving to the effect, or vice versa. Use this in speeches about events (the French Revolution), or actions (how a tennis player became a star), or to explain problems (why our city is running out of money).

Which method of organization is most appropriate for your topic? Some speeches rely on one type of organization, but most make use of several.

2. Follow Principles of Informing

The second step in getting your message across is to follow the principles of informing. You want people to listen to you and to remember what you say. So make what you say interesting, clear, and accurate. There are some basic principles behind all informational speeches.

Fulfill a need to know. The first principle of informing is to fulfill a need to know. How do you react when you hear this sentence? "Read this paragraph carefully because it will be on the test." You probably pay attention. In general, if you show people how your information makes an important difference in their lives, they will listen.

To do this well, you need to know your audience and its interests. The guidelines in Chapter 13 for learning about your audience should help. At this point, review your data on your audience—ages, genders, occupations, levels of education, and knowledge levels. Based on this data, what information do listeners want and need? If you're not sure, ask the organizers of your event or try to speak with audience members in advance.

Also consider the basic human needs of all people as identified by American psychologist Abraham Maslow. Maslow identified human need levels called Physical, Safety, Social, Ego, and Self. His theory is known as **Maslow's Hierarchy of Needs.** He believed that, starting with physical needs, a person must satisfy each need level before the next level can be approached. In other words, if your physical needs of food, water, and health aren't met, you won't be able to worry about your safety, social needs, ego, or self.

When you give a speech, start by addressing the audience on the level of its current needs. If a hurricane is approaching, don't expect listeners to care about job training. Their primary interest will be safety, Maslow's second level.

Maslow's Hierarchy of Needs
Physical Food, water, health
Safety Preparing for emergencies and the future
Social Love, friendship, acceptance
Ego Recognition by others: leadership, achievement
Self Recognition by self: meeting a challenge, creativity

Connect information to feelings. The second principle of informing is to connect information to your audience's feelings. You'll use facts, statistics, examples, and illustrations to connect with them intellectually. But many people will remember the emotion behind an event better than the facts and figures involved. So tie your information to their feelings. Use examples and stories that touch the audience's hearts.

Limit your main points. The third principle of informing is to limit your main points. Keep things simple. Complicated speeches can become confusing for the listener.

Repeat information. The fourth principle of informing is to repeat information. What is clear to you may not be clear to your audience. An old saying in speech class is, "Tell them what you're going to say, say it, and then tell them what you said." In other words, repeat things.

Checklist

How to Make Your Main Points

When you give a speech, imagine that you've invited listeners to a feast of information. Feed them with a fork, not a shovel. Slow down and repeat important points. Give them time to "swallow" before feeding them another biteful. Think in threes. Many experienced speakers suggest using three main points.

- ✓ Does my audience need to know this to understand my theme?

- ✓ Is this point clear and simple?

- ✓ Does it need to be stated separately, or could it be combined with another point?

- ✓ Am I stating each point so it shows a benefit for the audience?

AT THE RISK OF REPEATING MYSELF...

You'll want to stress the **theme,** or subject of your speech. Your theme is the central structure that connects your ideas. Your audience will retain a limited percentage of what you say. You want people to remember your thesis, or theme. Think: "If I had only one minute, what would I say?" That contains the basic idea you wish to get across.

Sidebar

Repetition

Winston Churchill, the leader of wartime Great Britain, wanted to inspire Britons to struggle on in World War II. He summed it up in a **slogan**— a catchy phrase. Then he repeated it. He repeated the initial phrase "We shall" to drive home his point. "We shall not flag or fail. We shall go on to the end. We shall fight in France. We shall fight on the seas and oceans. We shall fight with growing confidence and growing strength in the air. We shall defend our island, whatever the cost may be. We shall fight on the beaches. We shall fight on the landing grounds. We shall fight in the fields and the streets, we shall fight in the hills. We shall never surrender."

For guidelines on repetition, listen to speeches that others give. Read other famous speeches in the Handbook at the back of this textbook.

Everyday **COMMUNICATION**

It Sometimes Works Like Magic!

"I'm Louis Velasco, a junior in high school. At school, I'm involved in peer mentoring, volleyball, and model UN. Model UN is a discussion and debate group where students are assigned countries and topics as if they were delegates to the real United Nations. I also have a part-time job as a host at a local small restaurant. My speaking skills from model UN and peer mentoring have carried over to my job at the restaurant.

"Probably the most obvious speech skills I've used are pretty simple. I repeat something three times and speak slowly and clearly. It sometimes works like magic! For example, last week a restaurant patron asked for the Senior Discount. He obviously wasn't over 55. I politely told him the minimum age and asked for proof of age. He didn't have it, and he still demanded the discount. I told him the rule slowly and carefully three times. He finally gave up!

"I wouldn't have had the nerve to do this before I had practiced some of the speech techniques I've learned. I know that the repetition is for clarity, but it also gets across the message that you're not going to back down, and it doesn't insult anyone."

3. Polish the Speech

You've organized your information well and followed the principles of informing. The third step in getting your message across is to polish the speech, to work on the details that will make it develop smoothly. To polish your speech, you'll need to do a few things.

* **Use smooth transitions.** Rough spots often occur as you move from one section of your speech to another. One way to polish your speech is to make smooth **transitions,** or connections, between your ideas. Having a strong thesis and referring back to it helps the listener to move to the next part of that main idea. So does clear organization.

Two other strong transitional devices are repetition of key words or ideas and the use of transitional words and phrases. Repetition of your speech's theme and ideas helps to glue your speech together. Repetition also can be a very powerful transitional device. Here's an example.

". . . so we can see that Teresa made an excellent decision that time. The next time she tried, her decision was just as good."

Repeating the words *time* and *decision* connects the two sentences. Repeating the idea that Teresa made a good decision also helps make the connection. Note that a transitional phrase, "the next time," also was used.

Transitional Words and Phrases

Transitional words and phrases help keep a speech from sounding choppy and childish. Here are some common transitional words and phrases.

In This Situation	Use One of These Transitions
To present an example	for example, in particular, for instance, specifically, namely, another
To present a contrast	in contrast, while, but, although, though, on the other hand
To bring up a comparison	in comparison, not only . . . but also, similarly
To show a result	thus, therefore, as a result, consequently
To introduce a sequence	also, moreover, in addition, first, second, third, next, then, after, furthermore, soon

Being a Hero

GOAL

The goal of this activity is to practice using transitional devices to support various types of speech organization.

TASKS

1. Form groups of five. Each group will compose a short speech on the topic "Being a Hero." The most important goal is to link the sentences together well using transitional devices. One person records the group's sentences as they are composed.

2. In each group, the first person states the subject, "hero," in a sentence.

3. The second person names an example of a hero in a sentence but also must use a transitional device to connect the example to the first person's sentence.

4. Again using a transitional device, the third person compares a hero to something else. "Being a hero is like . . . ."

5. Using a transitional device, the fourth person presents a sequence of how-to steps on how to be a hero. This is challenging! Ask the group for help if needed.

6. Using a transitional device, the fifth person introduces the result of being a hero. If all of these are put together, you have a short speech on "Being a Hero."

7. Each group presents its completed short speech to the class.

8. The class decides which speech was most effective and why. What types of transitional devices were used?

OUTCOMES

What was the most challenging part of this activity? Which speech was most original? You used several techniques in this speech: definition, cause and effect, and process. Which do you think you used most effectively?

* **Avoid too much technical talk.** Another way to polish your speech is to avoid technical talk. Technical language can be a sneaky rough spot in a speech. Early home computer manuals were written by people who understood computers but weren't professional writers. They used so much **technical language**—the special vocabulary used in that field— without defining the terms that the average computer user was lost.

Especially when you know a lot about a subject, you're in danger of using words that your audience doesn't understand. Know your audience's knowledge level. If it's low, explain as much as possible in everyday words. Go slowly. Use examples, analogies, and visual aids to explain your concepts.

In short, don't try to impress your audience. Try to be understood.

What Are You Telling Me?

Here is a government bulletin that was going to be sent out in 1942 announcing a blackout order during World War II:

"Such preparation shall be made as will completely obscure all federal buildings and non-Federal buildings occupied by the Federal government during an air raid for any period of time from visibility by reason of internal or external illumination."

President Franklin D. Roosevelt rewrote the order in plain English:

"In the buildings where they have to keep the work going, tell them to put something across the windows."

---

* **Personalize the information.** As a final step in polishing your speech, personalize the information. Remember to show your audience the benefits of your words. If you're asking listeners to change their thinking or actions, what are the benefits to them? What are the negative results of not following your plans or ideas? What simple actions can they take now?

4. Keep an Eye on the Audience

While preparing the body of your speech, you've organized your information well, followed the principles of informing, and polished your speech. Now you're up there delivering your speech. A final step in getting your message across is to keep an eye on the audience. Your audience is watching and listening to you. Your job is to watch and listen to it, too, so you can make adjustments. Your audience will appreciate your responsiveness.

When you explain something, do people in your audience look confused or glassy-eyed? If so, back up and explain the last concept in simpler language. Give them everyday examples and analogies. Mentally adjust yourself to proceed more slowly with the rest of the speech or to eliminate any heavily technical information.

Are listeners getting restless? Are they talking to each other or looking at their watches? These are signs that you have lost their interest. Think about how to regain it. Maybe you've been talking too long. Reconnect with them by making a joke. Or summarize the remainder of your speech and open the floor to questions.

Try to anticipate these problems ahead of time. In speech class, you'll often get verbal and written feedback or comments and suggestions for each speech. You also can practice delivering your speech to a few friends. Watch their reactions and encourage honest criticism. Adjust your speech accordingly.

Ending a Speech

GOAL

The goal of this activity is to examine the effects of different ending techniques on a speech.

TASKS

1. Select a short speech that has been delivered previously in the class. Or choose one of the speeches in the Handbook, which begins on page 342.
2. Distribute it to the class.
3. Each student writes a different ending, in keeping with the original goal of the speech.
4. Form groups of four or five.
5. Within each group, reread the original speech, or have someone present it again.
6. Pass the alternative endings around your group, read them, and vote on the best one.
7. Each group presents its best new ending to the class.
8. As a class, discuss the endings and vote for the best one. Then discuss reasons that this ending won.

OUTCOMES

What effects do the new endings have? Were the new endings better or worse than the original? Did they change the meaning or focus of the speech?

❸ Conclusion of an Informative Speech

You've completed the body of your speech. Now it's time to conclude. The end of the speech is what the audience will remember. A weak ending can destroy a good speech.

Keep the conclusion brief and put out a strong signal that this is the conclusion. However, do not say "Last, but not least" or "I guess that's all." These are trite and unmemorable ways to end a speech.

Here are some techniques for ending your speech well:

* **Summarize your thesis and main supporting points.** Tell listeners what you've told them.
* **Remind the audience of the importance of the issue.** Repeat one of your most telling statistics.
* **Use an attention device mentioned earlier:** a dramatic statement, a rhetorical question, a relevant quotation, a joke or anecdote, a vivid description, or a contrast.
* **Urge your audience to take action.** "Tomorrow, vote for either candidate, but vote."
* **Warn your audience.** "The destruction of the ozone layer, taken to the extreme, means that you'd have to swim indoors or wear a lead body suit."
* **Predict the future.** "Within five years, most of America will be shopping on the Internet."
* **Use a "clincher" ending.** If you opened your speech with a sad story about a girl named Jennifer, end the speech with a reference to Jennifer: "We can't let this happen to any more Jennifers."

④ Conducting a Question-and-Answer Period

When a speech is over, audiences appreciate a chance to participate in a well-run question-and-answer period. Allowing questions during your speech can make the session more interactive and lively but questions also can interrupt your train of thought. You might prefer to ask the audience to hold questions until after the speech. To maintain some control over the questions, ask the audience to write questions on note cards. Collect them, and then choose the ones you wish to answer.

The best way to assure a good question-and-answer period is to give a stimulating and informative speech. This helps the listeners to get involved and gives them a basis for interesting questions. If you're well informed on your topic, you'll be ready to answer most questions they ask. If someone stumps you, you can answer, "That's an excellent question—so good that I don't know the answer. I'll find out and get back to you."

Prepare for a question-and-answer session in advance by writing a list of possible questions and answers.

Try to answer all questions that are asked, even if they seem silly or obvious. Rephrase all questions to make sure that you understand them. And remember:

* Don't be sarcastic.
* Don't lose your temper, even if an audience member does.
* Make sure you know what the question is. Ask to have it repeated if necessary.
* Keep your answers short.

I'm Glad You Asked That Question

GOAL

The goal of this activity is to practice forming and answering questions.

TASKS

1. Choose a partner.
2. Exchange previously written speeches with your partner. Read his or her speech and do a little research on the topic yourself.
3. Write five to ten questions that an audience might ask. Some audience members might be biased or downright hostile, so include a few questions that they might ask. Keep your language and ideas appropriate for the classroom.
4. In front of the class, ask your partner to answer some of your questions.
5. Repeat with other students and their partners.
6. As a class, analyze the results, using the questions below.

OUTCOMES

How can one deal with hostile questions? Which questions were easiest to answer? hardest? What is a good answer to a silly question? What was the most unexpected question? the best? Could the speaker answer all of the questions?

Informative Speech

A Chief Seattle gets the audience's attention and builds interest early on by using descriptive language.

B He previews the topic of the speech by informing the audience of his intentions and feelings.

Model

Chief Seattle Cautions Americans to Deal Justly with His People

Yonder sky, which has wept tears of compassion on our fathers for centuries untold, and which to us looks eternal, may change. Today it is fair; tomorrow it may be overcast with clouds. My words are like the stars that never set. What Seattle says, the great chief Washington can rely upon, with as much certainty as our paleface brothers can rely upon the return of the seasons. The son of the white chief says his father sends us greetings of friendship and good will. This is kind, for we know he has little need of our friendship in return, because his people are many. They are like the grass that covers the vast prairies, while my people are few, and resemble the scattering trees of a windswept plain.

The great, and I presume also good, white chief sends us word that he wants to buy our lands but is willing to allow us to reserve enough to live on comfortably. This indeed appears generous, for the red man no longer has rights that he need respect, and the offer may be wise, also, for we are no longer in need of a great country. There was a time when our people covered the whole land as the waves of a wind-ruffled sea cover its shell floor. But that time has long since passed away with the greatness of tribes almost forgotten. I will not mourn over our untimely decay, nor reproach my paleface brothers with hastening it, for we, too, may have been somewhat to blame.

When our young men grow angry at some real or imaginary wrong and disfigure their faces with black paint, their hearts, also, are disfigured and turn black, and then their cruelty is relentless and knows no bounds, and our old men are not able to restrain them.

But let us hope that hostilities between the red man and his paleface brothers may never return. We would have everything to lose and nothing to gain.

C The speech sends a clear message to the audience that Chief Seattle wants peaceful relations with his "paleface brothers."

True it is that revenge, with our young braves, is considered gain, even at the cost of their own lives, but old men who stay at home in times of war, and old women who have sons to lose, know better.

Our great father Washington . . . sends us word by his son, who no doubt is a great chief among his people, that if we do as he desires, he will protect us. His brave armies will be to us a bristling wall of strength, and his great ships of war will fill our harbors so that our ancient enemies far to the northward, the Simsians and Hydas, will no longer frighten our women and old men. Then he will be our father, and we will be his children,

But can this ever be? Your God loves your people and hates mine; he folds his strong arms lovingly around the white man and leads him as a father leads his infant son, but he has forsaken his red children; he makes your people wax strong every day, and soon they will fill the land; while our people are ebbing away like a fast receding tide that will never flow again.

The white man's God cannot love his red children, or he would protect them. They seem to be orphans and can look nowhere for help. How, then, can we become brothers? How can your father become our father and bring us prosperity and awaken in us dreams of returning greatness?

Your God seems to be partial. He came to the white man. We never saw him; never even heard his voice; he gave the white man laws, but he had no word for his red children, whose teeming millions filled this vast continent as the stars fill the firmament. No, we are two distinct races and must ever remain so. There is little in common between us. The ashes of our ancestors are sacred, and their final resting place is hallowed ground, while you wander away from the tombs of your fathers seemingly without regret.

Your religion was written on tables of stone by the iron finger of an angry God, lest you might forget it. The red man could never remember nor comprehend it.

continues ▶

Informative Speech

(continued)

D Chief Seattle compares his people with his audience.

E After listing reasons that Native Americans and white men are incompatible, Chief Seattle uses moving imagery to forecast his people's grim future.

Model

Our religion is the traditions of our ancestors, the dreams of our old men, given them by the great Spirit, and the visions of our sachems, and is written in the hearts of our people.

Your dead cease to love you and the homes of their nativity as soon as they pass the portals of the tomb. They wander far off beyond the stars, are soon forgotten, and never return. Our dead never forget the beautiful world that gave them being. They still love its winding rivers, its great mountains and sequestered vales, and they ever yearn in tenderest affection over the lonely-hearted living and often return to visit and comfort them.

Day and night cannot dwell together. The red man has ever fled the approach of the white man, as the changing mists on the mountain side flee before the blazing morning sun.

However, your proposition seems a just one, and I think my folks will accept it and will retire to the reservation you offer them, and we will dwell apart and in peace, for the words of the great white chief seem to be the voice of nature speaking to my people out of the thick darkness that is fast gathering around them like a dense fog floating inward from a midnight sea.

It matters but little where we pass the remainder of our days. They are not many. The Indian's night promises to be dark. No bright star hovers about the horizon. Sad-voiced winds moan in the distance. Some grim Nemesis of our race is on the red man's trail, and wherever he goes he will still hear the sure approaching footsteps of the fell destroyer and prepare to meet his doom, as does the wounded doe that hears the approaching footsteps of the hunter. A few more moons, a few more winters, and not one of all the mighty hosts that once filled this broad land or that now roam in fragmentary bands through these vast solitudes will remain to weep over the tombs of a people once as powerful and hopeful as your own.

But why should we repine? Why should I murmur at the fate of my people? Tribes are made up of individuals and are no better than

F Chief Seattle establishes credibility by setting forth demands and laying claim to the land.

G He concludes the speech concisely and powerfully.

they. Men come and go like the waves of the sea. A tear, a tamanamus, a dirge, and they are gone from our longing eyes forever. Even the white man, whose God walked and talked with him, as friend to friend, is not exempt from the common destiny. We may be brothers after all. We shall see.

We will ponder your proposition, and when we have decided we will tell you. But should we accept it, I here and now make this the first condition: that we will not be denied the privilege, without molestation, of visiting at the graves of our ancestors and friends. Every part of this country is sacred to my people. Every hillside, every valley, every plain and grove, has been hallowed by some fond memory or some sad experience of my tribe. Even the rocks that seem to lie dumb as they swelter in the sun along the silent seashore in solemn grandeur thrill with memories of past events connected with the fate of my people, and the very dust under your feet responds more lovingly to our footsteps than to yours, because it is the ashes of our ancestors, and our bare feet are conscious of the sympathetic touch, for the soil is rich with the life of our kindred.

The sable braves, and fond mothers, and glad-hearted maidens, and the little children who lived and rejoiced here, and whose very names are now forgotten, still love these solitudes, and their deep fastnesses at eventide grow shadowy with the presence of dusky spirits. And when the last red man shall have perished from the earth and his memory among the white men shall have become a myth, these shores shall swarm with the invisible dead of my tribe, and when your children's children shall think themselves alone in the field, the shop, upon the highway, or in the silence of the woods, they will not be alone.

In all the earth there is no place dedicated to solitude. At night, when the streets of your cities and villages shall be silent, and you think them deserted, they will throng with the returning hosts that once filled and still love this beautiful land. The white man will never be alone. Let him be just and deal kindly with my people, for the dead are not altogether powerless.

How to Prepare an Informative Speech

1. Plan your informative speech.

✓ Evaluate the speaking situation (time, occasion, audience, your goals).

✓ Choose a topic.

✓ Choose a type of speech (definition, description, informative process, directional process, or social ritual).

✓ Research the topic.

2. Plan your speech's beginning.

✓ Get the audience's attention.

✓ Build interest.

✓ Preview the topic.

✓ Apply the message to the audience.

✓ Establish your credibility.

3. Plan the body of your speech.

✓ Organize information by time order, spatial organization, comparison and contrast, classification, or cause and effect.

✓ Follow the principles of informing:
  * Fulfill a need to know.
  * Connect information to feelings.
  * Limit your main points.
  * Repeat information.

✓ Polish the speech:
  * Use smooth transitions.
  * Avoid too much technical talk.
  * Personalize the information.
  * Keep an eye on the audience.

4. Plan an effective conclusion.

5. Prepare for the question-and-answer period.

You have explored informative speaking and have learned about techniques and strategies to use in preparing and delivering this type of speech. You now know how to get your audience's attention—and how to keep it. You also know how to bring your speech to a strong conclusion and to field questions effectively. Your new skills will benefit you at school, in your community, and on the job. In an information society, it's important to be able to communicate with confidence and skill.

Speech

cause and effect—method or organization that explains events, actions, or problems by beginning with the cause and moving to the effect, or vice versa.

circular definition—explanation that uses a form of the word itself to describe it.

classification—method of organization that shows what makes up a group, then shows its parts.

comparison and contrast—method of organization that describes elements by explaining how they are alike and different.

definition speeches—speeches that tell the audience what something is or what it means.

demonstration and process speeches—speeches that tell the audience how to do something or how something is done.

description speeches—speeches that describe a person, place, thing, or event, concentrating on what something looks like, smells like, tastes like, sounds like, or feels like.

directional process speeches—speeches that give detailed information about processes so that listeners can replicate them.

extended definitions—detailed explanations that thoroughly explain the subject and incorporate the speaker's feelings.

free writing—writing without worrying about form or content.

informational process speeches—speeches that give information about how something happens or is done. But the listener is not expected to repeat the process.

continues ▶

more Speech Words to Know

informative speeches—speeches that present or describe information.

Maslow's Hierarchy of Needs—theory about the basic human needs that all people share, as identified by American psychologist Abraham Maslow.

process—series of actions that lead to a planned or expected outcome.

rhetorical question—question asked without expecting an answer.

slogan—short and easily remembered key phrase.

social ritual speeches—speeches given on special occasions.

spatial organization—method of organization that describes an object or geographical location in a logical sequence.

technical language—special vocabulary used in a field.

theme—subject of a speech.

thesis—main idea.

time order—method of organization that describes events or process steps in chronological order.

transitions—connections between ideas.

CHAPTER 10

Persuasion and Rhetoric

In this chapter, you will consider:

- **How does a persuasive speech differ from a speech to inform?**
- **What are three types of persuasive speeches?**
- **How do persuasive speakers appeal to the needs of the listeners?**
- **How do persuasive speakers communicate credibility?**
- **How do you organize a speech to persuade?**
- **How do you evaluate one?**

All day, every day, in all of the media, and in all areas of your life, you encounter persuasion. You also use persuasion to fill your own needs. In this chapter, you'll learn principles and techniques that will help you persuade more effectively. You'll discover the fundamental principles of persuasion and three types of persuasive speeches—questions of fact, questions of value, and questions of policy. You'll study three types of appeals for developing your central arguments—pathos (the listeners' needs), ethos (the speaker's credibility), and logos (reasoning). You'll learn how to argue to audiences that are positive, neutral, apathetic, or opposed. Finally, you'll find out how to appeal to basic human needs to sell your view, how to structure your argument, and how to organize and evaluate persuasive speeches.

Persuasion

Whenever you try to change how someone thinks, feels, or behaves, you are using **persuasion.** You may also use persuasion to strengthen a view, attitude, or pattern of behavior that already exists.

In today's society, attempts to persuade are inescapable. Wherever you look, you see and hear commercial messages—on billboards, on buses, on TV, on the Internet. You listen to persuasive arguments from your family, friends, teachers, bosses, co-workers, and telemarketers. You use persuasion yourself to get what you want and need from others. Persuasive skills can come in very handy in daily life.

Persuasive skills also can advance your career. Ability to communicate with and influence others are important components of business leadership. Training in persuasive speaking techniques can help you to critique proposals, advance new project or product ideas, land new clients, change working conditions or company policies, sell services and products to others, and more.

Comparison with Informative Speeches

In Chapter 9, you learned how to write informative speeches. Informative and persuasive speeches are similar in some ways. Both types of speeches should be structured carefully. Both types should focus on an objective. Both should utilize compelling evidence and an expressive delivery.

However, informative and persuasive speeches pursue different purposes. An informative speech provides information or explains a process, usually with an objective, emotionally neutral approach. The persuasive speech, on the other hand, tries to sell something—an idea, an attitude, or a plan of action. The persuasive speaker uses information, too, but structures it into an argument. The speaker's goal is to change the audience or to strengthen its commitment to something.

Three Types of Persuasive Speeches

A persuasive speech usually focuses on one primary issue, problem, or idea. This is the core of the speech. There are **three** types of persuasive speeches—questions of fact, questions of value, and questions of policy. A persuasive speech may be of one type or a combination of these types. Which type or types you use depends on the core issue being addressed.

❶ Question of Fact

A **question of fact** argument involves a real event or issue that can be viewed as either true or false.

For example, you may claim that school basketball game attendance this year is the best ever. Or you may argue that 50 people attended the last student council meeting. Both statements are either true or false. To prove either claim, you will need to define your terms and to supply strong and appropriate evidence.

Making Donations Personal

Tom Yang grew up in a family dedicated to community service. As a teenager, Tom donated part of his monthly allowance to a worldwide needy children's fund. Tom recalled that it really moved him to receive a photo of the child that he had helped.

Ten years later, Tom found himself in charge of music education programs for his city. He decided to use a similar means of persuasion to get people to donate money for the district's band and orchestra programs.

"Instead of asking people to simply contribute money to a program, we asked people to support a child in the band or orchestra by instrument and group. Instead of actual photos of children (which would make it too much of a popularity contest), we asked people to circle the number of chairs in a particular section of the band or orchestra they wanted to support.

"The results were fantastic. People apparently liked donating money to something specific. It personalized the process of giving for them. The campaign raised a whopping 42 percent more than the previous year. We're going to keep using this technique."

Here are some tips for arguing questions of fact:

* State your position clearly, making sure that you include all of the facts.
* Define all of your terms. This will help to avoid misunderstandings.
* Anticipate and refute opposing arguments.
* Provide ample, even excessive evidence to support your position.

Use evidence that is authoritative and universally accepted.

❷ Question of Value

A second type of persuasive argument deals with a **question of value**. A *value* is a strong opinion or attitude.

Everyone has values. Personal values are a person's most deeply felt beliefs about what is right and wrong, ethical and unscrupulous, moral and immoral, honest and dishonest. People often share values with others in their families, religious groups, and cultures. These collective values may be positive (equality, freedom of expression, patriotism) or negative (prejudice, isolationism).

People's values are deeply rooted. They can be difficult to change. Here are some tips on arguing questions of value:

* Know your audience well. Make sure you understand listeners' beliefs.
* Respect your audience's values and give them a fair hearing.
* Base your argument on a value that is important to this group.
* Use facts, testimonials, examples, and emotional appeals.
* Set realistic goals. Don't ask your listeners to abandon a value that is important to them. Instead, ask them to reconsider another value related to it. For example, rather than asking people to change their minds about a political candidate, ask them to reconsider some of the new legislation he or she proposes.

Types of Persuasion

The goal of this activity is to apply the different types of persuasion—question of fact, question of value, question of policy—to arguments appropriate for persuasive speeches.

TASKS

1. Form groups of three to six people.
2. Each group identifies the type of persuasion used for each of the topics below. Is this a question of fact, of value, of policy, or a combination?
3. Each group also writes a possible purpose statement for each of the topics listed below.

Topics:
* Preschoolers and computer use
* Internet taxation
* Off-campus lunch privileges for high school seniors
* Unsealing adoption records
* Attendance at school athletic events
* The educational value of part-time jobs
* The information society
* School proficiency tests

Example:
Topic: The importance of flu shots
Type of Persuasion: Question of fact
Purpose: To convince listeners that yearly flu shots are effective for 85 percent of those who get them each year.

4. The groups compare results and discuss any discrepancies.

OUTCOMES

What factors determined the type of persuasion that you selected for each topic? Could some topics be argued effectively with more than one type of persuasion?

❸ Question of Policy

The third type of persuasive argument is a **question of policy**. This type of argument proposes a change in an existing plan of action or in informal norms, regulations, or laws.

A policy argument uses both facts and values. For example, a speaker who favors stiffer penalties against graffiti (the policy) might use people's pride in their homes and businesses (a value) and the dollar amount spent to paint over graffiti (a fact) to argue for stronger legal penalties.

Here are some tips for arguing questions of policy:

* Argue from values that are important to your audience. Otherwise, people won't listen.
* Use facts to establish the need for a change.
* Anticipate and refute audience arguments.
* Use compelling evidence.
* Be sure that your facts and figures are current and relevant to the topic.

Aristotle's Pathos, Ethos, and Logos

To learn how to write powerful persuasive speeches, you can study those of history's great orators—such figures as Demosthenes, Pericles, Cicero, Edmund Burke, Patrick Henry, Frederick Douglass, Elizabeth Cady Stanton, Susan B. Anthony, and Winston Churchill. In the Handbook of this textbook, you'll find a great persuasive speech from Mohandas K. Gandhi, a great leader of India.

You also can learn persuasive techniques by studying *Rhetoric*, a work written by the famed Greek philosopher Aristotle (384–322 B.C.). Aristotle, one of the greatest thinkers who ever lived, was the student of Plato and the tutor of Alexander the Great. In his *Rhetoric*, Aristotle outlined principles of effective speaking that still are valid and relevant today.

In *Rhetoric*, Aristotle urged speakers to consider the rhetorical context, or **situation**—that is, the place, time, circumstances, and audience for a speech. He also identified **three** modes that persuasive speakers may use. Speakers may persuade an audience by:

1. Exciting emotions through connecting with the listeners' needs (pathos).
2. Establishing the speaker's credibility (ethos).
3. Satisfying the listeners' reason through proof (logos).

Pathos (Listeners' Needs)

Through **pathos**, the first mode of persuasion that Aristotle identified, a speaker excites a desired emotional response in the audience. Emotion is a powerful force that often arises spontaneously. Aristotle showed that a speaker may access this power by appealing to the needs of listeners.

TV commercials often are based on emotional appeals. The hard-won triumphs of heroic athletes inspire us to buy athletic shoes. Homey settings, stirring music, charming children, grannies, and pets sell us toothpaste, long-distance carriers, and greeting cards.

Persuasive speakers can use emotional appeals along with facts and logic to move audiences to a goal. To do this well, they need to know how to address different types of audiences and how to identify appropriate listener needs.

To engage an audience's emotions, you must know the audience. Basic information about the audience includes its members' ages, genders, occupations, educational levels, level of knowledge about your topic, and expectations for this event.

For a pathos appeal, in particular, you must know your audience's views and attitudes toward your topic. There are **four** general types of audiences—positive, neutral, apathetic, and opposed. Each type should be handled in a different way. (For more help in learning about your audience, see Chapter 13.)

❶ A Positive Audience

With a **positive audience**—one that shares and supports your position—you needn't spend time arguing for your basic views. Instead, consider how to harness the audience's positive energy. Use your speech to reinforce your listeners' common bonds, to deepen their commitment to the cause, and to stir them to new and positive action.

Use these strategies with a positive audience:

* Begin by stating your speech's purpose.
* Create warmth and a sense of community.
* Stress your common beliefs, ideas, and experiences.
* Use strong emotional appeals.
* Stir listeners to specific actions.
* Show that you appreciate their support.

❷ A Neutral Audience

A **neutral audience** might either be ignorant of or undecided about your topic. In either case, this audience probably isn't motivated to listen to you. You'll need to spend extra effort to get and keep its attention.

Use these strategies with a neutral audience:

* Wake up listeners with a powerful opening.
* Identify history, values, and goals that you share.
* Relate their arguments to their needs.
* Use strong and authoritative evidence.
* Establish your credentials.
* Hold their attention with high-interest material.

❸ An Apathetic Audience

An **apathetic audience** has no interest in your topic. Listeners see no connection between your topic and their lives. To excite their interest and gain their support, use the same strategies that you'd use for a neutral audience.

❹ An Opposed Audience

The biggest test for any public speaker is to stand before an **opposed audience**—that is, an audience that is not in agreement with you. Most people would prefer to avoid this experience. But it is a fact of life for most people in public office and for anyone who seeks to make big changes in the world.

When you know that your listeners are hostile, face your task with courage and humor. Try to gain their respect. Then establish a tiny patch of common ground between you and them. It is in this space that the audience can begin to listen.

With an opposed audience, try these strategies:

* Show that you know and respect the listeners' positions. Avoid confrontations.
* Establish common ground before introducing your argument.
* Gain their respect by sharing your qualifications, experience, background, and values.
* Build your argument carefully, taking into account their possible objections.
* Use evidence that they can't contradict.
* If appropriate, defuse tension by using humor.

With an opposed audience, don't expect miracles. People won't change their views as a result of one short speech. However, perhaps you will earn their respect and cause them to rethink some aspects of their position.

Maslow's Needs Hierarchy

The better you understand your listeners' needs—whether they need to be safe, to belong, to be respected, or something else—the greater your chances are to persuade them. Maslow's Hierarchy of Needs sheds light on this issue.

As you learned in Chapter 9, Abraham Maslow pinpointed five levels of basic needs that underlie human behavior—physical needs, safety needs, social needs, ego needs, and self needs. Maslow stated that humans are motivated to satisfy these five levels of needs only in ascending order. That is, a person's basic physical needs must be met before he or she cares about satisfying higher needs.

This concept makes sense. People who are starving care most of all about getting food. If you talk to them about self-esteem or self-fulfillment, they won't respond.

Maslow's five levels of needs are:

1. *Physical needs.* Which needs are most basic to human beings? Their physical needs for air, water, food, clothing, shelter, and health. Those who lack these things are powerfully motivated to get them. Those who lose these things are powerfully motivated to regain them.

   Speakers can appeal to their audience's physical needs when arguing for clean air, clean and plentiful water supplies, an uncontaminated and adequate food supply, fair and decent housing for all, health care, health insurance, and disease control.

2. *Safety needs.* According to Maslow, once people's physical needs are met, they are concerned with their safety and physical security.

Speakers can appeal to the need for safety and security when speaking of such topics as crime, drunk drivers, seat belts, security systems, sports equipment, highway accident rates, air travel, and insurance.

3. *Social needs.* When their physical and safety needs are met, people can focus on their needs for love, respect, and acceptance from others. Families, communities, and social and professional groups help satisfy these needs for human contact and friendship.

Speakers can appeal to social needs when arguing for better family relations, for balance between home and work lives, for better communication with others, or for participation on a committee.

4. *Ego needs.* Humans also have a need for self-esteem and self-respect. Advertisers appeal to this need for self-esteem in selling cars, clothing, cosmetics, jewelry, and hair color products. Though genuine self-respect has more to do with one's honesty, reliability, discipline, and other qualities, advertisers want people to believe that consumer products can make them feel better about themselves.

Persuasive speakers can appeal to people's need for self-esteem when asking people to volunteer, to make charitable donations, or when selling educational or training packages.

5. *Self needs.* According to Maslow, once all other needs are met, humans need self-actualization—a sense of having reached their highest potential. This is the highest need, appearing at the top of Maslow's hierarchy.

Speakers can appeal to this need by offering people ways to fulfill themselves, perhaps through job achievement, meeting special challenges, or making significant sacrifices.

Summary of Maslow's Hierarchy of Needs		
Need	**Description**	**Sample Appeal**
1. Physical	Air, water, food, clothing, shelter, health	Let's clean up the river.
2. Safety	Physical safety, security	Don't drink and drive. It puts everyone at risk.
3. Social	Love, respect, acceptance, need to belong	Here's how to survive a blind date.
4. Ego	Self-esteem, self-respect	Volunteer. Be a part of a team.
5. Self	Meaning in life, reaching your highest potential	Attend Harper University. Reach for the stars.

Ethos (Establishing Credibility)

Along with appeals to listeners' needs (pathos), Aristotle identified a second way a speaker can persuade others—through **ethos,** one's personal power or credibility. A credible speaker is knowledgeable and believable. He or she inspires trust. We all make decisions every day based on the credibility of a person who is speaking to us.

Personal Appearance

When you're speaking, all eyes are on you, and first impressions count. It's true that clothes can't guarantee success, but being dressed appropriately for the occasion goes a long way toward establishing your credibility with the audience. Would you buy a product or an idea from someone who looked as though he or she just woke up?

In general, listeners like speakers with whom they can identify and share something in common. In choosing what to wear, consider the audience and be careful not to overdress or underdress for the occasion.

Smooth Beginnings

Your body speaks before you utter a word. Make sure that your stance is straight and confident and that your expression is pleasant and genuinely interested. Introduce yourself and begin to speak slowly, maintaining good eye contact with everyone in the room.

Some speakers bob their heads up and down while reading their notes. Some swivel their heads rapidly from side to side when making eye contact. Practice moving your head slowly and naturally as you speak, so that people on both sides of the podium and at the front and back of the room know that you are aware of their presence.

Credentials

You need not be bashful. Let the audience know that it can trust you. Share your background, experience, or research in the field. Your credentials will go a long way toward establishing your credibility.

Make sure that you choose the most relevant parts of your background and experience to share. Too much information can overwhelm or bore your audience.

Enthusiasm

Enthusiasm is contagious. If you are excited about and sincerely believe in the ideas you're presenting, it is likely that the audience will be also.

Try to imagine hearing the speech you are giving, or tape record it. Do the words—and your voice inflection—communicate true excitement and enthusiasm?

Thorough Preparation

If you appear to be intelligent and well prepared, people will respond. Do your homework. Use up-to-date, relevant, and impeccably researched evidence to support each argument. Present your speech in a clear, organized way. Audiences who know the subject will listen especially closely.

If you're not an expert in a particular area, why pretend to be one? Audiences who know better will judge you harshly. You will win more support through honesty than you will by overstating what you really know.

Trustworthiness

What makes a person trustworthy? Qualities such as honesty, directness, sincerity, commitment, stability, respect for others, and personal character make a person seem trustworthy.

Make sure your approach to the subject is fair. If you are discussing a topic with two distinct points of view, a knowledgeable audience will trust you more for stating arguments for both sides without bias.

Checklist

How an Audience Will Judge You

- ✓ Personal appearance
- ✓ Presentation skills
- ✓ Knowledge and experience
- ✓ Enthusiasm
- ✓ Thorough preparation
- ✓ Trustworthiness

Persuasive Speech

A Churchill introduces key facts in emphatic parallel clauses. Germany has invaded neighboring countries.

B Churchill states the government's new policy in passionate, inspiring language.

Model

Winston Churchill

London, 13 May 1940

"I have nothing to offer but blood, toil, tears and sweat."

It must be remembered that we are in the preliminary stage of one the greatest battles in history, that we are in action at many points in Norway and in Holland, that we have to be prepared in the Mediterranean, that the air battle is continuous and that many preparations have to be made here at home. In this crisis I hope I may be pardoned if I do not address the House at any length today. I hope that any of my friends and colleagues, or former colleagues, who are affected by the political reconstruction, will make all allowance for any lack of ceremony with which it has been necessary to act. I would say to the House, as I said to those who have joined the Government: "I have nothing to offer but blood, toil, tears and sweat."

We have before us an ordeal of the most grievous kind. We have before us many, many long months of struggle and of suffering. You ask, what is our policy? I will say: It is to wage war, by sea, land and air, with all our might and with all the strength that God can give us: to wage war against a monstrous tyranny, never surpassed in the dark, lamentable catalogue of human crime. That is our policy. You ask, What is our aim? I can answer in one word: Victory– victory at all costs, victory in spite of all terror, victory, however long and hard the road may be; for without victory, there is no survival. Let that be realized; no survival for the British Empire; no survival for all that the British Empire has stood for, no survival for the urge and impulse of the ages, that mankind will move forward towards its goal. But I take up my task with buoyancy and hope. I feel sure that our cause will not be suffered to fail among men. At this time I feel entitled to claim the aid of all, and I say, "Come, then, let us go forward together with our united strength."

C Churchill uses repetition to appeal to his audience's sense of safety.

D This speech ends with a powerful appeal for courage and unity. Churchill's attitude inspires confidence in him as a leader.

Logos (Reasoning)

Aristotle advises persuasive speakers to engage listeners' emotions (pathos) and to establish their own credibility (ethos). But to convince or change an audience, a speaker's appeal also must contain Aristotle's third element, **logos.** The Greek word *logos* means reason, the faculty that allows people to think logically. Sophisticated audiences may distrust purely emotional appeals, but they'll find a well-constructed, sound, and logical argument hard to resist.

The Power of Logic

As Peggy Noonan writes in *Simply Speaking: How to Communicate Your Ideas with Style, Substance, and Clarity,* "Your speech doesn't need music, it needs logic. And the good news is logic can be very moving indeed."

A logos appeal requires sound arguments and the use of persuasive evidence. **Reasoning** is the process of drawing logical conclusions and formulating arguments from evidence. All persuasive speeches center around a basic **argument,** or rationale, for a position.

Once you have chosen the central argument (or arguments) of your speech, you begin to collect the **evidence,** or proof, necessary. Your evidence may include facts, examples, illustrations, personal experience, statistics, and the testimony of experts in the field. After clearly stating

your argument, you systematically build a substantive case, proving your argument through different types of evidence. Logic is the glue that binds together your argument, evidence, and conclusion.

Consider these **two** arguments.

1. Many people suffer from sleep deprivation, which affects their performance at school and work and their relationships with their families and friends. Possible evidence includes: medical statistics, expert opinions, school data, work injury statistics, anecdotal evidence, and personal examples.

2. Most accidents at home could be avoided if a few safety precautions were taken. Possible evidence includes: national fire and safety statistics, expert opinions, case histories, and research results.

How do you build a logical and effective persuasive argument? There are **three** main patterns of reasoning for persuasive speeches: inductive reasoning, deductive reasoning, and cause-effect reasoning. Which pattern you use depends upon the type of audience you are addressing.

❶ Inductive Reasoning

Inductive reasoning starts with specific facts or arguments, and then leads to a conclusion. For example:

Evidence:

* Research shows that blood pressure goes down when people pet their cats and dogs.

* Studies show that elderly people who own pets live longer.
* Surveys of pet owners list "personal happiness" as the main reason they own a pet.
* When my dog Otis runs to greet me or follows me around the house, it makes me feel good.

Generalization: Owning a pet can make you a happier, healthier person.

This type of reasoning is effective with opposed, neutral, and apathetic audiences who respond to inductive reasoning because it is "soft sell" persuasion. Instead of asking listeners to accept your whole argument, you're giving them one piece of evidence at a time. To establish common ground, begin with ideas, examples, and research that they can't refute. Then, through inductive reasoning, lead them, step by step, to your conclusion.

Here are some tips to help you construct a sound inductive argument:

* Use enough evidence and examples to prove your argument.
* Make sure that your evidence is authoritative.
* Organize your argument so that it leads logically to your conclusion.
* Use strong transitions between ideas so you don't lose your audience.
* Avoid sweeping generalizations. Use words such as *most*, *several*, and *often* rather than *all*, *every*, and *always*.

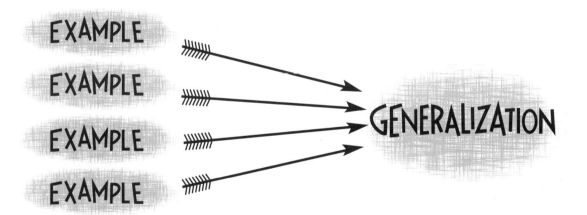

Marisela's Inductive Argument

Marisela and Tanya were best friends and, as usual, they had a great plan. This summer Marisela would go with Tanya and her family on a trip to Disney World. Marisela's problem was convincing her parents. She decided to try inductive reasoning.

"I began by thinking of the reasons that they might say no. I was too young. Tanya's parents wouldn't agree. I couldn't make enough money to pay for it. They couldn't afford to send me. I developed a strategy for dealing with each argument.

"I found a good time for us to talk when my parents were relaxed. I explained that, because I was getting older, I was assuming more responsibility at home, at school, and in my community. I reminded them that Tanya's parents really liked me. I said

that, to me, part of accepting responsibility was being able to make and follow a long-term plan. Mine was to make $300 by the beginning of the summer. I showed them a spreadsheet that detailed my plan to save $300 from my allowance, from babysitting, and from my part-time weekend job.

"Then came the request. 'Mom and Dad,' I said, 'It's for these reasons that I think you should say yes when I ask you whether I can please go with Tanya to Disney World this summer. Her parents have already said that it is fine with them.'

"I think my parents were amazed by my presentation. They just sat there, smiling. Then my dad said, 'Sounds like you've worked out the details in a very mature way, Marisela. Do us a favor. Please send us a postcard!'"

❷ Deductive Reasoning

Deductive reasoning, the opposite of inductive reasoning, starts with an argument or main premise, then produces specific evidence to support it. For example:

Generalization: Women's sports teams should be funded at the same level as men's teams.

Evidence:

* Women's teams generate revenue just as men's teams do.
* Women should have equal opportunities to participate in sports teams.
* Women's teams have been underfunded and neglected for years.

Generalization: The quality of life in our town will be better if the city built more parks as new housing developments are added.

Evidence:

* Parks provide places for families to enjoy the outdoors and play together.
* Parks beautify the community and provide a place for wildlife.
* Trees and plants filter the air and reduce toxins in the air.

Deductive reasoning is particularly effective with a positive audience that agrees with your position. Often used in sales pitches and business situations, it is simpler and more direct than inductive reasoning. A deductive approach can increase your credibility, since you're hiding nothing from the audience. Your argument is straightforward and easy to follow. People don't have to guess what you're driving at.

Here are some tips for constructing an effective deductive argument:

* Make sure it's the right approach for your audience. If listeners are hostile toward or suspicious of your argument, use an inductive approach.
* Define your conclusion clearly. Use terms that are precise.
* Spend time establishing your credibility.
* Use sound, ample, and interesting evidence.
* Make sure your argument doesn't contain logical fallacies or propaganda.

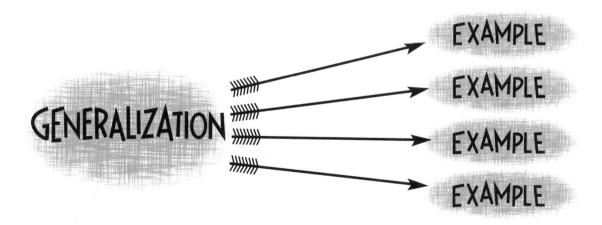

Ways of Showing a Cause-Effect Relationship	
Cause Chicago uses tons of salt on its icy streets and highways during the winter.	**Effect** Cars tend to rust quickly in Chicago.
Effect My grocery store is out of Brand X bread and muffins.	**Cause** The Brand X bakery workers went out on strike.

❸ Cause-Effect Reasoning

A third type of logical reasoning shows a cause-effect relationship. This type of reasoning can be used with any type of audience.

Persuasive speakers often use **cause-effect reasoning** in the following situations:

* To present scientific and historical evidence, such as the results of this year's flu epidemic or the causes of the Vietnam War.
* To motivate the audience to do something specific, such as approve a new city ordinance or install seat belts in school buses.
* To explain why something occurred, such as why 50 workers were laid off or why the rainforests are diminishing.
* To argue for strengthening practices that have positive outcomes, such as enforcement of parking violations.
* To argue against practices or policies with negative effects, such as price-fixing among utility companies.

You can structure a cause-effect argument in two ways—from one or more effects to a cause or from a cause to one or more effects.

Life is complicated. Real events and situations rarely have a single cause or a single effect. Most effects (like inner-city poverty) or events (like why you broke up with your boyfriend or girlfriend) have many causes. Most causes (like changing to a flat income tax) have more than one effect. Usually, things can be seen as a chain of events.

Here are some tips for constructing a sound cause-effect argument:

* Spend time on research and analysis. Get your facts straight.
* Consider which will be the most effective argument, beginning with the cause or beginning with effects.
* Make sure that your cause-effect relationships are sound. Two things that occur at once don't necessarily have a cause-effect relationship.
* Anticipate audience reactions and objections.
* Try your argument out on people that you respect. Some feedback might be helpful.
* Present solid evidence—but avoid overkill.
* Keep your presentation lively.
* Consider all possible outcomes of your argument.

Identify Methods of Reasoning

GOAL

The goal of this activity is to identify three methods of reasoning—inductive, deductive, and showing cause-effect.

TASKS

1. Form groups of three to six.

2. Each group considers the following arguments and decides (a) which type of reasoning—inductive, deductive, or cause-effect—the speaker used; and (b) the reason for this choice. A member of the group records the group's choices.

   Arguments:

   a. The flute has many advantages. It has a beautiful sound. It is easy to learn to play. It is easy to carry and to transport. You can play in orchestras and in marching and stage bands.

   b. Brand X is a superior car. You get more options for the money. It comes in great colors. It has a comfortable ride. It's highly rated by consumer magazines.

   c. I am a good student. I have perfect attendance. I always work for extra credit. I deserve to be on the honor roll.

   d. If you plan well and follow all these suggestions for preparing a speech, you will become a successful public speaker.

   e. Many Europeans object to American fast-food restaurants because they don't like their architectural "look," because they tend to undermine native cuisines, and because they're making some people fat.

   f. Our football team won the state championship last year. Almost all of the star players will return to the team this year. Our defensive line outweighs every defensive line in our league. We have a great chance to win the state championship this year.

3. Groups meet and compare their results, discussing any differences in opinion.

OUTCOMES

Were you able to tell the different types of reasoning used in each of the arguments? What clues did you use?

Faulty Reasoning

Not all argumentative methods are sound. Logical fallacies and propaganda are well-known types of faulty reasoning. They are unethical and misleading and don't follow sound principles for constructing an argument. An educated audience will easily identify and reject such arguments.

Logical Fallacies

Logical fallacies are flawed reasoning methods. They occur when evidence is inadequate or when arguments are irrelevant or inappropriate. If you're aware of the **seven** common logical fallacies described below, you will improve your skills both as a speaker and listener.

1. *Begging the question.* A speaker assumes a statement's truth or falsity without supplying proof. For example, "Our ineffective mayor should be replaced."

2. *Card-stacking.* A speaker mentions only the facts that will build the best case for his or her argument, ignoring other factors or evidence. For example, an advertisement for a sale on spring clothing doesn't mention that only 20 items are on sale.

3. *False premises.* A speaker begins with a false assumption that you assume is true. For example, "All other leading antacid remedies take 20 minutes to provide relief."

4. *Glittering generalities.* A speaker uses clichés; makes broad, sweeping, positive statements with little or no substance; or otherwise tries to make you accept something by associating it with things that you value. For example, "Good citizens will support new housing developments in our community."

5. *False generalizations.* Words such as *all, everywhere, everyone, always, never,* and *no one* signal that a broad generalization is being used. In some cases, a speaker offers a generalization that is based on incomplete or nonexistent evidence. For example, any statement that assumes all members of an ethnic, religious, or political group are the same in all or most respects is false.

6. *Non sequitur.* The conclusion does not follow from the evidence presented. For example, you argue that your neighborhood is dangerous, citing that you saw one or two "suspicious-looking" people walking around yesterday.

7. *Unrelated testimonials.* Authorities in one field are used to endorse a product or an idea that they lack expertise about. For example, a famous basketball player endorses a political candidate.

Propaganda

Propaganda is a form of persuasion that discourages people from making an independent choice. Propagandists offer a conclusion or opinion that lacks adequate evidence. Most propaganda targets the audience's emotions.

There are **five** common types of propaganda techniques.

1. *Transfer.* Transfer makes an illogical connection between unrelated things. For example, if politics is corrupt, this candidate also is corrupt.

2. *Bandwagon.* The bandwagon technique suggests that something is true because everyone else thinks that it is, as in the saying that "everyone is jumping on the bandwagon." For example, "Everyone is wearing GO-Jeans," so you should wear them too.

3. *Name calling.* A speaker uses emotionally charged, negative terms for a group or idea, without providing proof or examining the real issues. For example, calling someone a "loser" or a "racist" is meant to turn people against him or her.

4. *Loaded words and emotional appeals.* Language that evokes strong emotions can sway an argument. For example, "Men who didn't serve in the military are traitors to American values."

5. *Either/or.* Acting as though people have to make a choice between only two alternatives, when there may be many other possibilities. For example, "Without a college education, you're doomed to working at minimum wage all of your life."

Organizing a Persuasive Speech

You have many choices when you set out to organize your persuasive speech. Choose a method of organization that is appropriate to your audience and your goals.

Two of the most-used organizational formats are the problem-solution format and Monroe's Motivated Sequence format. Others include the sequential format, the labeling format, the comparison and contrast format, and the cause-effect format. You can also use these methods in combination.

Problem-Solution Format

The **problem-solution format** is one of the simplest organizational patterns for a persuasive speech. Using this format, you present a problem, then propose a solution.

Here are **two** examples.

1. *Problem:* The quality of our lives would improve now and in the future . . .

   Solution: . . . if more people recycled their garbage.

2. *Problem:* We would have less pollution and cleaner air . . .

   Solution: . . . if people carpooled, took public transportation, walked, or rode bikes to their jobs.

This format works well with apathetic or neutral audiences. You can use it when presenting an obvious problem with a clear solution or when you want the audience to take action of some kind.

Here are some tips for using the problem-solution format:

* Start by attracting the audience's attention.
* Describe the problem precisely and clearly.
* Be sure that your solution is both realistic and beneficial. If it can't be put into effect or if it creates other problems, it's not a good solution.
* Use strong and interesting evidence.
* Keep your main goal in mind.
* Work at holding the audience's attention.

Monroe's Motivated Sequence Format

Two speech professors from Purdue University, Douglas Ehninger and Alan Monroe, devised **Monroe's Motivated Sequence,** a popular format for persuasive speeches. This method structures a persuasive argument in a way that is highly motivational for audiences. For this reason, it is often used—and sometimes misused—in sales pitches.

Monroe's Motivated Sequence is based on research that suggests that people are likely to change if they are experiencing a state called cognitive dissonance. Cognitive dissonance is a feeling of conflict or anxiety that can occur when people hear something that conflicts with what they know and believe. For example, people who believe that school buses are safe can become very upset if they hear alarming school bus accident statistics. These people might be highly motivated to take action.

Monroe's sequence shows speakers how to attract audience attention, create cognitive dissonance, then motivate the audience to adopt the solution that is offered.

The sequence includes **five** steps: attention, need, satisfaction, visualization, and action.

1. *Attention.* In step 1, you attract and focus the attention of the audience. Be accurate but bold. The goal is to make the audience a bit unsettled or anxious about the problem you are describing. You can do this with a vivid case history, a riveting question, a quotation or example, or an arresting fact or statistic.

2. *Need.* In this step, you show the audience that the problem is their own. Use evidence to give them strong, compelling reasons to be concerned. Facts, statistics, quotations, and expert testimony are appropriate.

3. *Satisfaction.* Next, outline your solution to the problem. Explain the elements of the solution, and demonstrate why it will solve the problem and diminish the audience's worry. Address concerns that you think the audience will have about your plan.

4. *Visualization.* To help listeners see how the solution works, ask them to visualize a future as it would look when your solution is put into practice and the problem no longer exists. At the end of this step, move toward your summary and closing remarks.

5. Action. Your final step is a call to action. Inform the audience of actions you want it to take, inviting listeners to be part of the solution. A few clear, uncomplicated ideas are often all that are needed. In this step, you can provide contact information, directions for taking action (signing petitions, contacting politicians), and resources.

Sequential Format

The **sequential format** can be useful when the element of time is a factor in your argument. This simple organizational format presents events or elements in chronological order. For example, to persuade a committee to accept your proposal, you might structure the presentation so the audience can see concrete progress occurring at definite time periods during the process. A timeline can be a useful visual aid for a speech with a chronological organization.

Labeling Format

In a **labeling format,** the subheadings you create become the organizational tool. For example, if you are persuading a group to use a variety of saving strategies, you might discuss bank savings accounts, IRAs, tax-sheltered accounts, and 401K plans.

When using this format, make sure that you present elements in a parallel manner and use strong transitions. Otherwise, your speech might be confusing.

Comparison and Contrast Format

Content in the **comparison and contrast format** can be organized by topics, elements, pros and cons, or similarities and differences. Also called the pros and cons method, this structure is useful when you want the audience to assess the similarities and differences between two different strategies, candidates, solutions, or ideas. In this type of speech, you bounce back and forth between pros and cons or similarities and differences of each option, until it's clear that your solution is the only logical one.

This method requires that you do careful research. Your credibility will be at risk if you don't present both sides fairly and honestly.

Cause-Effect Format

Cause-effect format is useful when you are discussing a scientific or historical event with far-reaching consequences. You may choose to present the causes first, followed by the effects, or you may decide to begin with the effects and end with the causes.

Cause-effect organization can become complex. Devote time to careful outlining of your content, so the speech moves from beginning to end in a clear and logical manner.

School Commercial

GOAL

The goal of this activity is to create a commercial to promote your school.

TASKS

1. Form groups of three to six.
2. Each group writes a commercial promoting your school. Use one or more of the organizational methods described in this chapter. The commercial may be informative or entertaining and must have:
   * A minimum length of 150 words.
   * Creative or performance roles for all members of your group.
   * A slogan or jingle (catchy little song).
   * An equal part for everyone in the group.

* Some type of visual aid.
* Optional music and costumes.

Consider videotaping your commercial.

3. When finished, present the commercial to the class.
4. The class discusses the commercials, evaluating which were the most effective and why.

OUTCOMES

What persuasive techniques did your group use? Which format did you follow and why? Did you first establish a need and then show how features of your school fulfilled the need? What were some of the problems that you faced during creation? Do you think you might encounter similar problems when you create a speech to persuade? Why or why not?

Evaluating Persuasive Speeches

You've finished drafting a persuasive speech and you're ready to evaluate yourself. You also are being asked to judge other people's persuasive speeches in class. And you want information that helps you to evaluate the sales pitches and persuasive arguments that you're confronted with each day.

Evaluation Methods

Evaluation methods fall into **two** categories or types, qualitative and quantitative.

❶ Qualitative Evaluation

<u>Qualitative evaluation</u> involves judgments and observations rather than numbers and statistics. Comments that you make regarding how good or poor the speech was are considered qualitative evaluation. If members of the audience decide to try the speaker's suggestions for a new diet plan, this would be considered a positive qualitative evaluation. If audience members fail to sign the petition in the back of the room, this is a negative qualitative evaluation.

❷ Quantitative Evaluation

<u>Quantitative evaluation</u> uses objective standards such as evaluation forms or a numerical rating system to determine the effectiveness of a speech. In a numerical system, listeners may quantify their judgments of a speech by marking a scale from one to five or one to ten.

To determine whether listeners changed an attitude, belief, or behavior, try surveying them before and after a speech. The two surveys can then be compared to determine whether a change occurred.

Here is an example of a survey that might be used before and after a speech.

Audience Survey

Circle the number that best indicates the strength of your opinion on the following topic.

A high-protein diet will enable me to lose weight.

Disagree   **Strongly Disagree**

| 1 | 2 | 3 | 4 | 5 | 6 | 7 | 8 | 9 | 10 |

Agree   **Strongly Agree**

| 1 | 2 | 3 | 4 | 5 | 6 | 7 | 8 | 9 | 10 |

☐ **No Opinion**

How to Evaluate a Persuasive Speech

Situation

- ✓ Appropriate for the occasion?
- ✓ Within time limit?

Needs of listeners (pathos)

- ✓ Correctly identified audience attitude?
- ✓ Related issue to audience needs?
- ✓ Established common ground of agreement?
- ✓ Acknowledged other views?
- ✓ Stated what audience should do?
- ✓ Motivational appeals appropriate?

Personal credibility (ethos)

- ✓ Appearance appropriate?
- ✓ Knew subject?
- ✓ Cited credible and current evidence?
- ✓ Seemed well-organized and well-prepared?
- ✓ Shared interests and concerns with audience?
- ✓ Provided relevant personal information?
- ✓ Appeared truthful and sincere?
- ✓ Spoke with conviction and enthusiasm?

Reasoning and evidence (logos)

- ✓ Appropriate and effective organizational format?
- ✓ Clear central argument?
- ✓ Evidence honest, sound, ethical, believable, and relevant?
- ✓ Sound argument?
- ✓ Logical reasoning?
- ✓ Sufficient evidence?
- ✓ Arguments convincing?

Delivery

- ✓ Extemporaneous?
- ✓ Distracting mannerisms?
- ✓ Good enunciation and clear diction?
- ✓ Effective gestures, facial expression, and eye contact?
- ✓ Appropriate volume and pace?
- ✓ Smooth use of notes and visual aids?

Conclusion

- ✓ Adequate?
- ✓ Effective?

Overall effectiveness

- ✓ Clear message?
- ✓ Purpose accomplished?

The Evaluation Process

Evaluating persuasive speeches can be challenging. As an evaluator, it is important that you begin with a fair and unbiased attitude—even if you disagree with the speaker. Strive to be objective and to give the speaker constructive feedback. Your job is to help him or her improve.

Here are some guidelines for evaluating persuasive speeches:

* Don't take sides on an issue. Keep an objective, positive attitude.

* Consider all main areas of a persuasive speech—the situation, the speaker's purpose, the needs of listeners, personal credibility, reasoning and evidence, delivery, conclusion, and overall effectiveness. Use the checklist on page 194 to help your evaluation.
* Take notes as the speech proceeds.
* Be constructive. Offer suggestions for improvement.

For more details on evaluation, see Chapter 16.

Wrap-up

Persuasion is the process of changing or reinforcing attitudes, beliefs, or behaviors. The central argument of a persuasive speech may be a question of fact, a question of value, a question of policy, or some combination of these. Persuasive speakers use appeals to the listeners' needs (pathos), appeals based on the speaker's credibility (ethos), and appeals based on logic and reasoning (logos). To meet listener's needs, speakers can tailor their arguments to the audience's attitudes and appeal to the basic human needs defined by Abraham Maslow. To achieve credibility, speakers can use strategies ranging from personal appearance to thorough preparation. To appeal to listeners' logic, speakers can use inductive, deductive, or cause-effect reasoning to argue their main points. Persuasive speakers also can avoid common types of faulty reasoning that can destroy their credibility. There are several effective ways to structure a persuasive argument, including the problem-solution format and Monroe's Motivated Sequence. Quantitative and qualitative audience feedback can help speakers to learn whether a persuasive speech has been successful.

apathetic audience—audience that has no interest in your topic because its members may not see how it affects them.

argument—the rationale for a position in a persuasive speech.

cause-effect format—organizational format that presents causes followed by effects, or effects followed by the causes.

cause-effect reasoning—in persuasive speaking, type of logical reasoning that shows how one or more events caused another event or events to happen.

comparison and contrast format—organizational format that uses the pros and cons or similarities and differences of a topic as the organizing strategy.

deductive reasoning—thought process that moves from a general statement or principle to reach a specific conclusion and application to specific examples.

ethos—in Aristotle's thought, mode of persuasion that appeals based on the speaker's character or credibility.

evidence—the facts, examples, statistics, and expert opinions used to support the main points of an argument.

inductive reasoning—thought process that uses specific instances or examples to reach a general conclusion.

labeling format—organizational format that uses topic subheads as the organizing strategy.

logos—in Aristotle's thought, mode of persuasion that appeals to the listener's rationality.

Monroe's Motivated Sequence—five-step organizational pattern for a persuasive speech, in which the speaker uses the principle of cognitive dissonance to make an audience anxious about an immediate problem or need, then provides a solution.

neutral audience—type of audience in which listeners are neither for nor against your argument because they are either ignorant of or undecided about it.

opposed audience—type of audience in which listeners disagree with your position.

pathos—in Aristotle's thought, mode of persuasion that appeals to the listener's emotions by appealing to his or her needs.

persuasion—the process of changing or reinforcing attitudes, beliefs, or behaviors.

positive audience—type of audience in which listeners share and support your position.

problem-solution format—basic organizational pattern for a persuasive speech, in which a problem then its solution are presented.

qualitative evaluation—judgments of and observations about a speech.

quantitative evaluation—numerical rating of the effectiveness of a speech.

question of fact—problem, issue, or matter that can be viewed as true or false.

question of policy—problem, issue, or matter proposing a change in policy or plan of action.

question of value—problem, issue, or matter involving a strong opinion or attitude.

reasoning—process of drawing logical conclusions and formulating arguments from evidence.

sequential format—organizational format that presents the topic in the order in which events will occur.

situation—term used by Aristotle meaning the place, time, circumstances, and audience for a speech.

Other Types of Public Speaking

Although most speeches are given to inform, persuade, or entertain, some speeches are designed especially for specific occasions. These specially tailored speeches are as varied as the activities and the events of life. In this chapter, you'll discover how to write and deliver speeches of introduction, presentation, acceptance, and commemoration. You'll master the techniques of effective keynote, commencement, dedication, and entertainment speeches. And you'll find out how to give business reports, proposals, public relations speeches, and sales presentations. You'll even learn how to be ready for impromptu speeches. In short, you'll be prepared for almost any speech-giving occasion.

Preparing Other Types of Speeches

This chapter prepares you for life's special occasions by introducing you to speeches about people, speeches for special occasions, business speeches, and impromptu speeches. Preparing these speeches involves **four** steps:

❶ Evaluate the Situation

Speeches covered in this chapter may be delivered at building dedications, testimonial dinners, award ceremonies, memorial services, sales conferences, and other events. Your audience can range from a small family group at a funeral to thousands of professionals at a business conference. You might be speaking for a few minutes or an unlimited length of time. Listeners might expect to be informed, entertained, consoled, inspired, persuaded, or something else. Your tone could be dignified and formal, lighthearted, or profoundly sorrowful.

Obviously, your first task is to research and analyze the situation—the occasion, the location, the audience, the speech's length and tone, and your expected goal and content.

❷ Choose and Narrow the Topic

For special event speeches, your topic is often predetermined. The situation and type of speech often dictate a certain goal and approach. But at times you will choose your topic yourself or narrow it to a fixed time limit.

If you have topic choices, consider these questions. What is your goal for this speech? What do you want your audience to know, feel, think, or do? For more on how to narrow your topic, see the techniques described in Chapter 12.

❸ Gather Information

Most special occasion speeches require specific information, such as details about a person's life, facts about an occasion or award, knowledge of your competition, and more. After assessing your situation and narrowing your topic, spend time collecting appropriate information. Then identify your main points and outline your speech. What supporting material do you need to flesh out your main points? personal anecdotes? statistics? quotations? Spend the time necessary to collect the right information that fits your speech.

❹ Write and Rehearse the Speech

Next, begin to write. Observe appropriate time limits for the speech, deleting sections and ideas as needed. Rehearse your speech until you are comfortable with it, and then try it out on family and friends. Note their reactions. Does it hold their attention? Is it easy to follow? Is the point of the speech clear?

As you practice, imagine yourself at the event. Concentrate on your goal and the appropriate tone for the occasion. If you're selling a proposal, speak with enthusiasm. If you're delivering a testimonial, speak in a respectful but friendly tone of voice.

Speeches about People

Speeches about people recognize and honor the achievements of individuals and groups. Speeches about people include **four** types: introduction, presentation, acceptance, and commemoration.

❶ Speeches of Introduction

The first type of speech about people, a **speech of introduction,** prepares the audience to hear a speaker. These speeches may be delivered at formal banquets, club meetings, sports events, conferences, business meetings, or community events.

As famed motivational speaker Dale Carnegie said, ". . . an introduction ought to 'sell' the speaker." Your goals in an introduction are to engage the audience, to establish the speaker's credibility, and to create interest in and enthusiasm about the speech to come. For this brief speech, your tone should be sincere and respectful and your language either informal or formal, depending on the occasion.

Introductory Speech

In the beginning there was no Bonita Suarez.

It's hard to imagine that, since she has made such a profound and dynamic mark on this company in only two short years. In that short stretch of time, she has restructured each division with sensitivity and skill, all the while making us all feel involved in the process. She hired financial consultants to get the company back on track and marketing experts to help us to expand to overseas markets and to take advantage of e-commerce. Throughout our restructuring process, she kept the door—and her mind—open, always encouraging us to share our creative ideas.

In the beginning there was no Bonita Suarez, but thank goodness she is here now. Please join me in welcoming a woman who has done so much for this company—Bonita Suarez.

Structure your speech of introduction like this:

* If you are the first speaker, welcome the audience to this event.
* Briefly discuss this occasion and its importance.
* Spotlight the speaker, summarizing his or her background, qualifications, and special knowledge of this topic. Mention important highlights of his or her career and interesting personal anecdotes.
* If the speaker wishes, briefly introduce his or her topic and motivate the audience to learn about it.
* Conclude by reintroducing the speaker by name, then smoothly transition to his or her appearance on the stage.

Follow these general guidelines in your writing and delivery:

* Research your speaker well, collecting biographical information and anecdotes from the speaker or from other sources.
* Write out your entire text or memorize it. There's no need to be conversational with this speech.
* Make sure that your delivery is energetic and interesting.
* For a formal occasion, check ahead of time with the speaker about how you plan to cue him or her and whether or not you'll stay at the podium as he or she approaches.

Everyday COMMUNICATION

Caution: Preparation Needed!

Everyone knows a person like Jerry Kohler, who thought that he could give a speech of introduction without preparing in advance. Jerry was known for his ability to "think on his feet," so he decided to wait for inspiration and find the words at the moment he was asked to speak.

As a result, his speech went something like this:

Ladies and gentlemen, friends, colleagues, and first-time visitors. Welcome to the monthly meeting of Willamette Writers. We asked the governor to speak *(applause)*, but he had a schedule conflict and couldn't come. So, we asked Marla Lopez, recipient of last year's statewide writing award *(applause)* . . . but she had the flu. Then we tried to get a Nobel Prize winner, but of course that was impossible. So, instead, tonight we will hear . . . our own . . . Angie Jordan! *(silence)*.

Prepare and Deliver a Speech of Introduction

GOAL

The goal of this activity is to prepare and present a speech of introduction.

TASKS

1. Choose a subject for a speech of introduction—your favorite author, artist, musician, film star, or personal hero. Choose the event at which you'll introduce him or her.

2. Prepare and rehearse your speech of introduction, using the guidelines in this chapter.

3. Deliver your speech to the class for feedback and discussion.

4. As a class, discuss common difficulties that speakers had and how to avoid them.

OUTCOMES

Why do you think that advance preparation is helpful for this type of speech? Did class feedback help you to identify your strengths and areas that you need to improve?

❷ Speeches of Presentation

A second type of speech about people, a **speech of presentation**, honors an individual or group for special accomplishments, and then presents an award or honor.

Presentation speeches are given at many types of events, ranging from small Cub Scout meetings to industry galas such as the Academy Awards.

In this type of speech, your goals are to congratulate the award winner(s) and to lead the audience in a special tribute to this person or group. These speeches usually are brief. Your tone should be respectful and dignified, but your language may be formal or informal, depending upon the event.

Structure your presentation like this:

* Greet the audience and speak respectfully of this occasion.
* Focus on the award or honor to be presented, explaining why this honoree or group has earned it.
* Warmly congratulate the recipient(s) and urge the audience to join you in showing its appreciation.
* Present the award to the recipient.

Follow these general guidelines in your writing and delivery:

* Take time to prepare. Specific and little-known facts about the person or group will make the award more meaningful.

* Build your speech in a way that show-cases this person's or group's talents and accomplishments.
* Create a respectful mood and project genuine feeling.
* If the audience knows who is being honored, announce the name(s) first. If not, announce the name(s) at the end, building to a climactic finish.
* Be careful to observe the time limit. The audience wants to hear from the person being honored more than from the person giving the introduction.

❸ Speeches of Acceptance

In the third type of speech about people, a **speech of acceptance,** you are the honoree, formally expressing your heartfelt thanks for receiving an honor or award. Awards and honors usually are conferred at large conferences, meetings, and community events.

In an acceptance speech, your goals are to show your pleasure at receiving the award, to sincerely thank the audience, and to honor any who deserve to be

Example

Presentation Speech

This year's award for Most Valuable Employee goes to Marketing Director Kumiko Takemoto. For 25 years, Atlas Technologies has been presenting this award to outstanding honorees who have consistently demonstrated leadership, resourcefulness, initiative, and teamwork in helping Atlas achieve its business goals.

This year, we've all watched Kumiko Takemoto turn in a remarkable perform-ance. Her Productivity Task Force helped increase Atlas productivity levels by

25 percent. Her marketing campaigns for our new e-commerce system, "Ready-Sell," helped Atlas increase its market share 12 percent, topping all of our sales projections. Kumiko also helped us forge alliances with two start-up companies, which promise great things for the future.

We salute you, Kumiko, for your great success and thank you for your efforts on behalf of the company. Please join me in congratulating Kumiko Takemoto for earning this distinguished service award—Most Valuable Employee.

thanked for helping you. You usually are allowed only a few minutes for these speeches, so keep your speech short but sincere. Do your best to express your genuine thanks and gratitude.

Develop your acceptance speech this way:

* Communicate your great respect for this honor. Let the audience know how important and meaningful the award is to you.
* Sincerely thank the group or association for choosing you or your group.
* Recognize and honor others who helped you achieve this award—a teacher, a coach, your parents, a mentor, or your team members.
* If time permits, briefly explain how you became interested in this field or organization.
* Close by repeating your thanks and appreciation.

Follow these general guidelines in your writing and delivery:

* If you accept for a group, include them in your advance planning. If time permits, recognize them personally during your speech.
* Watch your language. Avoid slang and keep it appropriate to the occasion.
* Be humble. Refrain from telling people how talented and fabulous you are. Leave that for the person who introduced you.
* Avoid making political statements or trying to sell a point of view. Focus only on this event and this honor.

Acceptance Speech

To me, there are few honors greater than being honored by the people I work with every day. I am thrilled to receive the Most Valuable Employee Award. It's easy to be a good employee when you have such great management and such a wonderful team of people to support you. We've had lots of challenges this year, but for me this award seems magically to erase all those long hours to meet deadlines! I share this award with the rest of my marketing team. You're the greatest. Thank you all so much.

❹ Commemorative Speeches

The fourth type of speech about people, the **commemorative speech,** pays tribute to an individual or group. Testimonials and eulogies are both kinds of commemorative speeches.

Testimonials

Testimonial speeches acknowledge and honor living individuals or groups for their outstanding accomplishments, vision, heroism, or public service. Testimonial speeches usually are delivered at dinners or other special events that are organized especially to honor this person or group.

Dos and Don'ts of Presentation and Acceptance Speeches

GOAL

The goal of this activity is to identify the characteristics of good and bad presentation and acceptance speeches.

TASKS

1. Videotape or tape record presentation and acceptance speeches on a TV sports or entertainment award show such as the Oscars, Tonys, Emmys, Grammys, MTV Music Awards, or others. Include at least eight to ten presenters and award recipients and more if possible.

2. View or listen to the speeches as a class or in a group.

3. Discuss the speeches and vote for the best and worst presentation speech and the best and worst acceptance speech.

4. Make a list of good and bad features of the winning speeches.

OUTCOMES

What part did the structure of the speeches play in their overall quality? How important was tone? What did you notice about length and organization of the speeches?

These speeches may express appreciation to retiring or departing employees, to outgoing officers of an organization, or to someone who gave outstanding volunteer service or performed a courageous deed.

Testimonial Speeches

I've worked closely with Isaiah Washington for 10 years, first on the Technology Task Force and then on last year's Working for Success program. Isaiah truly provided outstanding leadership to those groups. Thanks almost solely to his knowledge, high standards, and persistence, Acceptance Software now has one of the most advanced products on the market. And—again thanks to Isaiah—it runs flawlessly. Because of people like Isaiah, we have prospered. It is my pleasure to express my sincere appreciation to Isaiah for his achievements.

On behalf of our clients and all of us at Acceptance Software, thank you, Isaiah.

* * * *

The outstanding work done by Lisa Pearl during her five years as president of the Women's Collaborative clearly warrants this special dinner in her honor. We owe much to Lisa. Because of her able efforts, this organization now is funded by more than 30 corporate partners and is able to help more than 800 abused women each year. We're delighted to pay tribute to Lisa for her extraordinary leadership of the Women's Collaborative.

The goal in a testimonial is to respectfully honor a person or group for special achievements. The speech can vary in length, and its tone might be formal or informal, depending upon the occasion.

Arrange a testimonial as follows:

* If you are the first speaker, welcome your listeners and talk about the special occasion that brings this audience together.
* Pay tribute to the achievements and special qualities of this person or group.
* Relate personal anecdotes and describe the personal qualities of the person(s) being honored.
* Explain why this honoree or group has earned the audience's respect and gratitude.
* Close with a personal statement to the honoree(s), offering your congratulations.

Follow these general guidelines in your writing and delivery:

* Research the recipient(s) carefully. Try to discover meaningful stories that will engage the audience and confer honor on the recipient(s).
* If you use humor, make sure that it is appropriate and that listeners will appreciate it.
* Don't overdo the praise. Wordy, overly emotional, or exaggerated tributes annoy the audience and embarrass the person(s) being honored.

Eulogies

A **eulogy** is a commemorative speech honoring someone who has died. During a eulogy, you pay tribute to the life and deeds of the deceased. Because eulogies are given at funerals or memorial services, emotions are intense; and giving a speech may be difficult for you

Your goals in this speech are to express your deep sorrow that this person has died, to remember his or her unique life and achievements, and to help the entire audience mourn this loss. The time you are allotted depends upon the length of the service and whether there are other speakers. Use a sincere, solemn, and reverent tone, but allow your genuine feelings to show.

Because funerals and memorial services usually come within a few days of someone's death, you may have little planning time for your eulogy. However, you'll want to include content along these lines:

* If this person was a relative or friend, express your personal grief and deep sense of loss. If you didn't know the person well, offer your sympathy to the family and friends.
* Share memories about this person's life—things that are meaningful to you personally and to the assembled group. Mention the person's unique qualities, achievements, and behavior or attitudes that were memorable for those who knew this person well. Use specific examples and anecdotes.
* Describe ways in which this person will live on in the memories of those who loved him or her, through his or her achievements, or in the afterlife.
* Close with a meaningful quotation or a short poem that conveys the sorrow that you and the audience share. If time permits, explain why you chose it.

Follow these guidelines in your writing and delivery:

* Though time might be short, gather information and specific anecdotes about this person from relatives and friends.
* If you share humorous stories, choose them and your words carefully so as not to convey disrespect or to offend anyone.
* If your emotions overwhelm you as you speak, don't worry about it. Lower your head and take time to recover. The audience will understand and sympathize.
* Be sensitive to the religious and cultural beliefs of the deceased, of his or her family, and of those attending the service.

Eulogy

In spring 1986, the space shuttle *Challenger* exploded just after takeoff, killing all aboard. President Ronald Reagan delivered a famous eulogy to the nation. Speechwriter Peggy Noonan prepared the speech, which President Reagan adapted to his own style. Here, from Peggy Noonan's *Simply Speaking*, are Reagan's remarks, that express grief and sorrow felt throughout the world.

Today is a day for mourning and remembering.

Nancy and I are pained to the core by the tragedy of the shuttle Challenger. *We know we share this pain with all of the people of our country. This is truly a national loss.*

. . . the Challenger *7, were aware of the dangers—and overcame them, and did their jobs brilliantly.*

We mourn seven heroes—Michael Smith, Dick Scobee, Judith Resnik, Ronald McNair, Ellison Onizuka, Gregory Jarvis, and Christa McAuliffe. We mourn their loss as a nation, together.

To the families of the seven: We cannot bear, as you do, the full impact of this tragedy—but we feel the loss, and we are thinking about you so very much. Your loved ones were daring and brave and they had that special grace, that special spirit that says, "Give me the challenge and I'll meet it with joy." They had a hunger to explore the universe and discover its truths. They wished to serve and they did—they served us all.

. . . The crew of the space shuttle Challenger *honored us by the manner in which they lived their lives. We will never forget them, nor the last time we saw them—this morning, as they prepared for their journey, and waved goodbye, and "slipped the surly bonds of earth" to "touch the face of God."*

Several days later, Noonan received a letter from an anonymous citizen. Noonan says she wishes that it had arrived before she finished writing the speech. The letter ended with the words "They left us looking heavenward."

Eulogy

A President Lincoln wrote the model eulogy in "The Gettysburg Address." He first expresses solemnly and sincerely the importance of the gathering—to honor the people who died for the nation.

Model

Abraham Lincoln's "Gettysburg Address"

". . . A new birth of freedom . . ."

Four score and seven years ago our fathers brought forth on this continent, a new nation, conceived in liberty, and dedicated to the proposition that all men are created equal.

Now we are engaged in a great civil war, testing whether that nation, or any nation so conceived and so dedicated, can long endure. We are met on a great battlefield of that war. We have come to dedicate a portion of that field, as a final resting place for those who here gave their lives that that nation might live. It is altogether fitting and proper that we should do this.

But, in a larger sense, we cannot dedicate— we cannot consecrate—we cannot hallow—this ground. The brave men, living and dead, who struggled here, have consecrated it, far above our poor power to add or detract. The world will little note, nor long remember, what we say here, but it can never forget what they did here. It is for us the living, rather, to be dedicated here to the unfinished work which they who fought here have thus far so nobly advanced. It is rather for us to be here dedicated to the great task remaining before us—that from these honored dead we take increased devotion to that cause for which they gave the last full measure of devotion—that we here highly resolve that these dead shall not have died in vain—that this nation, under God, shall have a new birth of freedom—and that government of the people, by the people, for the people, shall not perish from the earth.

B He explains that no one has died in vain, for each will be remembered for helping to shape and win freedom for the country for future generations.

Special Occasion Speeches

Your life will be filled with many special occasions—club events, family celebrations and reunions, organization meetings, sports events, graduations, weddings, special community celebrations, and the like. At many of these occasions, a speaker is the main attraction. At some point, the speaker might be you.

Consider the **four** types of special occasion speeches that follow:

❶ Keynote Speeches

The first type of special occasion speech, a **keynote speech,** opens an event or conference. The topic usually correlates with the subject or theme of the event. For example, a keynote address on "The Cost of Hunger" might kick off a conference on world hunger sponsored by the World Health Organization.

A keynote speech is a major speaking engagement. As a keynote speaker, your goal is to energize your listeners and make them enthusiastic about attending the coming conference. You're usually allowed 20 to 45 minutes to accomplish this task. A keynote speech may be informational, giving people facts or a perspective to think about. Or it may be persuasive, motivating people to care about something, to embrace a point of view, or to act. A keynote also may be entertaining, especially if the speaker is a well-known media personality. The tone for a keynote speech may be serious or light, depending on the event.

For help in writing an informative speech, see Chapter 9. For tips on persuasive speeches, see Chapter 10. For any serious keynote speech, the content of your speech might go as follows:

* Warmly greet and thank the person who introduced you.
* Engage audience interest and attention with an anecdote, quotation, case history, example, or statistic relevant to the topic.
* Focus on the topic of this conference and explain its value to audience members.
* Launch into your content. If it's an informative speech, this may include an overview of current events or developments in your field, an outline of common problems and possible solutions, or a proposed direction or vision for the future.
* Give an overview of the conference to come, inspiring the audience to take advantage of events surrounding the conference or meeting to follow.

Follow these guidelines in your writing and delivery:

* Attempt to write an exciting, vigorous speech. Your job is to motivate.
* Keep your content relevant to the conference topic, broad enough in scope to act as an overall introduction to the event, yet specific enough to interest and inspire the audience.
* Consider using high-interest media aids, including computer-based presentation programs, video, or multimedia.

❷ Commencement Speeches

Graduation from high school, trade school, college, or graduate school is a special milestone in anyone's life. Graduation ceremonies always include a second type of special occasion speech, a **commencement speech** that honors graduates and sends them out into the world. Someday you could be the prominent local or national politician or celebrity who gives a commencement speech.

The goals of a commencement speech are to lead the audience in commending the graduates for their achievements and in helping them to envision their futures. Since graduation ceremonies usually are long, a commencement speech typically takes about 15 or 20 minutes. Unless you're an entertainer, your tone should be serious and formal. Even if the graduates' future is challenging, project a positive attitude.

Sometimes the graduating class selects a theme that determines your topic. However, within general guidelines, graduation speakers usually may select their own topics. Your commencement speech might discuss important developments in your professional area of expertise. It also could discuss the role of technology, lifelong learning, the meaning of life, service to the community, stewardship for the planet, life after high school (or college), the changing face of careers and professions, or the importance of sound values in any area of life.

A commencement speech should proceed along these lines:

✱ Thank the person who introduced you and the institution that invited you to speak.

✱ Express your genuine pleasure at being invited to address this audience.

✱ Heartily congratulate graduates for reaching this milestone—completing their graduation requirements and meeting their educational goals.

✱ Talk about what graduation means—a point in time that marks the end of one period of life and the beginning of a new stage. Explain why this occasion should be thought about in a serious and respectful way. Relate anecdotes about what graduation meant to you.

✱ Launch into your own topic.

✱ Close with an inspirational message, quotation, or sendoff.

Themes to Personalize a Commencement Speech

* A review of people, events, and things that meant the most to graduates on their road to this day
* Comments on the importance of education
* Reflections on your own life, your unique experience, and the lessons you've learned
* A description of the meaning of adulthood, the new choices that graduates have, and the world that they are entering
* Some tips—humorous or serious—for graduates to take with them as they look to the future. These may include quotations, excerpts from famous speeches, or passages from well-known books.
* A vision of their positive, yet challenging, future

Follow these guidelines in your writing and delivery:

* Take time to write a unique, thoughtful, and fast-moving speech. Remember that you have an obligation to say something interesting.
* Avoid clichés and trite statements and expressions.

* Show your great respect for this institution and for the graduates.
* Honor the assembled family and friends who helped the graduates reach this difficult goal.

❸ Dedication Speeches

A third type of special occasion speech, the **dedication speech,** is delivered as part of a formal ceremony that unveils a public monument or opens a new building, a city park, or a community garden. The person for whom the park or building is being named might take part in the ceremony and even give the speech.

Your goals in a dedication speech are to focus on the significance of the occasion, the place being dedicated, and those who played a key role in the process. You'll usually be asked to speak for about 15 or 20 minutes. A dedication is a solemn event that calls for a formal speaking style.

Structure your dedication speech something like this:

* If you are the first speaker, welcome listeners and remind them of the event that has called them here.
* Honor the person for whom the park, public building, or center is being named. If this person or a family representative is present, introduce him or her to the audience and lead the audience in showing appreciation.
* Explain the significance of this occasion and the process that led to today's event. Include interesting and relevant anecdotes.

* Describe how this structure or center will be used and its importance to the community.
* Recognize and thank other key individuals—such as the architect, builder, major donors, and community volunteers—who helped make this dream a reality.
* Consider the symbolic meaning of the structure (for example, peace, freedom, or the power of people working together). Encourage those present to carry this message forward into their own lives.

Follow these guidelines in your writing and delivery:

* Spend time honoring those who brought this project about.
* Focus on the future and inspire your audience to support this effort as it moves forward.

❹ Speaking to Entertain

A fourth type of special occasion speech is a **speech to entertain.** This type of speech invites listeners to relax and enjoy themselves. Speeches to entertain are a popular diversion at meetings of clubs, community groups, and business organizations.

For this type of speech, your goal is solely to please and divert the audience. The speech's length will vary with the occasion. Its tone is light and informal.

A speech to entertain isn't necessarily a stand-up comedy routine (unless that's your specialty). At times, it will relate to the theme of an event. But usually you may choose any subject that will hold your listeners' interest and create a pleasant diversion. This might mean a satire of current politics, an account of a harrowing kayak trip, an imaginative tale, or an account of a funny experience you've had. Nearly everyone remembers favorite stories told by radio personality Garrison Keillor, newspaper columnist Dave Barry, or writer Bailey White, each of whom is a master at emphasizing what is most wacky, human, or interesting about the subject at hand.

Follow these guidelines in your writing and delivery:

* Select a topic that suits you, the event, and your audience.
* Avoid topics and language that could offend or embarrass your listeners.
* Try your speech on friends and family. Use their feedback to fine-tune your timing and delivery.
* Consider memorizing your speech. An entertaining speech should flow freely and seem spontaneous. You don't want to be fumbling with notes.
* Start the speech by setting a lighthearted tone. This prepares your audience to relax and enjoy themselves.
* Don't ramble. Your speech should have a subject and a point to make. Make sure that all of your jokes, stories, and comments relate to that subject and point and that they truly are funny.

Speaking for Business

In nearly every career, you work with other people, both coworkers and supervisors. Your future success depends to some extent on how well you convey information and ideas to these people. In business, the ability to communicate ranks very high on the list of required or most marketable job skills.

Four of the most common types of business speeches are reports, proposals, public relations speeches, and sales presentations.

❶ Reports

In the first type of business speech, a **report,** you summarize the current status of work you're directly involved with, either individually or as part of the team. A report also might analyze a problem with which you're dealing, offering a summary of progress to date as well as choices or recommendations for future action. Reports help to bring interested people up-to-date.

Nearly every type of job—from construction to graphic design to forestry to scientific research to store management—requires people to report to one another. Therefore, a report presents you with a good opportunity to show your talents and management potential.

In a report, your goal is to meet your audience's needs and to present information clearly and efficiently. Whether you're given a few minutes or an unlimited time period, your tone should always be serious, efficient, and professional.

Like any informational speech, a report contains an introduction, body, and conclusion. Organize your information so that the audience can easily follow your presentation. Begin by clearly stating the subject, then follow your outline, using statistics and other evidence when appropriate. End with a summary, next steps, or recommendations.

Follow these guidelines in your writing and delivery:

* Follow the basics of informational speeches provided in Chapter 9.
* Anticipate the informational needs of your audience. Make sure that you include all facts that listeners need.
* Organize your material tightly so it can be read or scanned quickly.
* If you're delivering bad news, don't try to hide it. Tell the truth, then outline your recommendations for next steps or for solutions to the problem.
* If a decision needs to be made, give the audience the information it needs to make that decision and/or outline a process that can lead to a positive outcome.
* Do your homework. Have all relevant facts at hand.
* Be prepared for any possible audience questions and concerns.

❷ Proposals

Another common type of business speech, the **proposal,** presents an idea, a plan, a project, or a vision for consideration by a group. You may deliver a proposal to your project team, to a committee or organization, to your boss, or to a management group.

The goals of proposals will differ, but your general goal is to sell your idea. Thus, a proposal follows the general guidelines for any persuasive speech. (See Chapter 10.) The length of a proposal will depend upon the complexity of the idea or plan and the time allotted in the business meeting. A proposal's tone always is serious and businesslike.

A proposal's content will vary. However, any proposal should contain a clear statement of the need that this proposal satisfies, the main points of the proposal itself, evidence that your solution will work, benefits of your solution, a plan for implementation, and, if relevant, a proposed budget and schedule.

Follow these guidelines in your writing and delivery:

* Gear your presentation to the audience. Will listeners be friendly? skeptical? hostile? curious?
* Identify exactly what you want to happen as a result of the meeting.
* Prepare thoroughly, with solid evidence to back up your assertions.
* Make your point clear. Don't keep the audience guessing.
* Intelligently identify the pros and cons of the issue, with thoughtful counterarguments for the cons you mention.
* Anticipate questions from the audience.
* Be passionate about your idea.
* Keep an eye on your listeners. If you're losing them, shift gears to a softer sell or try a little humor.

❸ Public Relations Speeches

A third type of business speech, the **public relations speech,** is an official communication from a group or organization to the public and the press. Public relations speeches are usually delivered by professional public relations (PR) spokespeople. PR speeches may announce organizational changes or new products, inform the public about the company's current status and activities, or explain how the company is handling a crisis.

Organizations that hire PR people need to address the public frequently. These include school districts, research institutions, colleges and universities, corporations, governmental agencies, and hospitals.

When giving a public relations speech, your general goal is to represent your organization in the best possible light. The audience will carefully assess your appearance, demeanor, and words to decide whether you—and your group— can be believed. Your speech's length will depend upon the situation, but its tone should be professional and businesslike.

The content of a public relations speech depends upon the situation. If you are speaking because of a crisis, acknowledge and restate the immediate problem, need, or situation and explain how your organization proposes to solve it.

Follow these guidelines in your writing and delivery:

* As you prepare, think through possible questions, objections, and arguments from the audience or press. This will help you deal with hostile questions in a confident, informed way.
* Clearly outline and emphasize key points.
* Project a calm, professional image. Never allow yourself to become angry, defensive, rude, or overwhelmed, even when facing a hostile or aggressive audience.

❹ Sales Presentations

A fourth type of business speech, the **sales presentation,** is designed to persuade an audience to do something specific—adopt an idea or proposal, buy a product, or hire a team or a company. In sales presentations, you often get just one chance. You want to make it count.

The ability to give formal and informal sales presentations with positive results is an important job skill. In many companies and in many types of jobs, it is the basis for promotion.

Your goal in any sales presentation is to convince your audience and to get results— an approval, a contract, or an order. The length of your presentation depends upon circumstances. It might range from a few minutes to more than hour. Your tone should be businesslike but enthusiastic.

Before a sales pitch, getting information about your audience is crucial. In addition to standard information about the audience, find answers to these questions:

* To whom will you be speaking?
* What are their positions?
* Who are the decision makers?
* What aspects of your proposal will each of them be most interested in?
* What type of evidence will be most helpful in convincing them (statistics, anecdotes, expert testimony, references)?
* What is their shared vision or goal for the company?
* Is the audience positive, neutral, apathetic, or opposed?

It will be equally important to know your competition. If you don't, you're not fully prepared to give a sales pitch.

Who are you up against? You'd better find out. Use industry keywords to search for competitive companies' Web sites. Visit trade shows for more information. Study their products and services. Talk to their clients and customers. What advantages or selling points do they offer? How does their company differ in services, approach, pricing, and product features from yours? How can you best convince this audience that your idea, product, or service is superior? This information helps you position your offer relative to theirs.

Content for a sales presentation will vary with your goal and objective. At times you may initiate the topic; on other occasions, the topic may be predetermined. Since a sales presentation is a persuasive speech, brush up on the basics in Chapter 10.

This standard sequence often is used in sales presentations:

* Identify the immediate concern, problem, or need of your audience.

* Show how your idea, service, or product will solve the identified problem or satisfy the identified concern or need. These become your "selling points."
* Present your selling points and quickly address and eliminate any potential arguments. State why, in each case, your product or service is the best one.
* In a short summary, reinforce the urgency of the problem and your idea as the logical and best solution.
* Ask the audience for a positive response of acceptance—a vote, a verbal agreement to continue the process, a purchase order, or a contract.

Follow these guidelines in your writing and delivery:

* Review basics about persuasive speeches in Chapter 10. Monroe's Motivated Sequence is particularly appropriate for sales pitches.
* Know your audience's attitude toward you, your company, and your objective. This will help you determine your approach. Good salespeople always spend time learning about their audience before they begin a presentation.
* Work on your personal credibility— always an important ingredient in a sales pitch.
* Avoid criticism of your competitors. A negative approach draws attention to them and makes you look defensive and weak.
* Watch your audience. If your listeners are growing impatient or hostile, alter your strategy.

* Listen to the audience's concerns and give honest answers. People like to work with those who listen to them.

After any business presentation, you will probably face questions from your listening audience. Here are some tips for fielding questions and answers:

* Listen carefully and appreciatively to audience questions and concerns.
* If the questions can't be heard by all, repeat them into the microphone.
* Give detailed and thoughtful answers.

* As possible, relate the questions back to your main selling points. This helps reinforce ideas that you want the audience to remember.
* Rephrase any negative question or comment. For example, if someone asks why your company hurts American working families by laying off workers, don't repeat the question. Instead, say something positive like, "Let me explain our company's long-term plan for American workers."
* Close on a positive, upbeat note.

The Presentation

GOAL

The goal of this activity is to create a presentation, giving you practice in making sales pitches.

TASKS

1. Choose a partner. Together you will write, videotape, and present an original TV presentation selling a product.

2. Choose a product from the list below, or think of one of your own.
   * Soft drink
   * Shampoo
   * Toothpaste
   * Cereal
   * Software
   * Deodorant

3. Invent a new name for your product and write a catchy phrase or tune to sell it.

4. Script the action and write the text for the presentation, following standard sales pitch sequence (minimum length: 100 words). Do not duplicate ideas on TV and radio. Use your product as a prop.

5. Videotape your presentation or present it live, using vocal energy, appropriate movement, and good eye contact.

6. View the presentations as a class and critique them. How effective are they as sales pitches?

OUTCOMES

Did you follow all the steps in the standard sales presentation sequence? What persuasive techniques did you use in your presentation? Were you able to establish a problem or need of the audience that your product could solve or fulfill?

Impromptu Speaking

Just before an important meeting, your boss stops by your cubicle. "Oh, by the way, I want you to give a ten-minute project report at the meeting this morning." You now are facing an **impromptu speech,** one that is given without advance notice or preparation.

Impromptu speeches can be intimidating, but they also are a reality. At some point, you'll probably be asked to give one, especially in the working world.

How to Handle an Impromptu Speech

When you're asked to give an impromptu speech, don't get flustered. The key things are that you organize your content and stay relaxed.

Follow these **three** steps for quick mental preparation, and you'll find that your impromptu speech can be very effective.

❶ Consider the Audience

* What do listeners already know about the topic?
* How do they feel about it?
* What is their mood?

❷ Organize Your Speech

* Identify your main point and two or three supporting points.
* Choose an appropriate organizational pattern (a chronological review of events; the pros and cons of each point; or order of interest, importance, complexity, or scope).
* Choose an interesting opening—a reference to a recent event, a personal reference, a preview of your main ideas, or a vivid description or metaphor.
* Plan your conclusion. Restate the topic or main idea, then conclude with a dynamic, upbeat ending sentence.

❸ Relax and Deliver the Speech

* Stand up, smile confidently, and make eye contact with your listeners.
* Don't panic or apologize for your lack of preparation.
* Talk to the audience as you would in conversation.
* Sit down and enjoy the applause.

Communication in Careers

Thinking on Your Feet

Anna Perez worked for a major advertising firm and hoped to rise through the ranks. After being passed over several times for a promotion, she became frustrated. She talked it over with an older colleague who observed that people who are promoted are usually highly articulate and able to think well on their feet.

Anna began to speak more often in meetings. As she explains it, "I realized that my shyness and lack of confidence was holding me back. So I decided to speak at least once in every meeting. As a meeting progressed, I'd pay intense attention to the subject and contribute my honest thoughts and reactions. At first, most of my comments were short. Then I noticed that others were looking to me for reactions. As I felt their respect and interest, I got bolder. Soon my boss was asking me to give speeches and presentations for the group.

"The funny thing is, the more I took part, the better I liked my job. But I still was surprised when my boss moved me up to Assistant Director of Advertising."

Impromptu Speech

A Patrick Henry arouses interest in his speech at the very start, expressing respect for his opponents, but promising to speak frankly.

B He clearly identifies the main point of the speech—that the "question of freedom or slavery" can only be answered by evaluating past experiences.

Model

Patrick Henry Ignites the American Revolution

Mr. President:

No man thinks more highly than I do of the patriotism, as well as abilities, of the very worthy gentlemen who have just addressed the House. But different men often see the same subject in different lights; and, therefore, I hope that it will not be thought disrespectful to those gentlemen, if, entertaining as I do opinions of a character very opposite to theirs, I shall speak forth my sentiments freely and without reserve. This is no time for ceremony. The question before the House is one of awful moment to this country. For my own part I consider it as nothing less than a question of freedom or slavery; and in proportion to the magnitude of the subject ought to be the freedom of the debate. It is only in this way that we can hope to arrive at truth, and fulfill the great responsibility which we hold to God and our country. Should I keep back my opinions at such a time, through fear of giving offense, I should consider myself as guilty of treason towards my country, and of an act of disloyalty towards the majesty of heaven, which I revere above all earthly kings.

Mr. President, it is natural to man to indulge in the illusions of hope. We are apt to shut our eyes against a painful truth, and listen to the song of that siren, till she transforms us into beasts. Is this the part of wise men, engaged in a great and arduous struggle for liberty? Are we disposed to be of the number of those who, having eyes, see not, and having ears, hear not, the things which so nearly concern their temporal salvation? For my part, whatever anguish of spirit it may cost, I am willing to know the whole truth–to know the worst and to provide for it.

I have but one lamp by which my feet are guided; and that is the lamp of experience. I know of no way of judging of the future but by the past. And judging by the past, I wish to know what there has been in the conduct of the British ministry for the last ten years, to justify those hopes with which gentlemen have been pleased to solace themselves and the House?

C Henry asks a series of provocative questions to establish that Britain intends to use force against the colonists.

D Using strong language and powerful parallel structure, Henry insists that the colonists have tried all means of reconciliation.

Is it that insidious smile with which our petition has been lately received? Trust it not, sir; it will prove a snare to your feet. Suffer not yourselves to be betrayed with a kiss.

Ask yourselves how this gracious reception of our petition comports with these warlike preparations which cover our waters and darken our land. Are fleets and armies necessary to a work of love and reconciliation? Have we shown ourselves so unwilling to be reconciled that force must be called in to win back our love? Let us not deceive ourselves, sir. These are the implements of war and subjugation—the last arguments to which kings resort. I ask gentlemen, sir, what means this martial array, if its purpose be not to force us to submission? Can gentlemen assign any other possible motives for it? Has Great Britain any enemy, in this quarter of the world, to call for all this accumulation of navies and armies? No, sir, she has none. They are meant for us; they can be meant for no other. They are sent over to bind and rivet upon us those chains which the British ministry have been so long forging.

And what have we to oppose to them? Shall we try argument? Sir, we have been trying that for the last ten years. Have we anything new to offer on the subject? Nothing. We have held the subject up in every light of which it is capable; but it has been all in vain. Shall we resort to entreaty and humble supplication? What terms shall we find which have not been already exhausted? Let us not, I beseech you, sir, deceive ourselves longer.

Sir, we have done everything that could be done to avert the storm which is now coming on. We have petitioned; we have remonstrated; we have supplicated; we have prostrated ourselves before the throne, and have implored its interposition to arrest the tyrannical hands of the ministry and Parliament. Our petitions have been slighted; our remonstrances have produced additional violence and insult; our supplications have been disregarded; and we have been spurned, with contempt, from the foot of the throne. In vain, after these things, may we indulge the fond hope of peace and reconciliation. There is no longer any room for hope.

continues ▶

Impromptu Speech (continued)

Model

If we wish to be free—if we mean to preserve inviolate those inestimable privileges for which we have been so long contending—if we mean not basely to abandon the noble struggle in which we have been so long engaged, and which we have pledged ourselves never to abandon until the glorious object of our contest shall be obtained, we must fight! I repeat it, sir, we must fight! An appeal to arms and to the God of Hosts is all that is left us!

They tell us, sir, that we are weak—unable to cope with so formidable an adversary. But when shall we be stronger? Will it be the next week, or the next year? Will it be when we are totally disarmed, and when a British guard shall be stationed in every house? Shall we gather strength by irresolution and inaction? Shall we acquire the means of effectual resistance, by lying supinely on our backs, and hugging the delusive phantom of hope, until our enemies shall have bound us hand and foot?

Sir, we are not weak, if we make a proper use of the means which the God of nature hath placed in our power. Three millions of people, armed in the holy cause of liberty, and in such a country as that which we possess, are invincible by any force which our enemy can send against us. Besides, sir, we shall not fight our battles alone. There is a just God who presides over the destinies of nations, and who will raise up friends to fight our battles for us. The battle, sir, is not to the strong alone; it is to the vigilant, the active, the brave. Besides, sir, we have no election. If we were base enough to desire it, it is now too late to retire from the contest. There is no retreat but in submission and slavery! Our chains are forged! Their clanking may be heard on the plains of Boston! The war is inevitable—and let it come! I repeat it, sir, let it come!

It is in vain, sir, to extenuate the matter. Gentlemen may cry, "Peace! Peace!–but there is no peace. The war is actually begun! The next gale that sweeps from the north will bring to our ears the clash of resounding arms! Our brethren are already in the field! Why stand we here idle? What is it that gentlemen wish? What would they have? Is life so dear, or peace so sweet, as to be purchased at the price of chains and slavery? Forbid it, Almighty God! I know not what course others may take; but as for me, give me liberty, or give me death!

E Henry validates his main point with supporting details and offers solutions to the plaguing question.

F He concludes the speech by restating the main idea and ending on a powerful and memorable note.

ACTIVITY

Giving and Evaluating Impromptu Speeches

GOAL

The goal of this activity is to provide practice in giving and evaluating impromptu speeches.

TASKS

1. Form groups of three to five.
2. Brainstorm to create speech topics that can be delivered in two to three minutes.
3. One person at a time chooses a topic and, in two to three minutes, prepares a short speech for delivery to the group, using the Checklist for impromptu speeches.
4. Each person delivers his or her speech.
5. Others in the group listen and evaluate.
6. After speeches are given, group members discuss everyone's performances.

OUTCOMES

What was the most challenging aspect of giving an impromptu speech? Which were the most memorable speeches in the group? What made these speeches stand out as good examples of impromptu speaking?

Checklist

How to Give an Impromptu Speech

✓ Analyze the audience:
  * Knowledge level
  * Attitudes toward subject
  * Mood
✓ Define the main point or main impression.
✓ Focus on two or three supporting points.
✓ Choose a pattern of organization:
  * Past, present, and future
  * Order of interest, importance, complexity, scope
  * Topic points 1, 2, and 3
  * Pros and cons
  * Another pattern
✓ Choose an opening for the speech:
  * Timely reference
  * Personal reference
  * Preview of your main ideas
  * Another opening
✓ Plan your conclusion:
  * Restating topic or main idea
  * Concluding with a dynamic, positive statement
✓ Relax and deliver the speech.

At some point, you're likely to give some of the specialized speeches discussed in this chapter. You may need to introduce a speaker, present an award, accept an honor, or give a testimonial or eulogy for someone. It's also possible that you'll give special occasion speeches such as keynote addresses, commencement speeches, dedication speeches, and entertaining speeches. If you enter a business career, you're certain to give reports and to present proposals. You also might give public relations speeches and sales presentations. Impromptu speeches are a common part of business and personal life, too. This chapter has given you techniques for synthesizing and applying your speaking skills to these situations. It hopefully has made you ready for almost any speaking occasion that comes your way.

Speech

commemorative speech—speech about people that pays tribute to an individual or group; includes testimonials and eulogies.

commencement speech—special occasion speech that honors graduates.

dedication speech—special occasion speech that is part of a formal ceremony that unveils a public monument or opens a new building, a city park, or a community garden.

eulogy—commemorative speech honoring someone who has died.

impromptu speech—speech that is given without advance notice or preparation.

keynote speech—special occasion speech that opens an event or conference.

proposal—business speech that presents an idea, a plan, a project, or a vision for consideration by a group.

public relations speech—business speech that is an official communication from a group or organization to the public and the press.

report—business speech that summarizes the current status of an individual or group project, analyzes a problem, and/or offers a summary of progress to date and choices or recommendations for future action.

sales presentation—business speech that is designed to persuade an audience to do something specific: adopt an idea or proposal, buy a product, or hire a team or a company.

speech of acceptance—speech about people in which an honoree formally expresses his or her thanks for an honor or award.

speech of introduction—speech about people that prepares the audience to hear a speaker.

speech of presentation—speech about people that honors an individual or group for special accomplishments, then presents an award or honor.

speech to entertain—special occasion speech that invites listeners to relax and enjoy themselves.

testimonial speech—commemorative speech acknowledging and honoring living individuals or groups for their outstanding accomplishments, vision, heroism, or public service.

CHAPTER 12

Researching a Speech

- How can you narrow your subject to a manageable topic?
- What kinds of personal, print, and electronic sources are available for researching?
- How can you record information most efficiently?
- How can you find and choose the best supporting material?
- What kinds of visual aids would make a speech more interesting and understandable?
- How should you credit other sources?

When planning a speech for school, work, or an organization, you will often need to conduct research. In this chapter you'll learn how to conduct research quickly and efficiently. You'll prepare for the process by reviewing your speaking situation, narrowing your topic, and writing a preliminary outline. You'll then consider which research resources to use. For some speeches, personal resources—such as your own experience, interviews, or surveys—are appropriate. For informative and persuasive speeches, you'll find what you need at the library: reference books, periodicals, print materials, and databases. The Internet also contains a wealth of excellent research resources. After you've selected resources, you will need to take careful notes, using a computer, photocopier, or note cards. When your research is complete, you'll select supporting materials and visual aids and choose a presentation method. As you write your speech, you'll want to be accurate and ethical in citing information taken from other sources.

Preparing for Research

Preliminary Steps

Whatever the occasion for your speech—a class, a committee meeting, your job, or a public event—plan to do some content research to deepen your factual base and add interesting support material. Most audiences enjoy concrete facts, statistics, quotes, anecdotes, and examples. So don't just make general statements about airline travel. Do some research and give information about how a pilot prepares for liftoff.

How much research should you do? That depends upon your speech's topic and length. For a short speech on strategies for saving money, you may need only a few facts, quotations, and methods proposed by experts. For a longer speech on e-commerce, for example, you'll need detailed background information, statistics, examples, and more.

The goal of this chapter is to help you approach research in an efficient, systematic way. Start with **three** preliminary steps—review your speaking situation, narrow your topic, and develop a preliminary outline. Then decide where to go for information—to personal sources, to library sources, to Internet sources, or to all three.

❶ Review Your Speaking Situation

To keep your research focused, begin by reviewing your speaking situation. Think about the following:

* The desired length of your speech
* The occasion
* Audience's ages, genders, education levels, and occupations
* Audience's knowledge of this topic
* Audience's attitudes toward this topic
* Audience's expectations of this speech

❷ Narrow Your Topic

Now consider the broad topic that you've chosen and the type of speech you'll deliver (speech to inform, to persuade, to entertain, or something else). Can you cover this topic well in the time allotted for your speech? Is your topic too complex for this audience? You may need to **narrow the topic** to something more manageable. A speech on "technology," for example, cannot be covered in a 15-minute speech. You need a narrower topic, such as "How to Choose a New Computer."

To narrow your topic, start by getting an overview of what it includes. Watch for a narrower topic area that inspires you. Try one or more of these strategies.

---

1. Review Situation ▶ **2. Narrow Topic** ▶ **3. Develop Outline**

---

* **Skim sources that list the main content divisions of your topic.** Look up your topic in encyclopedia articles and then examine the article's main content divisions and cross-references to other articles. Check books about your topic. Use tables of contents, indexes, and reference sections to see how your topic breaks down into subtopics in indexes such as *Facts on File* and the *Readers' Guide to Periodical Literature.* Scan sub-headings of your main topic, as well as article titles.

* **Interview someone with firsthand knowledge.** A university professor who specializes in urban studies could be a good source of information on urban poverty. A webmaster might be a good person to consult on e-commerce.

* **Conduct an Internet search.** Explore sites on your topic. The Internet is a good source for up-to-the-minute information in many areas, including hardware and software.

❸ Develop a Preliminary Outline

After narrowing your topic, create a **preliminary outline** of your speech. A preliminary outline is a guide for research rather than a final outline. In this outline, you try to list and organize all of the information you'll need for your speech. You'll revise this outline when you're finalizing your speech.

A typical preliminary outline includes three or four subheadings or main divisions. It might also include your ideas for supporting material. As you draft this outline, ask yourself whether your topic has any natural or logical divisions. Then ask yourself what your audience will want to know about the topic.

For example, say that you are writing an informational speech on the Underground Railroad, the network that helped African-American slaves to escape from the South before slavery was abolished. A logical way to approach this subject is with the standard information questions *who, what, when, where, why,* and *how.* You can shuffle those topics around in a way that is logical. Your preliminary outline might look like this:

I. Basic Facts about the Underground Railroad
 A. What was it?
 B. When was it active?
 C. Where was it active?
 D. How did it work?
II. People of the Underground Railroad
 A. Who escaped?
 B. Who helped them escape?
III. Dangers of the Underground Railroad
 A. What were the laws at the time?
 B. What were the dangers?
IV. Stories of Escapes
 V. Importance of the Underground Railroad

When you've completed your research, you'll rearrange the information so your speech is as exciting as possible. For example, to get the audience involved, you might start with one of the personal escape stories or with a profile of Harriet Tubman, the escaped slave who repeatedly risked her life to help other slaves.

Choose Sources of Information

After assessing your situation, narrowing your topic, and writing a preliminary outline, think about where you'll go for information. Your choice, again, depends upon your topic. There are **three** main <u>sources</u> for research information:

1. **Personal sources** include personal experience, interviews, and surveys.

2. **School, public, and university libraries** offer print resources, such as reference books, fiction and nonfiction books, periodicals, trade and professional journals, and pamphlets; nonprint sources, such as videotapes, audiotapes, and CDs; and online resources, such as library databases and microfiche, as well as Internet access.

3. **Internet sources** include online encyclopedias, online references, and specialized information sites.

Preparing for Research

GOAL

The goal of this activity is to help you to prepare for research by summarizing your situation, narrowing your topic, and devising a systematic and efficient research strategy. If you wish, work with a partner.

TASKS

Complete each step of the activity using a topic for a speech that you will be giving. Write your answers on a separate piece of paper.

1. Broad topic
2. Type of speech (inform, persuade, entertain, other)
3. The speaking situation
   * Length of speech
   * Occasion

   * Audience
     –Ages
     –Genders
     –Levels of education
     –Occupations
     –Knowledge about my topic
     –Attitude toward my topic
4. Expectations of this speech
5. Types of support and evidence needed
6. My narrowed topic
7. Preliminary outline
8. Sources I plan to use for research

OUTCOMES

Did you gain ideas for limiting your topic? Did main points become evident as you investigated different indexes and listings? How did your topic change as you examined various listings?

Personal Research Sources

When researching your speech, be sure to consider **personal sources.** Are there areas in your own experience that relate to your topic? Whom might you interview who could provide interesting or useful information? Would a survey or opinion poll be useful?

Personal Experience

Speeches often deal with subjects of special interest to the speaker. Include yourself as a potential expert. You may have knowledge or experience in a skill such as dog training or snowboarding. You may have a hobby, such as making candles or collecting sports cards. You may have firsthand knowledge about fixing computers, designing Web sites, or babysitting.

Whatever your area of expertise, if it is relevant to your topic, include it. Think about the examples and personal stories or anecdotes you can use to support some or all of your main points. A speaker's firsthand knowledge always increases his or her respect and credibility in the eyes of the audience.

Interviews

People are rich sources of information. Older people are often generous in sharing their own experiences. Businesspeople are often willing to talk about the challenges and rewards of their professions. Artists and people in public service can be valuable resources. Even some of your friends might be well informed on a topic relevant to your speech.

Here are some ways to find the names of knowledgeable people to interview, either in person or by phone or e-mail.

* Ask appropriate adults for referrals.
* Contact associations with an interest in or knowledge of your topic.
* Inquire at your local community college or university.
* Try city and business directories, the Yellow Pages, and the *Donnelley Directory.* Government, school, and community resource listings might be helpful.

When you have chosen someone to interview, telephone him or her to request a phone or personal appointment. Briefly and politely explain who you are, why you want an interview, and how long you expect the interview to take. Set up an appointment. If one person turns you down, ask him or her for referrals for other people who might be able to help you.

Before the actual interview, educate yourself by gathering background information on the person, company, or issue. Use the accompanying checklist as a guide.

How to Conduct an Interview

1. **Arrive with two pens or pencils, a notebook, or a laptop computer.** If you want to take photos or tape the interview, ask permission first. If taping, check the microphone and audio level before you start. Bring along an extra tape and battery and take notes anyway, as a backup.

2. **Have a list of questions ready,** but don't be tied to them. Listen carefully to the person you are interviewing. Allow some questions to arise from the information you hear.

3. **Keep track of each question** on your list as it is asked. Ask for clarification or added information if needed.

4. **Ask to see primary source materials** if relevant. Examples of the person's work or a collection, for example, might add to your understanding and appreciation of the topic.

5. Before ending the interview, **make sure you have all the information you need.** Thank the person warmly for his or her time.

6. **Work with your notes and tape** within a few days, while the interview is fresh in your mind.

7. **Write a handwritten thank-you note** to the person within one day of the interview.

Surveys

Many people—marketing analysts, authors, political pollsters, and product developers—use opinion polls and surveys as sources of research. You can use them, too. An informal poll or survey can give you current information or opinions on your speech topic.

To create a survey or questionnaire, think first about the information you want. Then design questions that will give you that information. Make your survey fun, creative, and informative to take. Design one that is easy for respondents to use and for you to tally and analyze.

Make copies and distribute the surveys to people whose opinions you want. If you mail them, be sure to include a stamped, self-addressed envelope for each person's reply. Include a short, friendly letter requesting a response. Faxed replies may be an option in some cases.

Follow these guidelines for developing your survey questions:

* Outline the data that you need.
* Write one simple question for each piece of information.

* Limit your survey to 10 or 15 questions, a mix of multiple-choice and short-answer formats.
* Keep all questions brief, objective, and easy to follow.
* Try your survey out on target audience members. Use feedback to finalize the survey.

Using the Library

When you begin to research a speech topic, the library is a perfect place to start. There you can find general reference sources to get you started and more specific resources to fill in details and supporting material.

If your speech requires a lot of research, set aside enough time to do a careful, thorough job. Start with background information about your topic and examine a variety of resources. In some cases, you'll take extensive notes. In other cases, you'll skim. In all cases, take careful, complete notes. Be sure to gather plenty of information to satisfy your preliminary outline.

The following sections will help you make the most of your research efforts.

Reference Section

The **reference section** of the library is a good place to start any research project. It contains both general and specialized reference materials. Librarians in the reference section can direct you to specific reference books and help you learn to use them.

General Reference Books

General references include encyclopedias, almanacs and yearbooks, atlases, dictionaries, biographical references, geographical references, bibliographies, and more. These resources not only give you information, they can direct you to other useful materials.

Sidebar

Dictionaries of Quotations

Well-chosen quotations get your audience's attention quickly and forcefully. Use quotations to stress an important idea or to open or close a speech memorably.

Most collections of quotations index them by subject and by speaker. You'll find quotations in such sources as:

* *Bartlett's Familiar Quotations*
* *Baseball's Greatest Quotations*
* *The Penguin Dictionary of Modern Humorous Quotations*
* *Dictionary of Outrageous Quotations*
* *Columbia Dictionary of Quotations*
* *The Manager's Book of Quotations* (business quotes)

Check your local library, a bookstore, or the Web.

General Reference Books		
Type of Work	**Description**	**Examples**
Indexes to Reference Works	list general and specialized reference books in specific fields	*The Guide to Reference Books*
General Encyclopedias	provide general information and summaries	*Encyclopedia Britannica* *Encyclopedia Americana* *Collier's Encyclopedia* *Compton's Encyclopedia* *The New Columbia Encyclopedia* *Random House Encyclopedia* *World Book Encyclopedia*
Almanacs and Yearbooks	give brief descriptions of the year's events and/or data in many categories	*World Almanac and Book of Facts* *Information Please Almanac* *Statesman's Yearbook* *Statistical Abstract*
Atlases	supply maps and geographical information	*Rand McNally World Atlas* *National Geographic Atlas of the World*
Dictionaries	contain definitions of words and information on spelling and usage	*American Heritage Dictionary* *Webster's New World Dictionary*
Biographical Reference Books	provide information about famous people's lives, works, and other achievements	*American National Biography* *Dictionary of American Biography* *Who's Who in America* *Current Biography* *Who's News and Why*
Bibliographies	supply lists of books	*Books in Print* *Book Review Digest*

Specialized Reference Books

After consulting general reference sources for background information, it's time to investigate some specialized references. The library's reference section holds reference sources on almost any topic. Ask the reference librarian for help in finding the sources that you need.

Check the chart below for some examples of specialized reference books.

Specialized Reference Books	
Business and Economics	*Encyclopedia of Economics* *Handbook of Modern Marketing*
Film and Television	*International Encyclopedia of Film* *International Television Almanac*
History and Political Science	*The Women's Chronology* *Encyclopedia of American Facts and Dates*
Literature	*Twentieth Century Authors* *The Oxford Companion to American Literature* *Granger's Index to Poetry*
Music	*International Cyclopedia of Music and Musicians*
Mythology	*Bulfinch's Mythology* *Brewer's Dictionary of Phrase and Fable*
Religion and Philosophy	*A Reader's Guide to the Great Religions* *The Concise Encyclopedia of Western Philosophy and Philosophers*
Social Sciences	*Dictionary of Education* *International Encyclopedia of the Social Sciences*
Technology and Science	*Encyclopedia of Chemistry* *Encyclopedia of Computer Science and Technology* *The Larousse Encyclopedia of Animal Life*

Sample *Readers' Guide* Entry

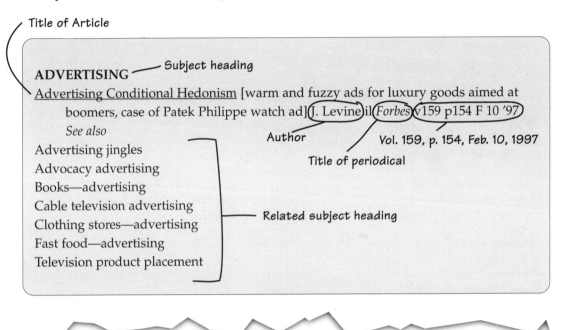

Title of Article

ADVERTISING — Subject heading
Advertising Conditional Hedonism [warm and fuzzy ads for luxury goods aimed at
boomers, case of Patek Philippe watch ad] J. Levine il *Forbes* v159 p154 F 10 '97
See also   Author   Vol. 159, p. 154, Feb. 10, 1997
Advertising jingles   Title of periodical
Advocacy advertising
Books—advertising
Cable television advertising
Clothing stores—advertising   Related subject heading
Fast food—advertising
Television product placement

Periodicals

Periodicals are magazines, journals, and newspapers that are published on a regular basis. Periodical indexes such as the *Readers' Guide to Periodical Literature* usually are found in a library's reference section. This alphabetical guide lists articles from many periodicals. Libraries may have the *Readers' Guide* in print, on microfilm or microfiche, or in a database.

For information on sports injuries, you would search in the *Readers' Guide* by subject listing. You'd need the periodical title, volume number, and date. Then you would request the magazine issues that you want from the librarian. Although libraries carry current and past issues of many magazines, they may also have the information on microfilm or microfiche.

Some libraries also offer online periodical databases. Users can search for the information they need and then read abstracts or complete texts of articles on screen, print the text, or e-mail it to their home computer.

The accompanying chart lists some of the many standard periodicals that most libraries carry. University and large public libraries typically have the widest selection.

Periodicals	
Newspapers	**Art and Leisure**
International World Tribune The New York Times Christian Science Monitor The Wall Street Journal	American Indian Art Fine Woodworking Opera News Guitar Player
Sports and Outdoors	**General Interest**
Field and Stream Sports Illustrated Snowboarder Outsider	Ebony Mother Earth News Life The New Yorker
Food, Nutrition, and Health	**Business, Economics, and Finance**
Yoga Journal Cooking Light New Age Journal Prevention	Money Business Week Kiplinger's Personal Finance Entrepreneur
Politics and Social Issues	**Computers and Technology**
Futurist The Nation Atlantic Monthly The New Republic	MacWorld TAP (Palm Pilot Computers) PC World Technology Review

Print Materials

Outside the reference area, the library contains both fiction and nonfiction materials. These can supply information, statistics, examples, facts, poetry selections, film quotations, and fictional selections that support your topic.

The Library Catalog

To find books and nonprint resources on your topic, start with the **library catalog**. This is an alphabetical index of all resources in the library. The catalog might be on cards, in a computer database, or on microfiche. The library catalog lists all resources in the library in at least **three** ways—by author, title, and subject.

1. *Author* entries list all books by one author.
2. *Title* entries list information about a particular book.
3. *Subject* entries list all resources on a subject (books, CD-ROMs, brochures, documents, tapes, and so on).

Many computerized card catalogs also list materials from other libraries, either locally or statewide. You can obtain these off-site materials through Interlibrary Loan (ILL).

If you find a book that looks promising, note its author, title, and call number. A **call number** is a letter and number code assigned to that resource according to the library's classification system. You'll use this call number to find the book that you need. In both the Dewey Decimal System and the Library of Congress system, non-fiction books follow a number system. Fiction books are organized alphabetically by the last name of the author.

Example

Card Catalog Entries

LC Control Number: 98037257
Type of Material: Book (Print, Microform, Electronic, etc.)
Brief Description: Sleep disorders sourcebook : basic consumer health information about sleep and its disorders including insomnia, sleepwalking, sleep apnea, restless leg syndrome, and narcolepsy, along with data about shiftwork and its effects, information on the societal costs of sleep deprivation, descriptions of treatment options, a glossary of terms, and resource listing for additional help / edited by Jenifer Swanson.
1st ed.
Detroit, MI : Omnigraphics, © 1999.
xii, 439 p. : 24 cm.

CALL NUMBER: RC547 S536 1999
Copy 1
—Request in: Book Service: Jefferson (Main Eur Hisp LHG) or Adams 5th fl
—Status: Not Charged

CALL NUMBER: RC547 S536 1999
Copy 1
—Request in: Reference - Science Reading Room (Adams, 5th Floor)
—Status: Not Charged

Electronic Databases

Many libraries allow you to access **computerized databases** of books, periodicals, and other materials. Like a card catalog, a computerized database includes title, author, and publisher information for each entry. Such databases often contain information about books or other materials not owned by the library you are using.

Some libraries provide a periodical database for users. From a dedicated computer, you can often search, pull up, and read an abstract or the full text of any article you select.

Some specialized databases offer information on the arts, medicine, history, current events, and science. GEOBASE, for example, indexes ecological, geographic, and geological articles. Others contain a variety of topics. A reference librarian can help you access these files.

If your library does not have the book or periodical you need, you may be able to obtain it through interlibrary loan. It takes several weeks to get the requested materials and a fee may be involved, but it may be worth it.

All of these resources may sound a bit complicated to use and keep straight. But you should consult the reference librarian for help. Once he or she has shown you a few basic resources, you have a valuable way to access mountains of information.

Checklist

How to Evaluate Resources

1. **How current is this information?** Check its publication date in the library catalog or the book's copyright date.

2. **What are the author's or source's credentials?** Who is the author? Is he or she an expert on this subject? Check the library catalog to see how many works on this topic he or she has written. Check his or her credentials on the book jacket or in the book's introduction. Look him or her up in biographical sources. Try to find out whether anyone else uses this author as an expert.

3. **Is the data correct?** Fact-check a few dates or pieces of information. If the data aligns with other current, respected, and authoritative sources, it probably is reliable.

4. **Is the tone objective?** If the author or source has a definite point of view, he or she may distort facts and information. Compare the facts and information to other sources.

5. **Are the arguments solid and well-supported?** Check to be sure evidence or facts are used to back up the arguments. If arguments are presented with scant information to back them up, then move on. You don't want to make the same mistake in your speech.

Using the Internet

In the 1950s, the U.S. Department of Defense created the **Internet**—a matrix of networks connecting computers worldwide. The military wanted an information system that could survive a strong outside attack. But a more public side of the Internet soon came into existence—the **World Wide Web,** a system of interconnected Web sites and files that can be accessed through browser software.

Today the Internet and World Wide Web represent the world's busiest public communication system, information resource, and commercial hub. According to an NEC Research Institute study, in July 1999, there were about 2.8 million public Web sites and more than 800 million pages of information.

Advantages of Web Research

Using the Web as a tool for research has many advantages. It:

* Allows easy access, 24 hours a day.
* Provides up-to-the-minute, breaking news, from sites that update several times each day.
* Assures availability of worldwide resources. English is the official language of the Web, so many foreign Web sites include an English version of their information.
* Contains free information. Most of the information on the Web is available to anyone at no charge.
* Assures efficient access to and transfer of information through search engines, file saving, and printing.

Types of Resources Available

Almost any subject can be researched on the Web. Here is a general sampling of some of the research resources it offers.

Online encyclopedias. Major encyclopedias include *Britannica Online, Catholic Encyclopedia, Encyclopedia of Women's History,* and more. For a nominal fee, *Britannica Online* offers searches of the entire text of its multivolume encyclopedia. It also contains more than 3,000 additional articles, 12,000 graphics, 30,000 links to high-quality sites, maps and statistics, and more.

Museums and galleries. Almost every major museum and gallery has a Web site. Some cultural sites offer Web tours—examples include the Smithsonian, the British Museum, the Louvre, and the Uffizi Gallery. The site for New York City's Metropolitan Museum of Art, for example, now displays 3,500 artworks and plans to offer more than 7,000 by 2002. Someday, its entire collection of 2,000,000 works will be online.

Colleges and universities. All major colleges and universities now offer Web sites. Many have created useful research resources, such as Web resource lists, special exhibits, collections of documents, reports on archaeological projects, and so on.

News and politics. Newspapers, magazines, and radio/TV networks all have active Web sites. Look on the Web for *The Washington Post, C-Span, The BBC, CNN, ABC, NBC, CBS,* and *The Discovery Channel.* All news sources are online, some with specialized reports and searchable databases. Most resources are free, but a few charge a small fee for database searches.

Businesses. According to a 1999 study, 83 percent of Web sites were business sites. Nearly every major corporation has a Web site. Most small businesses have them, too.

Election information. Major political parties have Web sites, and so do candidates. Objective watchdog groups, such as Vote-Smart and The League of Women Voters, offer biographies and voting records of thousands of elected officials and candidates. Voter.com displays real-time election results as the votes come in.

Government agencies. Almost every United States government agency has a Web site, and many of them have good indexes to help you find your way around.

Interesting sites include NASA, the statistics database of the Census Bureau, the countries' fact database at the CIA, the White House, Congress, the Thomas Register (legislative information), and the Library of Congress.

Partisan organizations and foundations. Groups with specific points of view—such as Common Cause and the American Civil Liberties Union (ACLU)—have Web sites that offer detailed information on causes that interest them. Foundations have sites, too.

Public opinion polls. If you're curious about public opinion on an issue, you can find many sites with opinion polls, including the Gallup Organization and Harris.

Search Engines

Web Search • Category Search • News Search • Photo Search • Audio/Video Search

Search Web Sites:

| spider | **Search** | Search Home • Help |
| | | Advanced Search |

Top 10 Web Site Results for: **Spider**

- Discovery Online. Expeditions -- Spiders!
  URL: htp://www.discovery.com/exp/spiders/spiders.html
  Discovery Online Expeditions

- Nick's Spiders of Britain and Europe
  URL: htp://members.xoom.com/nickspiders/main.html
  Welcome to Nick's Spiders Welcome to Nick Loven's web site dedicated to pictures and photographs of British and European Spiders...

- Spider Resources
  URL: htp://seamonkey.ed.asu.edu/~hixson/index/spiders.html
  Spider Resources Learn About Spiders with Us Click on the addresses below and travel to sites with rich information about spiders. Have fun on your journey and see what you can learn.

Using Search Engines

The term **search engine** usually describes Internet-based true search engines and directories. HotBot is an example of a true search engine. It uses a "spider" or "crawler" that electronically visits and updates sites periodically. Yahoo, on the other hand, is a directory that was created by humans.

To find information on the Web, start with a search engine or directory. At the search prompt, simply enter a keyword (one or more terms that describe your topic), then click on the Go or Start button. (Use the search engine's Tips on Searching section to help limit your searches.) The search engine or directory then produces a list of sites that it finds on that topic. Click on the underlined links that interest you to explore the sites.

Hundreds of search engines are available, but they have their limitations. For one thing, the Web is growing too fast. A July 1999 NEC Research Institute study indicated that the most comprehensive search engine (Northern Light) covered only 16 percent of the 800 million public Web pages available at that time. Others (including popular search engines such as Yahoo) covered even fewer pages.

Try the same keywords in several search engines; you may be surprised at the differences in the results. Some search engines provide prescreened and rated lists for the topics they index and "specialize" in, such as museums, historical periods, and others.

Watch also for specialized sites that are simply collections of links to other sites. The Librarians' Index to the Internet is like a Web-based reference room, full of links to pre-approved sites in many categories. Sites such as these can help make your searches quick, efficient, and reliable.

Whenever you find a valuable and reliable site for your topic, see whether it offers a Links or Internet Resources section. These links can lead you to still other valuable sites on your topic.

Evaluating Internet Sources

The quality and reliability of Web information varies greatly. Some information is absolutely reliable, and other information is pure fiction. Be a discerning Web user. Question everything and never take information you find at face value. Use the accompanying checklist to screen every site that you use.

Checklist

How to Evaluate a Web Site's Reliability

Ask yourself these questions to determine a Web site's reliability.

1. Who sponsors the site? Check the site's copyright notice or its Who We Are section. If a site's publisher is reputable—a college or university, publisher, newspaper, museum, corporation, or agency—the site itself is probably reliable. Sites run by individuals are more suspect, since their credentials are unknown.

2. How current is the site's information? Check the copyright date or last update notice on the Home Page. Avoid sites that haven't been updated recently. The facts may be erroneous or outdated.

3. Do the facts check out? Check the site's facts, dates, spellings, and other information against other reliable sources that you have found.

4. Is the site selling an idea or a product, perspective, or philosophy? If so, what is the point of view? Since anyone can put "information" on the Web, you must evaluate its truth and quality. Read a site carefully to discern its overall purpose, perspective, and goal.

5. How well-organized, complete, and well-designed is the site? A sloppy, unattractive, incomplete site full of typos is also likely to be careless about facts. Be careful.

Recording Information

You've gathered your research resources and you're ready to take notes. Naturally, you want to do this as quickly and accurately as possible.

You may choose to gather information using a computer, a handheld scanner, a photocopier, or the traditional note card method. An overview of these methods follows. Whatever method you choose, be well-organized and work systematically. As you skim for information, maintain focus on your purpose and topic. Devise an organized system to record your information. You want to avoid those painful, time-consuming trips back to the library to dig out the information that you forgot.

Computers, Scanners, and Photocopiers

A notebook computer, a handheld scanner, or a photocopy machine can aid the process of note taking.

Notebook Computers and Scanners

You can take notes directly into your notebook computer, using a word processing or database program. This can save you writing time, since you won't have to type handwritten notes into your computer later. Another alternative is a pen-sized text scanner, an innovative and inexpensive device that can hold 1,000–2,000 pages of text. You can take this device to the library, scan information into it, and then transfer the text to your computer at home. Be careful: these new scanners are limited in some ways. Getting good results requires care.

Don't let the ease of using technology make you careless. Remember that for every source that you use and for every note that you take, you need complete bibliographical information and note information. See the sections on bibliography cards and note cards that follow for a complete list of data needed.

Photocopy Machines

Most libraries have photocopy machines. Though copies cost money, you can save time by copying pages of reference sources, books, and periodicals that you need, and then doing your reading at home.

However, don't forget bibliographical information and page citations for every source that you copy. Either hand-write all bibliographical information on copies that you make or photocopy the information on the front and back of a book's title page.

Note Cards

You may decide to use the traditional note card system for taking notes. Note cards are easy to organize and use.

Many researchers at all levels take notes on three-by-five-inch or four-by-six-inch cards. Most note takers create two kinds of cards: **bibliography cards** and note cards.

❶ Bibliography Cards

Bibliography cards record important facts about your sources. For each source that you use—whether it's an encyclopedia, book, periodical, or Web site—create one bibliography card. Here's what the cards should include:

✱ **For a book:** the call number, author or editor name(s), book title, place of publication, publisher, and copyright date. (For this information, see the book's spine and the front and back of its title page.)

✱ **For a periodical:** the author of the article, the article title, name of newspaper or magazine, date of publication, and page numbers. (For this information, see the article itself and the magazine cover.)

✱ **For a Web site:** the Web site title, the site address (or URL), and site section name that you're using. (For this information, see the site's Home Page.)

Example

Bibliography Card

(Put call number here for books)   #7—(card number)

Levine, J. *Rock Music, A to Z.* New York: Barefoot Press, 1999.

    (author, book title, place of publication, publisher, publication date)

Note Card

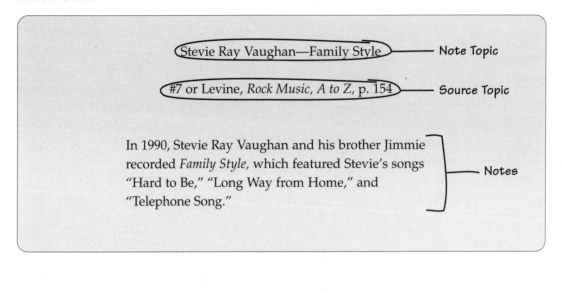

Stevie Ray Vaughan—Family Style — Note Topic

#7 or Levine, *Rock Music, A to Z*, p. 154 — Source Topic

In 1990, Stevie Ray Vaughan and his brother Jimmie recorded *Family Style*, which featured Stevie's songs "Hard to Be," "Long Way from Home," and "Telephone Song." — Notes

❷ Note Cards

Note cards contain the actual information you're gathering from sources. Write a note for each individual topic or piece of information you find. Each note card includes these items:

* **The source of the note.** Use a short reference—the author's last name, the title, or a number—since you already have complete information on your bibliography card.
* **The topic of the note.** Key this to headings in your preliminary outline.

* **The information itself.** Include no more than one idea, fact, or example on a card. Either paraphrase the material (restate it in your own words) or use quotation marks for any phrases of the author's that you record. This will help you to avoid plagiarism. Plagiarism is theft of the ideas and words of others, a form of intellectual dishonesty that also is illegal. (See the section on plagiarism later in this chapter.)

Taking Notes

Here are **six** steps for making your note taking efficient and systematic:

1. **Assemble materials for note taking,** including your preliminary outline.

2. **Locate a potential information source** (book, magazine, newspaper article, or Web site).

3. **Review your preliminary outline** to help you recall information that you need.

4. **Skim the source** for this information. In a book, use the table of contents and index. In a magazine or newspaper, scan the boldfaced headers. In a Web site, check section names and topic links.

5. **Take notes as you read.** If you find useful information in this source, record this source's bibliographical information. If you're using bibliography cards, use a separate card for each source. Write a note card for each individual topic, using direct quotes for any quoted material. Include the topic, note, source title, and page(s).

6. **Repeat the process** until you have all of the notes and supporting material that you need.

Taking Notes

GOAL

The goal of this activity is to help you learn the skill of efficient note taking. Focus on your purpose and topic, work quickly, decide what is important and unimportant, and be accurate.

TASKS

1. Choose a partner. Each of you will do this activity independently, and then check each other's work.

2. Gather note-taking materials, your preliminary outline, and other notes.

3. Find relevant sources—books, articles, pamphlets, Web sites, and so on.

4. Evaluate the reliability of these sources.

5. Choose at least three sources for note taking.

6. Make a bibliography card or entry for each source.

7. Make at least nine note cards from the three sources.

8. Swap finished materials with your partner. Check each other's bibliography cards and note taking against the guidelines given here.

OUTCOMES

How well did you follow the guidelines for note taking? Did you learn more about your subject? Were you able to narrow your topic further? Were you able to identify several main points and some supporting details that will develop those points?

Supporting Material

As your research progresses, the final focus and organization of your speech will emerge. If your speech's topic and purpose have changed, review all of your research notes. Then reorganize your speech again. Create a new outline that fits your new approach and makes good use of the research materials that you found.

The **support material** that you gather will help you to develop your main point and add interesting ideas and details to your speech. Often the support material is what makes a speech lively and interesting to the audience

Here are some frequently used types of support materials:

* Facts and statistics
* Direct quotations
* Analogies and definitions
* Examples and descriptions
* Stories and personal anecdotes
* Visual aids

Facts and Statistics

Facts are information based on evidence. **Statistics** are numbers that express information. It's a fact that novelist Herman Melville was born in New York City in 1819. It's a statistic that, in 1999, so-called "heavy users" spent $66 billion of the $110 billion spent on fast food in the United States.

Facts and statistics will underscore your main points and are an important part of any speech to persuade or to inform. They add interest and credibility to your discussion. They also can help to persuade audiences ("Three out of four doctors recommend Brand X aspirin"). Statistics come in the form of percentages, averages, or ratios. Or they may describe profit margins, population growth, or a decrease in forested land.

Here are tips for using facts and statistics:

* Keep statistics simple and to a minimum. Numbers can sway an audience, or they can put listeners to sleep.
* Use current, trustworthy sources such as newspapers, almanacs, independent survey organizations, government publications, and so forth.
* Be careful how you read sources. A "50 percent increase in dropouts" can mean an increase from two to three students.
* Compare or connect statistics with something to help the audience feel the effect. For example, "The amount of trash collected from our city in one year would form a mountain X miles high."
* Use visual aids, such as graphs, to help the audience understand numerical data.

Direct Quotations

Speakers often use **direct quotations**— cited passages that are repeated in a person's own words—in a speech. To find quotations, look in the reference section of the library. Many standard and specialized dictionaries of quotations are listed on page 231.

Direct quotations help to get the audience's attention, to support a conclusion, to dramatically make a point, or to close a speech. A well-chosen literary quotation can move listeners emotionally and help them to remember your speech for a long time. Direct quotes by respected authorities in a field add credibility to a speech.

Here are tips for using quotations:

* Know your audience and choose your quotations carefully.
* Short quotations, used sparingly, are more inspiring and memorable than long ones.

Analogies and Definitions

An **analogy** is a comparison based on similarities between things that otherwise are dissimilar. "Debt is like a leaky roof" is an analogy. A **definition** is a statement explaining the meaning of a word or phrase. Analogies and definitions can help clarify new or confusing information in a speech.

Simple analogies use something that is familiar to help explain the unfamiliar. A good analogy conveys a mental picture and entices the audience to listen closely.

Definitions are important simply to clarify terms. In a speech on conservation, for example, you'd want to begin by telling the audience exactly what you mean by that term. Giving a definition helps to build common understandings.

Here are tips for using analogies and definitions:

* Use analogies to add a creative spark to the opening or closing of a speech.
* Include short definitions to help increase your credibility.
* Cite definitions from the dictionary or suggest your own. Make sure that you state which source you are using.

Examples and Descriptions

In almost any piece of writing, it is clear **examples** and vivid **descriptions** that make the ideas come alive. The use of **hypothetical examples**—examples of something that did not happen but which possibly could happen in the future—also are useful in some situations.

Examples and descriptions give the audience concrete images to aid understanding and pique interest. If rather than simply discussing women's suffrage, you vividly describe the lives of Elizabeth Cady Stanton and Susan B. Anthony, the audience will get a clearer mental picture.

Here are tips for using examples and descriptions:

* Choose typical, relevant examples.
* Whenever possible, use personal examples.
* Back up hypothetical examples with facts, statistics, or expert testimony.
* Warn the audience if your example is a hypothetical example. Use words such as, "Imagine that . . ." so listeners don't take you literally.

Stories and Personal Anecdotes

You might begin a speech with a **story,** a description of something that happened to you or to someone else; or a personal **anecdote,** a short narrative. Stories and anecdotes help to make a speech memorable. They are especially useful when you want to draw out the audience's emotions.

Personal stories and anecdotes permit the listener to enter into a different place or time and to experience someone else's feelings or responses more fully. They also can help establish a common bond of experience between speaker and audience. Stories and anecdotes can help make a topic such as "investment strategies" personal and more meaningful.

Here are tips for using stories and personal anecdotes:

* Try not to ramble on too long. The audience will become restless.
* Make sure that you tie your story or anecdote skillfully into your speech topic. Otherwise, people will become confused.

Visual Aids

Visual aids are special types of support materials that show facts, statistics, or ideas to aid understanding or increase interest. Used wisely, visual aids can give strong support to your main arguments.

You can choose from many types of visuals. Examples are pictures, objects, models, graphs and charts, diagrams, slides, overhead transparencies, and videotapes. Whatever you use, be sure that everyone in the audience has a full view and that your figures and words are bold and clear enough for everyone to see plainly. See Chapter 13 and the Handbook for more information on creating effective visual aids.

People have different ways of learning. In this visually oriented culture, many people remember what they see better than what they hear. If they can both see and hear, a point is even more memorable. Even a simple diagram or pie chart drawn on a white board can help the audience understand a point. Listeners may forget the statistics that describe last year's huge leap in sales, but they'll remember the sharp upward angle on a line graph for weeks to come.

Here are tips for using visual aids:

* Don't overuse visual aids but rather use them to highlight your key points.
* Test your visuals by asking, "Will this visual make it easier for my listeners to understand and enjoy my talk?"

Bar Graph

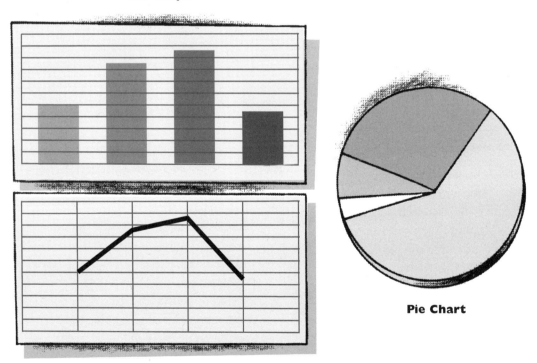

Pie Chart

Line Graph

How to Evaluate Support Material

Examples

✓ Uses examples that are appropriate, clear, and relevant for the speech, the audience, and the occasion.

✓ Uses interesting and vivid examples.

Sources

✓ Uses reliable, credible sources that the audience knows and trusts.

✓ Checked to see that source information is unbiased.

✓ Cites sources for statistics and direct quotations.

Quality of Support Materials

✓ Cites typical or representative evidence, rather than an exception.

✓ Proofed all examples and visual aids for spelling and factual correctness.

Types of Support Materials

✓ Uses visual aids sparingly.

✓ Chose the best type of visual aid or support material to get each point across.

Facts and Statistics

✓ Uses relevant facts to back up each argument.

✓ Selected statistics to quantify and validate main points.

✓ Uses statistical terminology and measures correctly.

Using Technology

Technology provides almost unlimited possibilities for enhancing your speech. However, the high-tech aids that you choose should fit the occasion and your speech's goal. If you're speaking to eight people in a cafeteria lounge, a big projection system is simply not appropriate. Also, think of your audience's comfort. You probably should not expect more than two or three people to crowd around to view a presentation on your notebook computer screen. Either get a projection system or give them individual screen printouts that they can view in the comfort of their own chairs.

At best, high-tech presentation aids will add interest and clarity to your speech. At worst, the equipment will cause hassles for you, or your audience will be confused by too many dazzling graphic images and lose the point of the whole presentation.

Technology-assisted presentations generally fall into **two** categories:

1. *Text/graphics presentation packages.* These packages are designed to help you create and run presentations with text, photos, drawings, diagrams, flowcharts, and other visuals. Programs like these can accompany your entire talk. When selected well and presented smoothly, computer presentations clarify your speech and give it a professional polish.

2. *Multimedia presentation packages.* Multimedia presentations incorporate a wide variety of components—images, animated sequences, video, sound, and branching hypertext. These sophisticated, speaker-controlled presentations can even route live to the Internet.

For more information on technological aids, see the Handbook.

Support Materials

GOAL

The goal of this activity is to help you select a variety of support materials that develop your main points as well as build interest for your audience.

TASKS

1. Choose a partner. Each of you will perform the activity separately, and then evaluate each other's work.

2. Use the preliminary outline that you created in the first activity in this chapter. If you haven't yet created one, do so at this time.

3. From your notes, select engaging facts, descriptions, examples, quotes, statistics, or other support materials that will explain your main points.

4. Insert two or three supporting items under each main point. Include ideas for visuals.

5. Check the quality of your support materials by using the guidelines above.

6. Swap outlines with your partner. Evaluate each other's work. Try to determine which points are well-supported and which need better support.

OUTCOMES

Did you find one to three support items for each main point? Did you include visuals? Does each support item under each point directly relate to that point? Do all of your examples, illustrations, and so forth meet the criteria outlined in this chapter?

Accuracy and Ethics

All material from outside sources that you use in your speech must be properly handled and properly credited.

Fabrication

Fabrication is inventing information as if it came from an actual source. Fabrication is lying. Lying about information in a speech can destroy your credibility and harm your reputation.

Plagiarism (Deliberate and Careless)

Plagiarism is the act of taking another person's words or ideas and representing them as your own. Under copyright laws, all words, ideas, and visuals found in books, magazines, Web sites, and other publications are the property of their authors or publishers. If you use someone else's exact words or ideas, you must give the author proper credit and use quotation marks for direct quotations. Failure to do this is both illegal and intellectually dishonest. Whether it happens on purpose or out of carelessness, it is still plagiarism.

To avoid plagiarism, start handling sources properly in the note-taking stage. Either take notes in your own words or use direct quotes to indicate even short phrases in the author's words. Also be very careful to record appropriate bibliographical information and to cite your sources when you speak. In a speech, you can give credit to your source by saying something like, "As President John F. Kennedy said in his famous speech . . ." or "According to Brandow's 1997 landmark deforestation study. . . ."

Some facts require no source citations. This is because they are considered to be common knowledge—that is, facts that are known to most educated people. For example, most people know that President John F. Kennedy was assassinated on November 22, 1963. There is no need to cite a source for this fact. But, if you discussed various assassination theories, you would need to cite your sources.

Copyright laws also protect information and visuals from Web sites. You can save and print out this material, but you must handle it as you would handle materials from a book.

How to Credit Sources

Attributing is the act of naming the source of your quotation, fact, or anecdote. Every time you use a person's exact words or phrases, or paraphrase his or her ideas, you are required to credit the source. In a speech, you can simply tell the audience the source of the information. This may include the author, title of the publication, or other description that will identify and give formal credit to your source. Source citations in a speech show the audience that you are careful and trustworthy. Listeners will appreciate the fact that you've done research and credited your sources properly.

Wrap-up

After reviewing your speaking situation, focusing your research, narrowing your topic, and developing a preliminary outline, you'll be ready to choose sources. Whenever you are getting ready for a presentation to an audience, look to your own experiences first. Use your personal experience, interviews, and surveys. Use the library and the Internet for collecting in-depth information. The library's reference section can help you to explore your topic and find supporting materials. Periodicals, electronic databases, and print materials can fill in background and details. The Internet also is a universe of information that can be tapped into easily and quickly through search engines. All information—whether taken from print materials or Web sites—needs to be scrutinized for accuracy and reliability. Whether you take notes using a computer, a scanner, a photocopier, or note cards, be systematic and organized. As you work, watch for vivid descriptions, examples, quotations, and statistics that directly relate to your main points. Think about ways to present your material visually. People remember better when they see as well as hear information. Finally, be sure that you attribute information to appropriate sources.

Speech

analogy—infers the similarities (or differences) between two things.

anecdote—short narrative.

attributing—identifying the source from which you got your information or quotation.

bibliography cards—note cards for each source of information. Each card includes all bibliographical information for that source.

call number—letter and number code assigned to a resource according to the library's classification system.

computerized databases—bibliographic computer files of articles, reports, and, less often, books.

definition—statement explaining the meaning of a word or phrase.

descriptions—verbal accounts or portrayals.

direct quotations—cited passages that are repeated in a person's own words.

examples—illustrations.

fabrication—making up information as if it came from an actual source.

facts—information based on evidence.

hypothetical example—example of something that did not happen but which could happen in the future.

continues ▶

Internet—matrix of networks that connect computers around the world.

library catalog—index of all the books and other materials housed in the library, whether in card, microfiche, or computer file form.

narrow the topic—taking a general subject and reducing it to a smaller, more specific topic to fit the time limits for a speech.

periodicals—magazines and journals published at regular intervals during a year.

personal sources—personal experience, interviews, and surveys.

plagiarism—act of presenting another person's words or ideas as your own.

preliminary outline—informal outline of speech information, made as a guide to research.

reference section—part of the library that contains reference materials ranging from general sources to specialized ones.

search engine—computer software designed to locate Web sites on the Internet.

source—anything from which you have gotten information.

statistics—numbers that express information.

story—description of something that happened to you or to someone else.

support material—information that is used to explain or develop a main point.

visual aids—support material developed for the audience to see.

World Wide Web—system of interconnected Web sites and files accessible through browser software.

CHAPTER 13

Preparing a Speech

In this chapter, you will consider:

- **What is the focus and purpose of your speech?**
- **Who is your audience?**
- **What do they know about your subject?**
- **How do you create a framework for your talk?**
- **What should you include in the body of your speech?**
- **What is the best way to rehearse your speech?**

You have gathered information for your speech by reviewing your own experience, conducting interviews, administering surveys, and researching your topic at the library or on the Internet. Now you are ready to prepare the speech itself. In this chapter, you'll discover how to prepare a speech through a series of simple steps. First, you'll learn a process for selecting and narrowing your speech topic. Next, you'll find out how to analyze your audience, focusing on basic data and the audience's attitudes and knowledge of your subject. Then you'll review steps in researching and outlining your speech. Finally, you'll review tips for rehearsing your speech and choosing media aids.

Select and Clarify a Topic

The first step in preparing a speech is selecting your topic—and it is probably the most crucial step.

Select a Topic

Preparing a speech begins with crafting a perfect topic. When you choose a topic, you need to consider three factors: your own experiences and interests; the occasion; and the makeup, knowledge, attitude, and expectations of your audience.

Always consider yourself when choosing a speech topic. The best public speaking topics reflect your personal experience and interests. If you choose to speak on topics that matter to you personally, your enthusiasm will help to involve the audience.

The occasion and the audience can have decisive influence on your topic. If you're speaking at a basketball banquet, you'll obviously address a topic related to team interests. If you're addressing your school at a community assembly, you'll certainly choose a topic related to your community.

If you're free to choose your own topic, you can use a variety of methods: your own experience, brainstorming, listening and reading, scanning indexes, and talking to people.

Use Your Own Experience

Creative writers always are advised to "write about what they know." It also makes sense to "speak about what you know." Ask yourself some questions. Is there anything in your experience so far—your childhood, your travels, your areas of expertise, your work experience, or your favorite recreations and hobbies—that might make a good speech for this audience and this occasion? If topics within your experience don't seem appropriate, choose a subject that you'd like to know more about and then research it.

Brainstorm

A idea-generating technique called **brainstorming** can be used to create a long list of possible speech topics. Here's a review of how to brainstorm.

First, review your own interests, the occasion, and what you know about the audience. Then, with paper and pencil or the computer, start writing down topic ideas. Don't analyze them as you go. Just write down every idea that occurs to you, as fast as you can. Generate as many ideas as possible.

When you run out of ideas, stop writing. Now analyze your list. Select the ideas that seem the most promising and that best fit the occasion.

Listen and Read

Newspapers, magazines, and radio and television programs can spark many ideas for speech topics, so stay alert. If you see an interesting topic, learn more about it. Use research to fill in the gaps of your knowledge.

Scan Indexes and the Internet

As discussed in Chapter 12, a library's encyclopedias, books, and periodical indexes can serve as good sources of speech ideas. Look up the topics that interest you. Search for headings or article titles that suggest good topics.

The Internet is a good source of speech topics, too. For example, look at a site such as the one for the Gallup Organization (www.gallup.com), which surveys public opinion. Or, you could search for sites on subjects that you're considering. Look for specialized areas of those topics that would suit your occasion and audience.

Talk to People

Talk to your family and friends and even to subject area experts about possible speech ideas. If possible, talk to people who will be in your audience. What issues and concerns are on their minds? If you learn that audience members are worried about neighborhood crime or about rising costs of housing, you've opened up important new topic areas for your speech.

Narrow the Topic

Say that you've been asked to prepare a ten-minute speech and have chosen the general topic "music." Suddenly, you panic. How can you possibly handle this subject well in ten short minutes? You probably can't. But there is no need to discard the idea. Simply narrow the topic.

Stairstep Method

In the stairstep method, you begin by constructing a series of steps. On the bottom step, write your general speech topic, "music." With each step up, narrow the topic. The following figure shows how the topic of music can be narrowed to something more specific.

Mind Mapping

A mind map, or web, is called a graphic organizer because it helps you to explore an idea in a pictorial way. Begin by writing a main idea—this time, the narrowed topic "blues music"—in an oval in the middle of your paper. Then let your mind explore different facets of this topic. Place them in circles, connecting them to the main topic or to each other. One benefit of mind mapping is that it allows you to explore many related ideas of a topic simultaneously. Then you can choose the most interesting part of your mind map for your speech topic.

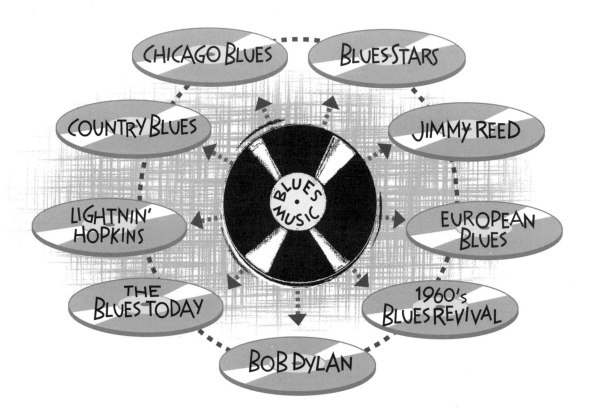

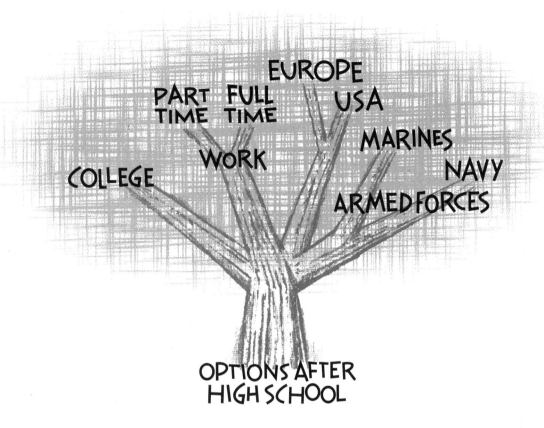

EUROPE

PART FULL
TIME TIME

USA

MARINES

WORK

NAVY

COLLEGE

ARMED FORCES

OPTIONS AFTER
HIGH SCHOOL

Spider Outlining

A spider outline, also called a spider diagram, is another graphic organizer. It resembles a mind map, but it tends to branch out from the bottom concept, like the branches of a tree. This structure works well when you want to narrow a topic that may have causes and effects (such as "stress-related illnesses and children") or pros and cons (such as "options after high school").

Begin by writing your general topic, "options after high school," on paper or on the computer. Below it, think of main topic branches. You might think of four: college or other school, work, travel, and armed forces. Write them in separate columns below the topic.

If the travel option is most interesting to you, try narrowing that topic even more. You might narrow it according to an area of possible travel or look at it from another angle—for example, a world tour for $1,500. Then branch out to identify the pros and cons of that option or other options that interest you more.

When you finish, simply highlight the portions that you wish to explore in your speech.

Plus and Minus Spreadsheet

Another method for narrowing a topic is a plus and minus spreadsheet. This is especially useful when the topic is controversial or when you want to narrow your topic to a specific position in an argument—for example, buying versus leasing a car.

List your issue at the top, then create a computer spreadsheet with two columns, one labeled Pluses (or Pros) and the other Minuses (or Cons). Brainstorm a list of as many pros and cons of the issue as you can. When you are finished, choose the most compelling positive or negative points on which to focus your speech.

This method of narrowing a topic is helpful overall, because, in a controversial topic, it is important to identify both sides of the argument. Keep adding to your spreadsheet as you begin your research. It also will provide you with useful background information for a question-and-answer period.

Narrow Your Topic

GOAL

The goal of this activity is to narrow topics and practice turning broad topics into specific ones.

TASKS

1. Collect and bring to class current newspapers, news magazines, or TV listings.

2. Form groups of four to five.

3. List at least five to eight potential speech topics from stories in these sources.

4. Narrow three broad subjects into workable topics for a three- to five-minute informative speech. Use one of the narrowing techniques described in this chapter.

5. Each group presents to the class its narrowed topics and the process it used to arrive at them.

6. The class discusses the results, including whether the process was used properly and whether topics are sufficiently narrowed for three- to five-minute speeches.

OUTCOMES

Did working with others help you with the narrowing process? What ideas for topics did you get for your own speeches?

Determine a Speech's Purpose

After choosing and narrowing your speech topic, you need to determine your controlling purpose. Is it to inform, to persuade, to entertain, or all three?

Many speeches have more than one purpose. An entertaining speech can also persuade. An informative speech can be entertaining. TV commercials and infomercials combine all three purposes. They impart information in an entertaining way while attempting to sell you a product or service.

In the business world, most presentations both inform and persuade. Entertainment is rarely the main purpose, unless it is an after-dinner speech. Businesspeople deliver many informative reports, such as problem analyses, research summaries, or project reports. Their goals frequently are to persuade the audience to change its behavior, attitudes, or beliefs. For instance, they may want management to approve plans for a project, choose a particular outside consultant, or grant the department a budget increase.

Focus on a Specific Purpose

After you identify the main purpose of your speech—to inform, persuade, entertain, or a combination of all of them—take a moment to think about that purpose. If you're speaking to the school's Music Booster Club about next year's budget, clearly identify your main objective. Do you want them to approve a budget increase for new band uniforms? Or are you presenting a plan for increasing Booster Club membership? Without a clear objective, you'll get off track and the audience will be confused about what you want them to do and why.

Write a Purpose Statement

A **purpose statement** defines the main goal or objective for the speech. Take time to write a statement of purpose before you begin. It will help you to keep the topic, the audience, and your primary purpose in mind as you research and write your speech. For example:

"My objective is to inform (result) the board of directors (audience) about progress on my project (topic)."

"My objective is to persuade (result) upper management (audience) to approve a 10 percent increase in my department's budget (topic)."

Components of a Statement of Purpose		
Audience	**Topic**	**Desired Result or Purpose**
Booster Club	Next year's budget	I want a 10 percent increase.

Analyze the Audience

When writing a speech, focus on the audience. Your listeners are a crucial element in your success. Your effectiveness will depend upon how well your speech anticipates the audience's experiences, needs, attitudes, and expectations.

Knowledge about your audience should guide every step of your preparation—research, organizing your content, choosing arguments and supporting materials, and determining whether humor is appropriate. The process of studying your audience is called **audience analysis.**

To learn about your audience, ask those who organized the event, try asking questions of potential audience members, or do research. In general, there are **four** types of information you need about your audience: basic data, knowledge of the topic, audience attitude, and audience goal.

❶ Basic Data

No two members of an audience are alike, but they will likely share some general characteristics. The statistical characteristics of a population (that is, age, gender, occupation, and level of education) are called **demographics.** Information about audience demographics can help you prepare relevant examples or present meaningful arguments that will be persuasive to your listeners.

In all cases, the trick is to be sensitive to the needs and interests of your audience without stereotyping them by those very characteristics.

Age. Knowing the age range of your listeners will enable you to gear your topic to them. An audience of middle school students generally will have different attitudes, experiences, concerns, knowledge, and interests than an audience of working parents or retired people. Be sure to avoid stereotyping, but consider age when choosing personal anecdotes, quotations, examples, and your opening and closing statements.

Gender. Gender classification refers to the male/female breakdown of your audience. This won't greatly affect your topic choices, but it's important to choose examples that are gender-neutral (not stereotyped). No matter what the gender of your audience, you should use respectful and unbiased language in your speech.

Select examples and illustrations that will be meaningful to your audience. If you are giving a speech on healthy living to an audience of teenage girls, it seems appropriate to mention eating disorders, since that is a frequent problem for that group. When speaking to teenage boys, it might make sense to mention dangers of smoking or chewing tobacco. However, don't assume that one group lacks interest in the issues of the other.

Occupation. Learn as much as possible about your listeners' occupations. This can help you to make some general assumptions about a group's interests, values, lifestyles, and general attitudes. Consider, for example, the differences between an audience of Internet specialists, skilled laborers, restaurant owners, corporate executives, and politicians. Even so, some issues such as job security and basic health concerns may be shared across many occupations.

Level of Education. Knowing the educational level of your audience is helpful in determining the vocabulary, informational content, and examples used in your speech. An audience with less formal education may require more background information on some topics (for example, Web browsers) than a better-educated audience will. To determine an adult audience's education level, ask the organizers of the event.

❷ Knowledge of the Topic

The basic audience data you collect may suggest what audience members already know about the subject. You can also find this out by talking with the event's organizers.

If audience knowledge of your subject is high, you can skip some basic information. For example, if you are speaking about surfing to a group of experienced surfers, you won't pull out a surfboard or discuss basic techniques. Instead you'll present something

that increases their knowledge and expertise, such as advanced techniques used by world champions or a new type of wetsuit.

On the other hand, if your audience knows little or nothing about your topic, you will need to include basic information in your speech. For example, if you're talking about video games to people who have never played them, you should cover the basics. Avoid information and techniques that are appropriate only for experts.

❸ Audience Attitude

As discussed in Chapter 10, an audience will generally be either positive, neutral, apathetic, or opposed to the topic of your speech. To determine audience attitudes, ask yourself these questions: Will my listeners be for or against me? What do they value? What are their needs? How can I relate my goal to the concerns of my audience?

Knowing the climate ahead of time gives you the opportunity to create a speech that will maintain the audience's positive attitude, create interest and concern, wake listeners up, or win them over.

Practice Analyzing Your Audience

GOAL

The goal of this activity is to practice analyzing your audience.

TASKS

1. Form groups of four or five.
2. Within each group, choose a speaking scenario from the options below or choose another.

   * You are the emcee for the MTV Music Awards or another awards program.
   * You are speaking to the PTA about beginning a school breakfast program.
   * You are a famous celebrity talking to your fans.
   * You are an architect explaining a revolutionary new building design to a potential client.
   * You are a high school senior asking the faculty to allow you to substitute an upcoming Asian travel experience for a required graduation course.

3. Use the Checklist on the next page to analyze the audience expected for your chosen speaking situation. Record all answers.

4. Share your group's audience profile with the class. Discuss similarities, differences, and stumbling blocks.

5. Discuss how these characteristics would influence choices for objectives and supporting material.

OUTCOMES

Did this exercise help you to focus on your audience and select your material?

❹ Audience Goal

What is the overall goal of your speech? What do you want the audience to do, believe, or understand at the end of your speech? Think about what the audience has to gain from your speech. Taken together, these aims define the **audience goal**. Here are **three** possible goals you might want for your audience:

1. **Take action.** I want the audience to approve funds for Stage Two of the museum remodeling plan.

2. **Believe my words.** I want the audience to be convinced that the arts are essential to any healthy educational program.

3. **Understand an idea or a process.** I want the audience to be informed of new graduation requirements.

Of course, goals are often interrelated. For example, if you are presenting a speech on the importance of the arts in education, your goals may be both to inform your audience of the benefits of such a program and to persuade listeners to take an action such as approving funding.

How to Analyze Your Audience

Make notes on this checklist and keep it close at hand as you research and write your speech.

Who is my audience?

✓ Age

✓ Gender

✓ Occupation

✓ Levels of education

✓ Special circumstances, needs, or values

✓ Knowledge level of the topic or issue

What is the attitude of my audience?

✓ Attitude toward my topic (positive, neutral, apathetic, opposed)

✓ Openness to me personally (open, neutral, apathetic, opposed)

What are my objectives with this audience?

✓ Main goal

✓ Support material, arguments, and examples to include

✓ Support material, arguments, and examples to avoid

Preparing a Speech

A The goal is described in the title.

B Dr. King focuses his audience on one fact, using parallel structure and repetition for emphasis.

Model

Martin Luther King, Jr.

Washington, DC, 28 August 1963

"I have a dream"

Five score years ago, a great American, in whose symbolic shadow we stand, signed the Emancipation Proclamation. This momentous decree came as a great beacon light of hope to millions of Negro slaves who had been seared in the flames of withering injustice. It came as a joyous daybreak to end the long night of captivity.

But one hundred years later, we must face the tragic fact that the Negro is still not free. One hundred years later, the life of the Negro is still sadly crippled by the manacles of segregation and the chains of discrimination. One hundred years later, the Negro lives on a lonely island of poverty in the midst of a vast ocean of material prosperity. One hundred years later, the Negro is still languished in the corners of American society and finds himself an exile in his own land. So we have come here today to dramatize an appalling condition.

In a sense we have come to our nation's Capital to cash a check. When the architects of our republic wrote the magnificent words of the Constitution and the Declaration of Independence, they were signing a promissory note to which every American was to fall heir. This note was a promise that all men would be guaranteed the unalienable rights of life, liberty, and the pursuit of happiness.

It is obvious today that America has defaulted on this promissory note insofar as her citizens of color are concerned. Instead of honoring this sacred obligation, America has given the Negro people a bad check; a check which has come back marked "insufficient funds." But we refuse to believe that the bank of justice is bankrupt. We refuse to believe that there are insufficient funds in the great vaults of opportunity of this nation. So we have come to cash this check–a check that will give us upon demand the riches of freedom and the security of justice. We have also come to this hallowed spot to remind America of the fierce urgency of *now*. This is no time to engage in the luxury of cooling off or to take the tranquilizing drug of gradualism.

C Dr. King appeals to his audience—freedom marchers in Washington—with a series of goals.

Now is the time to make real the promises of Democracy.

Now is the time to rise from the dark and desolate valley of segregation to the sunlit path of racial justice.

Now is the time to open the doors of opportunity to all of God's children.

Now is the time to lift our nation from the quicksands of racial injustice to the solid rock of brotherhood.

It would be fatal for the nation to overlook the urgency of the moment and to underestimate the determination of the Negro. This sweltering summer of the Negro's legitimate discontent will not pass until there is an invigorating autumn of freedom and equality. Nineteen sixty-three is not an end, but a beginning. Those who hope that the Negro needed to blow off steam and will now be content will have a rude awakening if the nation returns to business as usual. There will be neither rest nor tranquillity in America until the Negro is granted his citizenship rights. The whirlwinds of revolt will continue to shake the foundations of our nation until the bright day of justice emerges.

But there is something that I must say to my people who stand on the warm threshold which leads into the palace of justice. In the process of gaining our rightful place we must not be guilty of wrongful deeds. Let us not seek to satisfy our thirst for freedom by drinking from the cup of bitterness and hatred. We must forever conduct our struggle on the high plane of dignity and discipline, We must not allow our creative protest to degenerate into physical violence. Again and again we must rise to the majestic heights of meeting physical force with soul force. The marvelous new militancy which has engulfed the Negro community must not lead us to a distrust of all white people, for many of our white brothers, as evidenced by their presence here today, have come to realize that their destiny is tied up with our destiny and their freedom is inextricably bound to our freedom. We cannot walk alone.

And as we walk, we must make the pledge that we shall march ahead. We cannot turn back. There are those who are asking the devotees of civil rights, "When will you be satisfied?"

continues ▶

Preparing a Speech
(continued)

D Dr. King moves into the core of his speech, a vision of tomorrow's freedoms.

Model

We can never be satisfied as long as the Negro is the victim of the unspeakable horrors of police brutality. We can never be satisfied as long as our bodies, heavy with the fatigue of travel, cannot gain lodging in the motels of the highways and the hotels of the cities. We cannot be satisfied as long as the Negro's basic mobility is from a smaller ghetto to a larger one. We can never be satisfied as long as a Negro in Mississippi cannot vote and a Negro in New York believes he has nothing for which to vote. No, no, we are not satisfied, and we will not be satisfied until justice rolls down like waters and righteousness like a mighty stream.

I am not unmindful that some of you have come here out of great trials and tribulations. Some of you have come fresh from narrow jail cells. Some of you have come from areas where your quest for freedom left you battered by the storms of persecution and staggered by the winds of police brutality. You have been the veterans of creative suffering. Continue to work with the faith that unearned suffering is redemptive.

Go back to Mississippi, go back to Alabama, go back to South Carolina, go back to Georgia, go back to Louisiana, go back to the slums and ghettos of our northern cities, knowing that somehow this situation can and will be changed. Let us not wallow in the valley of despair.

I say to you today, my friends, that in spite of the difficulties and frustrations of the moment I still have a dream. It is a dream deeply rooted in the American dream.

I have a dream that one day this nation will rise up and live out the true meaning of its creed: "We hold these truths to be self-evident; that all men are created equal."

I have a dream that one day on the red hills of Georgia the sons of former slaves and the sons of former slaveowners will be able to sit down together at the table of brotherhood.

I have a dream that one day even the state of Mississippi, a desert state sweltering with the heat of injustice and oppression, will be transformed into an oasis of freedom and justice.

I have a dream that my four little children will one day live in a nation where they will not be judged by the color of their skin but by the content of their character.

I have a dream today.

I have a dream that one day the state of Alabama, whose governor's lips are presently dripping with the words of interposition and nullification, will be transformed into a situation where little black boys and black girls will

E Dr. King repeats his purpose statement throughout the speech, giving it focus and lasting resonance.

F Dr. King builds to a climax with a final series of exhortations to his audience.

be able to join hands with little white boys and white girls and walk together as sisters and brothers.

I have a dream today.

I have a dream that one day every valley shall be exalted, every hill and mountain shall be made low, the rough places will be made plains, and the crooked places will be made straight, and the glory of the Lord shall be revealed, and all flesh shall see it together.

This is our hope. This is the faith with which I return to the South. With this faith we will be able to hew out of the mountain of despair a stone of hope. With this faith we will be able to transform the jangling discords of our nation into a beautiful symphony of brotherhood. With this faith we will be able to work together, to pray together, to struggle together, to go to jail together, to stand up for freedom together, knowing that we will be free one day.

This will be the day when all of God's children will be able sing with new meaning

My country, 'tis of thee,
Sweet land of liberty,
Of thee I sing:
Land where my fathers died,
Land of the pilgrims' pride,
From every mountainside

Let freedom ring.

And if America is to be a great nation this must become true. So let freedom ring from the prodigious hilltops of New Hampshire. Let freedom ring from the mighty mountains of New York. Let freedom ring from the heightening Alleghenies of Pennsylvania!

Let freedom ring from the snowcapped Rockies of Colorado!

Let freedom ring from the curvaceous peaks of California!

But not only that; let freedom ring from Stone Mountain of Georgia!

Let freedom ring from Lookout Mountain of Tennessee!

Let freedom ring from every hill and molehill of Mississippi. From every mountainside, let freedom ring.

When we let freedom ring, when we let it ring from every village and every hamlet, from every state and every city, we will be able to speed up that day when all of God's children, black men and white men, Jews and Gentiles, Protestants and Catholics, will be able to join hands and sing in the words of the old Negro spiritual, "Free at last! free at last! thank God almighty, we are free at last!"

Research the Topic

Now that you've selected and narrowed your topic and analyzed your audience, you are ready to consider the type of information and support material needed to back up the main points of your speech. Refer to Chapter 12 for information on using your personal experience, the library, and the Internet to research your topic.

After you complete your research, use your notes to write background information and support material for your main points. Support material may include definitions, examples, statistics, anecdotes, analogies, quotations, and more. As a general rule, it's wise to collect more support material than you think you'll need. That way, you can choose the very best examples as you begin to write and discard the rest.

Make sure that you vary the type of support material that you use. If your speech is full of nothing but facts, or quotations, or statistics, you are sure to lose your audience. Your audience analysis can guide you in deciding which type of support material would work best for each part of your speech.

Start with What You Know

Adding something of yourself—a personal story or anecdote—will greatly enhance any speech. Even though you may add factual support information, personal references will make your speech come alive for your listening audience.

Consider your topic and ask what you can add to it. Here are some questions to guide you:

1. What personal experiences and associations do I have with this topic?
2. Where, when, how, and from whom did I gain this experience?
3. How do I feel about the topic, on the basis of my own knowledge and experience?
4. What experiences have my family, friends, or acquaintances had that relate to the topic?

Adding yourself to your speech makes the speech yours—and unlike anyone else's speech on the same topic. A speaker on family communication quickly captivated his audience in the first two sentences of his speech with the words, "Last week my father told me that he has a serious illness. I realized that it was the first serious, personal conversation we've ever had."

Use Research to Support

After your research is completed, you are ready to select the best type of supporting material for each part of your speech. Look over the support material notes you made earlier. Are there any gaps? Fill them in now.

Speech coach Liyan Wilder advises you to ask yourself **three** questions about each example, fact, quote, or anecdote that you have identified:

1. **Does it help to explain my point?** Make sure that each supporting element that you add amplifies your point in some way.

2. **Will listeners understand it?** If they can't understand or relate to the fact or example you present, it won't have the effectiveness you want.

3. **Does it truly interest me?** Make each piece of support material that you use count. Avoid dull quotations or unimpressive statistics. They will hurt more than they will help.

Checklist

How to Select Support Material

The support material I selected . . .

✓ Clarifies and supports the speech's main idea and purpose.

✓ Represents different types of support material throughout the speech.

✓ Is memorable and appealing.

✓ Reflects my interests and experiences.

✓ Will be understandable and appealing to my audience.

Create a Final Outline

In preparing your speech to this point, you have worked to:

* Select and narrow your topic.
* Identify your main purpose—to entertain, inform, or persuade.
* Analyze your audience.
* Create a statement of purpose.
* Identify personal experiences that will add interest to your topic.
* Conduct any needed research.
* Consider the types of support material you might use.

Now you're ready to create a final outline for your speech.

Central Idea Statement

As you completed your research, you worked from a preliminary outline. Now you'll begin to draft a final speech outline that incorporates the materials you've found. You'll probably make several drafts of your outline before it is final.

To begin your outline, you will construct a **central idea statement.** The central idea statement is closely related to your purpose statement. The purpose statement summarizes the main objective of your speech. The central idea statement goes a step farther. It includes the wording of exactly what you intend to say to the audience. Whereas the purpose statement serves as a guide for you during speech preparation, the central idea statement is what you actually say to the audience, at the beginning and the end of your speech.

Here are examples of a purpose statement and a central idea statement:

* **Purpose statement:** After my speech, audience members will choose to participate in the Stop Violence Now march to City Hall scheduled on Martin Luther King, Jr.'s, birthday.
* **Central idea statement:** By participating in the Stop Violence Now march to City Hall on Monday, we can show our intention to promote nonviolence in all areas of our lives.

The following guidelines can help you put your central idea into words.

1. Express one idea in sentence form.
2. Be precise in your wording.
3. Target the audience's needs and interests.
4. Be sure the statement fits the occasion.
5. Try not to overgeneralize.

Headings and Subheadings

The central idea statement should guide the final organization of your speech. If it truly summarizes your speech in one sentence, it probably also suggests natural divisions, reasons, or steps to create the body of your speech.

Main Headings

The **main headings** of your speech are your main points. After reviewing your final statement of purpose and central idea statement, ask yourself:

* Does the central idea include a time frame or process? If so, the main events or the main steps of the process make logical main headings. Here is an example.

How to Shampoo Your Dog
I. Find and Organize a Good Place
II. Persuade the Dog
III. Shampoo the Dog
IV. Care for the Dog Afterwards

* Does the central idea involve space? For a speech on the "21st Century House," moving from room to room provides a logical list of main points as you write your speech.

The 21st Century House
I. Living and dining rooms
II. Kitchen
III. Bedrooms and baths

* Does the central idea involve a number of reasons, pro or con? For example, it would make sense to organize a speech on "The Benefits of Taking Healthy Risks" around those reasons.

Benefits of Taking Healthy Risks
I. What Are Healthy Risks?
II. Examples of Healthy Risks
III. Why Take Healthy Risks?
IV. What Happens if You Don't Take Risks?

Supporting Material

You've identified the main points of your speech; now it's time to flesh out each of your main headings. To do this you will add **subheadings,** or **supporting material,** placed under the main heads of your outline to explain, develop, prove, or elaborate on these main ideas. Here you'll draw on the material you've collected, including personal experience, definitions, and supporting information from your research.

Choose the best, most compelling, and most interesting information you have collected. To do this, ask yourself: What kind of material is needed to support this main point? If you're explaining a concept that's unfamiliar, the audience may need an analogy, facts, a definition, and a series of examples. If you're supporting an argument, the audience probably needs facts, statistics, and expert testimony. If you're describing an unfamiliar landscape, listeners probably need a simple description, anecdote, analogy, and visual aid.

Some common types of support materials are shown in this table.

Types of Support Material		
Support Material	**Definition**	**Use to . . .**
Fact	Information based on evidence	Explain background, establish problem, support argument, increase credibility
Statistic	Number that expresses information	Establish problem, support argument, add interest, increase credibility
Direct Quotation	Cited passages that are repeated in a person's own words	Open/close speech, support argument, add interest
Analogy	Suggests the similarities or differences between two things	Explain a difficult new concept, idea, or object
Definition	A statement explaining the meaning of a word or phrase	Clarify your terms, set up argument
Example	An illustration of something	Clarify your point, support argument, add life to speech
Description	Verbal account or portrayal	Create mental picture, add life to speech
Story	Description of something that happened to you or someone else	Create mental picture, illustrate point, entertain
Personal Anecdote	Short narrative	Create mental picture, illustrate point, entertain
Visual Aid	Special types of support	Aid understanding, increase interest

Outline Formats

You are familiar with the format used for outlines. Below is an example of the Topic Outline format you'll use to organize your speeches. You state your central idea at the top. You list your main headings under Roman numerals, with main supporting points listed beneath them with capital letters and the next level of points listed with numbers.

The next page shows the same speech organized as a Sentence Outline. When outlining your speech, consistently use either a Topic Outline or Sentence Outline format.

Example

Topic Outline:
Electric Vehicles (EVs)

Central Idea Statement: Get a jump on the future and envision yourself in an electric vehicle (EV).

I. Opening

II. EVs in the Past

  A. The First EV

    1. Photo of Vehicle

    2. Information about Vehicle

    3. The Vehicle's Invention

      a. Who Invented It and Why

      b. Story of Mrs. Henry Ford

  B. What Happened to This Vehicle

III. EVs in the Present

  A. Gas-Powered Autos in the U.S.

    1. Statistics: How Many

    2. Why They Became Popular (quote news article)

    3. Description of Clogged Freeways at Rush Hour

    4. List of Phenomena Related to Cars (phones, drive-ins, and drive-throughs)

  B. Problems Caused by Gas-Powered Autos

    1. Oil Consumption/Natural Resources Drain (statistics)

    2. Pollution and Health Problems, Environment

IV. EVs in the Future

  A. Why EVs?

    1. Chart of Comparisons with Gas-Powered Cars

    2. Short Scenarios/Audience Participation: Take the Car or the EV?

  B. Family of the Future (hypothetical story)

  C. The Future Today

    1. 2000 EVs in New Car Lots (quote magazine article)

    2. Photos of EVs on Sale Now

V. Closing

Sentence Outline:
Electric Vehicles (EVs)

Central Idea Statement: Get a jump on the future and envision yourself in an electric vehicle (EV).

I. Introduce the topic.

II. Review the history of electric vehicles.

    A. Discuss the first electric vehicle.

        1. Show a photo of this vehicle.

        2. Give basic information about this vehicle.

        3. Discuss the EV's invention.

            a. Explain who invented it and why.

            b. Tell the story of Mrs. Henry Ford.

    B. Explain what happened to this vehicle.

III. Talk about EVs in the present.

    A. Discuss gas-powered autos in the U.S.

        1. Give statistics about how many, etc.

        2. Quote news article explaining why they became popular.

        3. Describe clogged freeways at rush hour.

        4. List the phenomena related to cars—cell phones, drive-ins, and drive-throughs, etc.

    B. Describe problems caused by gas-powered autos.

        1. Use statistics to explain U.S. oil consumption and the natural resources drain.

        2. Describe pollution and the resulting health and environmental problems.

IV. Imagine EVs in the future.

    A. Explain why EVs are important.

        1. Show chart comparing them to gas-powered cars.

        2. Describe short scenarios, with audience participation: "Take the car or the EV?"

    B. Tell hypothetical story of the family of the future.

    C. Show how the future has become the present.

        1. Quote magazine article showing the new EVs hitting the car lots.

        2. Show photos of EVs on sale now.

V. Conclude the speech.

Outline Template

I.

  A.

  B.

    1.

    2.

      a.

      b.

II.

  A.

  B.

    1.

    2.

Developing Your Speech Outline

GOAL

The goal of this activity is to develop an outline for a speech.

TASKS

1. Be sure you have completed these preliminary steps:
   * Analyzed the audience
   * Defined the speaking situation or occasion
   * Narrowed your topic
   * Reviewed your personal qualifications for speaking on the topic
   * Written down the reason your audience should care about your topic

2. Next, jot down your topic.

3. Write your purpose statement and central idea statement, using guidelines in this chapter.

4. Examine your central idea and ask, "Are there natural divisions, reasons, or steps in my statement?"

5. In answer to the question above, list three or four main points or headings that you want to use in your speech. Use the type of speech outline you see on page 274.

6. Select supporting information for your main points, as explained in this chapter.

7. Write down ideas for your speech's opening.

8. Write the outline of your speech, using different types of supporting materials for each subhead.

9. Write the conclusion to your speech.

10. Finalize your speech's opening.

OUTCOMES

Were you able to fill in the outline successfully? Were you able to distinguish between your purpose statement (to guide the speaker) and your central idea statement (to guide the audience's understanding)? Do you need to select more supporting material? Are your examples, descriptions, and other supporting material lively and interesting? Is everything you used relevant to the overall purpose of your speech?

The Importance of Rehearsing

Martina Tull and Kira Brandow create book series for children. Last winter they flew across the country to pitch their idea for a brand new book series to an important publisher.

They started preparing weeks in advance. They defined their goals, outlined their presentation, created and duplicated professional-looking handouts, and selected strong work samples. They then scripted the presentation, dividing up speaking roles. They practiced in front of each other many times, critiquing each other's style and delivery and smoothing out the transitions. They carefully timed the presentation and rehearsed everything from the introduction and conclusion to questions they might be asked.

As luck would have it, their carefully laid plans went awry. Martina recalled, "Three canceled flights over 12 hours due to bad weather made us almost a day late in getting there. We had to rent a car and drive for six hours to arrive before the publisher's closing time on Friday."

When they finally drove into the parking lot, time was short. The company president was waiting at the front door and led them up to a conference room full of people. "We had absolutely no time to think, relax, or prepare for even one minute," said Kira. "Within ten minutes of getting out of the car, we had already begun to talk. Luckily, we had practiced so much that we could focus and do a good job. And the publisher bought the series."

Rehearse a Speech

Experts in public speaking recommend various ways to rehearse and deliver your speech. You will have to decide which method suits you best.

Choose a Method of Delivery

Before you rehearse your speech, you'll need to choose a method of delivery. **Four** common methods of delivery are the extemporaneous method, the manuscript method, the memorization method, and the impromptu method. Most speakers use the extemporaneous method, which employs note cards as prompts. For detailed information on methods of delivery, see Chapter 15.

Plan the Pattern of Ideas

As in written composition, ideas are developed in speeches through patterns of organization. There are many ways to organize a speech, depending on the type of speech, your subject, and your main idea. (For organization of an informative speech or persuasive speech, refer to Chapters 9 and 10.)

Structuring your ideas into a speech is similar to constructing a house. A set of house plans shows how the building materials go together. The pattern for organizing your speech shows how supporting materials can be arranged.

Earlier in this chapter, we discussed composing the central idea statement. Just as you used that statement to form your main points, you can use the central idea to plan the pattern of organization for your speech. Select the pattern that best suits your topic and central idea.

Rehearse the Speech

Rehearsing a speech is a sure path to confidence. Here are some tips on rehearsing from the experts.

Tip 1: Rehearse Aloud

As you practice by yourself and in front of others using a mirror or videotape, watch for:

* Speed (too fast, too slow)
* Volume (too loud, too soft)
* Eye contact (looking down at paper, looking at one person or at one side of the room only)
* Pauses (pauses too long, no pauses)
* Clarity (mumbling, stumbling over words, swallowing the ends of sentences)
* Verbal pauses (um, like, ah)
* Annoying mannerisms (jingling keys, brushing hair back)
* Gestures (unforced, too theatrical)
* Emphasis (natural, phony, monotone)
* Expression and demeanor (friendly, stiff, excited, bored)

Sidebar

Keep in mind . . . Experts disagree on whether practicing in front of a mirror is a good thing. Some experts feel that it gives you a chance to see yourself. Others feel that it's too distracting and can be discouraging for a speaker, who then loses confidence.

Tip 2: Ask for Feedback

* Ask family and friends for their impressions and advice on your content and delivery.
* Revise as desired on the basis of their feedback.

Sidebar

Keep in mind . . . Try to choose family members and friends who sincerely want to help and whose feedback you can trust. In the end, this is your speech. You can decide what feedback to use and what to ignore.

Tip 3: Time Your Speech

* Time the entire speech to make sure it fits in the time allotted.
* Time each main part, or section, of your speech.

Sidebar

Keep in mind . . . In almost any actual speaking situation, the timing will be a bit different than the practice sessions. Especially for a long speech, knowing the approximate length of each main segment will enable you to adjust as necessary as you are giving your speech.

Tip 4: Simulate Actual Conditions

* For one rehearsal, dress in the clothes you will wear.
* Practice walking on and off the stage to a podium.
* If you will be using a handheld microphone, practice with one.
* Practice using all visual aids.
* Run through your speech from beginning to end with no stops.
* If relevant, practice your question-and-answer session.

Later you will learn more about polishing your delivery and what to check before your presentation.

Sidebar

Keep in mind . . . Practicing a speech is a lot like practicing a piano solo. Experts caution that if you practice only the beginning of your speech, the ending will receive less practice and will be weak. Force yourself to go straight through your speech without restarting.

Motivating Volunteers

Sue and Akili are in charge of planning the senior graduation party. Their first challenge is motivating other students to volunteer their time. They've been given 15 minutes after a senior assembly to drum up students' interest.

Sue knows a lot about motivation, since she is captain of the women's basketball team. Akili's strengths are his sense of humor and his organizational experience. Sue and Akili decide that they want to see at least 25 students sign up on the spot for party committees. They script their presentation and then do a trial run, using a few friends and a teacher as their audience. They decide on a multimedia approach. Akili collects old photos for a five-minute slide show, "Graduation Parties You Would NOT Want to Attend!" These include 1950 family reunions and costumed pet parades. With Akili's comical narration, these slides get the students'

attention. Then Sue follows with a five-minute presentation of party ideas that she and Akili know will excite students. She uses great background music to help students get in the mood for a really fun senior party.

For the last five minutes of the presentation, Akili and Sue take turns describing the kind of committee volunteers that are needed, then invite students to sign up. They use an overhead projector to display committee names and their activities. Meanwhile, audience volunteers pass out small round tags on which students can write their names. Sue and Akili ask students to drop their tags in specially marked jars, one for each committee, as they leave the auditorium. They think this will be more fun and efficient than sign-up sheets.

To their amazement, 58 students dropped tags in jars. Sue and Akili will have more than enough volunteers. They attribute their success to planning, presentation, and practice.

Media Aids

Most people can remember a speaker's thoughts and ideas more easily if pictorial images accompany them. In a speech, a chart or photograph often is the most eloquent way to make a point.

Types of Media Aids

If you want to enhance your speech by using media aids, there are many types from which to choose. They include pictures; objects and models; graphs, charts, and diagrams; slides; overhead transparencies; videotapes; and sound effects, CDs, and tapes. Refer to the Handbook for more comprehensive information on media aids.

Pictures

A drawing or photograph gives your audience a graphic, detailed look at something you are describing. This can add impact to your point. However, consider the size of your audience when using drawings and photographs. For a small audience, hold up a large drawing or photo. For a large audience, scan it into a computerized slide show format.

Objects and Models

When you want people to know what something actually looks like, consider using an object or model. Objects are the "real thing"—for example, a Civil War uniform. Models are three-dimensional replicas of a real thing, such as an architect's scale model of a building.

Objects and models can be fascinating to an audience and can be highly memorable. They also have great power to communicate. However, limit the time that these aids are available to the audience, so they don't distract from the rest of your speech.

Graphs, Charts, and Diagrams

Graphs and charts are visual representations of numerical information. They make it easy for an audience to understand numerical comparisons and contrasts, upturns and downturns, results, and trends over time. Diagrams help to explain complex or abstract procedures and processes in a compact way.

Using Media Aids
In speeches, media aids are often used to:
Introduce a new concept.
Focus the audience's attention.
Reinforce a main idea.
Help summarize your main points.
Present complicated or mathematical information.
Add clarity, interest, and vitality.

Graphs, charts, and diagrams give an audience large amounts of information quickly and in a compact form so the speaker does not have to take time to describe them in words. Instead, he or she can focus on the significance of the information presented.

Slides

Slides of drawings, photographs, or other material provide an audience with concrete images for abstract ideas or concepts that may be hard to explain in words. Slides are colorful and easy to see, even for large audiences. They are useful when you want the topic to have a deep and lasting emotional effect on the audience. Slides also can help a presenter explain a lot of information quickly, because they can be flashed on a screen briefly before moving on to the the next point.

Overhead Transparencies

Transparencies are easy to prepare and use with just a little practice. They can be created by hand or with a computer and printer. Speakers sometimes use them to accompany an entire talk.

Transparencies must be very readable, so use print that is large and legible and keep your design uncomplicated. One advantage of using a computer is that you can establish a uniform font and point size throughout a set of transparencies. The equipment needed to show transparencies is widely available and generally is relatively modest in cost.

Videotapes

Videotapes present moving images along with color and sound. They offer a way to explain complex processes in an engaging way. Or they allow you to share real-life examples and events. Video clips often are used during special presentations to chronicle the life events of a person being honored. One drawback to using videotapes is the advance planning and the cost of getting projection equipment.

Sound Effects, CDs, and Tapes

Sound effects, CDs, and tapes can energize a speech and emphasize important ideas. Music can supply an illustration, emphasize an idea, provide an example, or add emotional impact. CDs and music tapes can create a mood during all or part of a presentation.

Preparing Media Aids

Speech experts advise that you use restraint and common sense when creating visual aids. If you try to include too many—and too many kinds—of visual aids in your presentation, you will appear to be leading a three-ring circus. Soon the

audience will be more fascinated with the logistics of your presentation than with the points you are trying to get across.

Select the best way to emphasize each main point in your speech. Often words alone will suffice. When a media aid will enhance understanding or interest, choose the best type to convey that point.

Here are some guidelines to help you create strong media aids to support your speech topic. Careful selection may culminate in a presentation that will be remembered for a long time to come.

* Limit the complexity of visuals. Text should be easy to read even from the back of the room and limited to five to six words per line for no more than five to six lines.
* Offer only one idea or concept per visual.
* Emphasize your points by using color.
* Use bulleted and numbered lists whenever possible.
* Rely on charts or graphs to present complicated numerical data.
* Clearly title and label each media aid.
* Proofread each visual aid carefully.

If you plan to use media aids, rehearse your speech several times while using them.

Checklist

How to Put a Speech Together

☑ Write a purpose statement.

☑ Write a central idea statement.

☑ Choose a pattern of organization.
   * Time and process
   * Spatial
   * Topical
   * Problem-solution

☑ Create a speech outline.
   * Sentence
   * Word or phrase

☑ Create a strong introduction.
   * Gets attention
   * Introduces subject
   * Arouses interest
   * Establishes credibility
   * Previews main ideas

   * Startling statement
   * Rhetorical question
   * Humor
   * Quotation

☑ Make transitions in your speech.
   * Between important points
   * Introduces and summarizes
   * Short and interesting
   * Attention-getting, statistics, or humor
   * Varied
   * Gestures and movement

☑ Write a conclusion.
   * Summarizes main points
   * Restates main goal
   * Motivates audience
   * Gives closure

Wrap-up

Preparing a speech can be simple and efficient, using the process presented in this chapter. Begin by selecting and narrowing your topic. This helps you to define your purpose statement. Then carefully analyze your audience, paying attention to basic demographic data as well as to listeners' attitudes and knowledge levels. This process assists you in formulating a central idea statement, which expresses your main idea as well as the audience result that you want. Next, do research to assemble supporting materials. Once your materials are assembled, outline your speech, using your central idea statement to suggest main topic headings. Arrange supporting material—such as examples, definitions, statistics, and analogies—in an interesting and varied way in your subheadings. Then rehearse your speech and, if appropriate, add media aids.

Speech

audience analysis—determines the characteristics of listeners.

audience goal—a statement of what the speaker wants the audience to do, say, or think at the end of the speech; also includes its value to the audience.

brainstorming—technique used to generate a lot of possible ideas or solutions in a short time.

central idea statement—a summary of the speech in one sentence for the purpose of guiding the audience's understanding; usually spoken in the speech's introduction and conclusion.

demographics—statistical information about a population that describes population characteristics, such as ages, genders, occupations, and level of education.

main headings—main points of a speech outline; supported by subordinate points.

problem-solution pattern—the arrangement of material to develop a main idea in which one part of the speech explains the problem and the other part suggests a solution.

purpose statement—a sentence to guide the speaker in preparing the speech; specifies the subject, the audience, and the desired result of the speech.

subheadings—information placed into more specific categories under main heads of an outline.

supporting material—information used to develop, prove, explain, or elaborate on main ideas.

CHAPTER 14

Effective Language

In this chapter, you will consider:

- **How does spoken language differ from written language?**
- **What are the most important ways of achieving clarity in a speech?**
- **How can you make your speech writing more emphatic?**
- **What devices can you use to add color, interest, and vividness to your speech?**
- **How can you avoid cultural insensitivity in your speech writing?**

You have thought, you have planned, and you have researched. It is time for you to sit down and write your speech. This chapter explains the goals and techniques of effective speechwriting. Listeners have different needs than readers. In spoken language, you strive for clarity, emphasis, vividness, and cultural sensitivity. In this chapter, you will learn a variety of techniques that will help you to achieve these goals. You also will learn to avoid common language problems, such as euphemisms, clichés, stereotypes, slang, and incorrect grammar and usage.

Spoken versus Written Language

Communicating through a speech is different from communicating through writing. With written language, readers can go back and reread anything they didn't catch the first time. But a listening audience can't back up and "re-listen." Your audience needs to understand what you are saying as you speak. There are no instant replays.

A strong, memorable speech has four main characteristics: clarity, emphasis, vividness, and cultural sensitivity. In this chapter, you'll learn how to achieve all of them.

Clarity

Spoken language requires exactness. You only have one chance to get your point across. Give yourself time to revise and tighten up your speech several times. Omit points or examples that add confusion rather than clarity. Make sure that every point leads clearly to your main objective.

You can achieve clarity in four ways—through simple language, specific and concrete wording, repetition of the main idea, and elimination of unnecessary words.

Spoken versus Written Language	
Characteristics of Spoken Language	**Characteristics of Written Language**
Tone is usually informal and personal.	Tone usually is precise and formal.
Text can be altered as it is delivered.	Text cannot be spontaneously altered.
Voice inflections and pauses can add interest and appeal.	Dependent on wording and phrasing to add interest and appeal.
Requires clear organization and structure so audience can understand main points the first time.	Benefits from careful organization and structure, but the audience can reread unclear sections if needed.
May be enhanced by the use of audio and visual aids.	Written presentations include visuals only.
Power to persuade influenced by ideas presented, the speaker's delivery, and the speaker's credibility.	Power to persuade depends on the credibility of the ideas presented and the credentials of the author.
Speaker can use fewer words and phrases and more repetition to establish a rhythmic flow to the presentation.	Written presentations typically use a more complex sentence structure and structured format with few repetitions.
Uses averages and rounded off numerical data.	Can use precise statistics and other numerical data.

❶ Simple Language

To make your speech easy to understand, choose the best possible words to get your point across. Use short words, vivid phrases, and sentences in active voice.

Plain English

Speak plain English, using a conversational tone and simple words. Too many academic, formal, or foreign words make your speech sound stuffy and uninteresting. Choose the simplest word to get your point across—*trouble* rather than *adversity*, *talk* rather than *confer*, *try* rather than *endeavor*, *because* rather than *due to the fact that*. Use your thesaurus to find interesting descriptive words.

Vivid Phrases

Make every word count. Avoid clichés (discussed later in this chapter) such as "make a world of difference" or "try to put your best foot forward." Use vivid, descriptive language that keeps your audience awake and eager to hear more.

Active Sentences

Use active rather than passive voice. Active voice heightens interest and aids understanding because there are fewer unnecessary words to wade through. For example, say "This speaker avoids passive voice" rather than "Passive voice is avoided by this speaker." Also avoid *-ing* verb forms. Instead of "The bear was seen *shuffling* through our campsite," substitute "The bear *shuffled* through our campsite."

❷ Specific and Concrete Wording

You also can achieve clarity in your speeches by using specific and concrete wording. A **concrete word** such as *sparrow* points to a specific, visible thing and creates an immediate mental picture. An **abstract word** such as *bird* expresses a general concept or idea. The word *nectarine* is concrete; the word *food* is abstract. The terms *hockey puck, face mask, shin guards,* and *hockey stick* are concrete, referring to specific equipment used in a specific sport. The term *sports equipment* is abstract and general, referring to items used in all sports.

Think of a pyramid, like the one below, with abstract words appearing at the bottom. As you ascend the pyramid, the words become more concrete and specific.

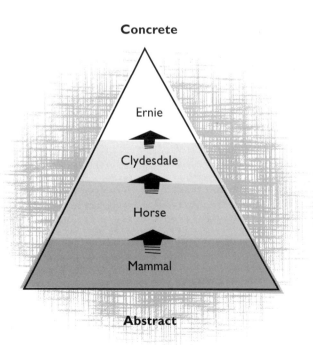

Concrete

Ernie

Clydesdale

Horse

Mammal

Abstract

Avoid using vague descriptive words such as *very*, *slightly*, and *extremely*. Use only words and phrases that say precisely what you mean.

❸ Repetition of the Main Idea

Many professional speechwriters use this time-honored, three-part formula in presenting their ideas. In the *introduction*, briefly explain what you will be telling the audience. In the *body* of the speech, describe it in detail. In the *conclusion*, summarize what you just told them. That way your listeners are three times more likely to remember what you said.

❹ Elimination of Unnecessary Words

You also can achieve clarity by removing unnecessary words. Too many words dilute your meaning and make your speech hard to follow. One way to do this is to limit such words as *very* or *quite* that quickly drain energy from the point you are trying to make. To revise a wordy sentence, isolate your key ideas. Then pack as much of their meaning as possible into the key parts of the sentence—the subject, the verb, and the object.

Removing Unnecessary Words

Wordy	Less Wordy
Of all the speakers that we heard in today's program, I thought the last was the best one.	Today's last speaker was the best.
When I am supposed to be doing homework, I have a tendency to call my girlfriend.	Instead of doing homework, I often call my girlfriend.
A few of the employees who were just hired seemed to be wandering around the main lobby of the office.	A few new employees wandered around the office's main lobby.

Clarifying Your Speech's Language

GOAL

The goal of this activity is to help you clarify your speech's language by making it shorter and simpler, and more specific and concrete, by adding restatement of your main ideas, and by eliminating unnecessary words.

TASKS

1. Find or write a first draft of a three- to five-page speech that you plan to give.
2. Choose a partner and exchange your speech drafts.
3. Each person evaluates the clarity of his or her partner's language. Use guide-lines listed under **GOAL**. Is the language short and simple? Is it specific and concrete? Does it restate the main idea? Are there unnecessary words?
4. Each person revises the other's speech for greater clarity, as described under **GOAL**.
5. Partners return the revised drafts and discuss the results.

OUTCOMES

Did your partner improve your speech? In what ways? In what areas do you need to work to achieve greater clarity in your speechwriting?

Emphasis

Emphasis is forcefulness of expression that gives importance to something. Emphasis can help an audience to remember a speech for a long time. You can add emphasis through variety and contrast, rhetorical questions, language techniques, and repetition.

❶ Variety and Contrast

In general, short sentences are snappier and more apt to be remembered. But variety is necessary, too. Otherwise, the constant drone will lull people to sleep. To keep your audience's attention, vary your sentence length between long, explanatory sentences and short, forceful ones.

An excerpt from an 1852 speech by Frederick Douglass, an escaped slave who became a famous abolitionist, illustrates how to vary rhythm by contrasting sentence lengths.

Fellow citizens, I will not enlarge further on your national inconsistencies. The existence of slavery in this country brands your republicanism as a sham, your humanity as a base pretense, and your Christianity as a lie. It destroys your moral power abroad, it corrupts your politicians at home. It saps the foundations of religion; it makes your name a hissing and a byword to a mocking earth. . . .

It's also wise to vary your sentence structure. If most of your sentences are written in a subject-verb-object pattern, try using some introductory phrases and clauses as in the example below.

A Monotonous Sentence Pattern

William Shakespeare was born in Stratford-upon-Avon in 1564. Stratford-upon-Avon is a small town 75 miles northwest of London. His father was a glovemaker. His name was John Shakespeare. His mother was the daughter of a prosperous farmer. Her name was Mary Arden. He went to public school until he was 14. He was 18 when he married Anne Hathaway. She was a woman of 26.

Revised for Structural Variety

In 1564, William Shakespeare was born in Stratford-upon-Avon, a small town 75 miles northwest of London. His father, John Shakespeare, made gloves. His mother, Mary Arden, was the daughter of a prosperous farmer. Until he was 14, Shakespeare attended public school. At 18, he married 26-year-old Anne Hathaway.

---

❷ Rhetorical Questions

Another way to achieve emphasis is through use of **rhetorical questions**—questions that are asked with no expectations of an answer. Rhetorical questions invite an audience to think. Here are some examples of rhetorical questions.

✱ "What do we mean by freedom and justice for all?"

✱ "How can we save these endangered animals?"

Speakers use rhetorical questions to focus attention on the topic and to challenge the audience. Rhetorical questions can turn a drowsy audience into active, energized participants.

❸ Language Techniques

Language techniques, or rhetorical techniques, create memorable wording and eloquent phrasing in a speech. Famous speakers such as John F. Kennedy, Winston Churchill, and Martin Luther King, Jr., employed many of these techniques. There are seven techniques that can make a speech memorable. They are parallelism, antithesis, groups of three, inversion, order of climax, alliteration, and repetition.

Parallelism

When you use **parallelism,** you repeat sentence structures—words, phrases, clauses, and sentences—to help emphasize your content. Parallel patterns help make your main points easy to understand and remember. Often parallelism exists in groups of three.

✱ "We will gather up our intellects, our hearts, and our courage."
✱ "With this act, we are regaining our self-respect as citizens. We are regaining justice."

Winston Churchill's speeches are full of parallel structures. So is Martin Luther King, Jr.'s "I Have a Dream" speech.

Antithesis

Antithesis is another type of parallel structure. In this language technique, the beginning and ending of the sentence provide a contrast. President John F. Kennedy used antithesis in two 1961 addresses, his Inaugural Address and an address to the United Nations. Notice that the first example ends with the most uplifting idea, while the second example does the opposite. In general, antitheses usually are stronger when they end positively.

* "And so, my fellow Americans: ask not what your country can do for you—ask what you can do for your country."
* "Mankind must put an end to war or war will put an end to mankind."

Antithesis also works best when you include roughly the same number of words in each half of the sentence.

* "She symbolized the hope of peace encased within the despair of war."
* ". . . I can never remember whether it snowed for six days and six nights when I was twelve or twelve days and twelve nights when I was six." (Dylan Thomas)

Groups of Three

Groups of three abound in nature, daily life, advertising, children's games, and folktales. Races begin with "On your mark, get set, go!" We eat "morning, noon, and night" and promise someone "the sun, the moon, and the stars." In children's literature we have the *Three Little Pigs* and *Goldilocks and the Three Bears.*

Speakers often use groups of three for emphasis. To make your speech more powerful, try breaking some of your points into threes.

* ". . . government of the people, by the people, for the people. . . ." (Abraham Lincoln)
* "Our games were exciting, heart-wrenching, . . . and the best place to spend Friday nights!"

Inversion

In **inversion** a phrase or sentence is flipped in a way that we are unused to hearing. Because it is an unfamiliar pattern, it sparks interest and makes an audience take notice. Be careful not to overuse inversion or it will quickly lose its power.

* "Anyone can take life from man, but no one death. . . . " (Lucius Annaeus Seneca)

Order of Climax

Climax ordering is a technique that is used to build emphasis into your speech. This moment may cause your audience to sit in hushed silence, to applaud wildly, or to gasp in recognition of a truth.

When climax ordering is appropriate, arrange your points in order of increasing strength or importance. Say, for example, that your speech describes the Black Death, an epidemic in medieval Europe. You might begin by describing a single case, then trace the plague's spread within one city, then to other cities, and finally to all of Europe.

Alliteration

In **alliteration,** many words in a passage begin with the same sound (usually an initial consonant). Alliteration, if not over-used, can add interest to a title and add rhythm and feeling to your speech.
"Love's Labour Lost"
"Flashbacks from Our Forefathers"
"Parting is such sweet sorrow."

Repetition

You are often part of an audience, so you know what audience members do. They daydream, doodle on a piece of paper, whisper to their neighbor, and think about what they will do when they leave.

Repetition of important words or phrases is one way to get an audience's attention, to make them stop and listen. Repetition of a phrase or an idea can make your speech sound eloquent, even profound.

* "Where is the Life we have lost in living? Where is the wisdom we have lost in knowledge? Where is the knowledge we have lost in information?" (T. S. Eliot)
* Martin Luther King, Jr., used the phrase "let freedom ring" ten times in only slightly more sentences at the end of his famous 1963 "I Have a Dream" speech. See the Handbook.

Figures of Speech

Speakers can help listeners to feel their words by using figures of speech. **Figures of speech** create visual images and lend special emotional meaning to your words. They use words in a nonliteral way or with altered word patterns to make a vivid, and often memorable, description or comparison.

Five common figures of speech are similes, metaphors, personification, hyperbole, understatement, and irony.

❶ Similes and Metaphors

Similes and metaphors are devices commonly used in many types of writing, including poetry. They also can be effective in speeches, because they help the audience to understand one idea or object by comparing it with another familiar image.

A **simile** uses the words *like* or *as* to directly compare two different things.

* "The autumn leaves tumbled across the road *like* small boys in yellow slickers."
* "The hard rain felt *as* bruising *as* buckshot."
* "O my love's like a red, red rose." (Robert Burns)

A **metaphor** directly compares two different things, but without using the words *like* or *as*. One thing is represented as *being* the other thing.

* "All the world's a stage." (Shakespeare)
* "A shadow has fallen upon the scene . . . an iron curtain has descended across the Continent." (Winston Churchill)
* "His painting transported him to a new geography of space."

Extended metaphors or similes are longer, more elaborate comparisons. Public speakers often use extended metaphors or similes to give the audience a visual or concrete framework for an idea.

Tips for Using Similes and Metaphors

Don't overdo it! If you do, your audience will focus on your images rather than on your message.

Don't use someone else's metaphors. Overused metaphors are called *clichés*. Examples include "it was carved in stone" and "raining cats and dogs." Instead, create your own meaningful comparisons.

Don't mix metaphors unless you are trying to give a humorous speech! An example is, "She was as shy as a daisy in sheep's clothing.

Everyday COMMUNICATION

Using an Extended Metaphor

Juanita is recruiting tutors for an adult literacy program. In her talk she compares the plight of an adult who cannot read to being in a hurricane.

Imagine yourself camped on a remote beach, happily collecting shells and swimming in the ocean. Suddenly, the sky darkens and the wind picks up. You run for your tent, hoping to wait out the storm. After a few hours, the fierce wind and rain rip it into shreds. In the dark now, you look for shelter. You find a rocky cave at the edge of the water. You are out of the rain, but soon the storm and the tides bring the ocean in

to where you are perched, on a ledge a couple feet up from the ground. The rain pounds outside and the winds rage at hurricane force.

You are hanging onto your tiny rock perch, wet, cold, hungry, and alone. You can't climb any higher to avoid the water and the wind and rain are too powerful to venture out to try to find a safer place. You feel that you are doomed.

But suddenly you hear voices and can vaguely make out a lantern of some kind. Can it be that a rescue crew will save you before the tide washes you away? Yes! Someone is here to help you. You now know that you will be all right.

Now just imagine. You can offer that kind of lifeline for a person who cannot read.

❷ Personification

Personification gives human characteristics or qualities to nonhuman ideas or entities.

* "Mother Earth"
* "The crowd swallowed him up."

Like other literary devices and language tricks, personification can add something special to a speech if used thoughtfully and sparingly.

❸ Hyperbole

Hyperbole is an exaggeration, either mild or extreme. In both cases, hyperbole is meant to help make a point and shouldn't be taken literally.

* "If I have to keep this secret one more minute, I'll explode."
* "Our competitors have everything going for them except a viable product and a plan for selling it."

❹ Understatement

Understatement deliberately downplays a person, idea, or object in order to call attention to it. As in irony, understatement says, in effect, that the opposite is true.

* "As a playwright, Shakespeare wasn't half bad."
* "Take your time in considering whether you want this all-expenses-paid vacation."

❺ Irony

When a speaker uses **irony**, he or she means the opposite of what is said. In writing, the reader detects irony through written clues. In a speech, the audience detects irony through verbal cues and the speaker's slightly sarcastic tone of voice. Listen to the vocal inflections that might be heard in each of these examples:

* "Other than the poor service, lousy food, and ridiculously high prices, I loved eating there."
* "The new manager with no experience rattled off a list of things we needed to change."

Word clues in these examples—such as "poor service, lousy food, and ridiculously high prices," "new manager with no experience," and "rattled off a list of things"—show that the statements are not meant to be taken literally.

Cultural Sensitivity

Whether you are at school, at work, or in your own neighborhood, you may see a much wider variety of people around you than your parents and grandparents did when they were your age. In addition, many people have the opportunity to travel to faraway places now. We are fortunate to live in a world where we can experience so many different types of people, beliefs, and cultures. We need to learn to respect individual differences.

A listening audience for a speech can be as diverse as the world around you. To communicate, you need to speak a "language" they understand. How can you make sure that you communicate with your audience in an appropriate, respectful way?

Cultural Differences

Before giving a speech in a place or to a group with whom you are unfamiliar, do some research. Find out as much as you can about the culture and issues of this area. Read the local papers. Talk to people in shops and on the streets. Observe the ways that they interact.

Remember that what is appropriate in one cultural setting may have a totally different meaning in another. Learn the basics. How do people greet one another? In Asian countries, hearty American handshakes and backslapping are not appropriate. Be respectful and imitate your host culture's customs, bowing respectfully to those you meet.

Avoid using stereotypes of geographical areas, too. People in Chicago are tired of hearing about gangsters. Those who live in the Northwest dislike jokes about the rain. In general, people are proud of where they live and don't like "outsiders" criticizing their state, region, or country. Attacking your audience's beliefs or attitudes is a surefire way to create a hostile audience for your speech.

Keys to Cultural Sensitivity

When speaking to an audience that may be culturally unfamiliar to you, use these strategies.

* **Have someone from the target audience read your speech** to see whether you have communicated your ideas in a respectful and understandable way. Revise your speech based on the feedback you receive.

* **Be polite and gracious. Follow the rules.** Observe how other people act and respond when they are introduced and when they say hello, good-bye, and thank you. Cultures can differ greatly in these customs.

* **Avoid slang, most jokes, and all stereotypes** when speaking to an audience that is culturally unfamiliar to you. What is commonly understood in one culture or region may be unknown or interpreted much differently in another.

* **Avoid speaking as a "member" of an ethnic, religious, or other group (even in spirit) if you're not.** "I'm one of you" or "I know just how you feel" sound presumptuous and may cause the audience to withhold their support.

* **Create understanding between you and your audience** by sharing aspects of your own life and where you live. Emphasize things you may have in common, such as concern for the environment, hobbies or interests, love of family or children, or concerns or hopes for the future.

* **Avoid mixed messages or cultural misunderstandings** that may result in hurt feelings, mistrust, or anger. If you offend inadvertently, apologize sincerely. Most audiences will appreciate and respect you for your honesty.

* **Watch for clues to understanding— or misunderstanding.** Audience questions, body language, and feedback during your speech may give you clues to whether your speech is being understood.

Common Language Problems

Common language problems in speeches include euphemisms, clichés, stereotypes, slang, and incorrect usage and grammar.

❶ Euphemisms

A **euphemism** is a polite and often affected word or phrase that is used in place of a word that the speaker thinks might be offensive. Euphemisms tend to be more "politically correct."

Euphemism	Plain English
economically disadvantaged	poor
little people	children
inventory shrinkage	theft
downsized	fired
passed away	died
between jobs	unemployed

Identifying Euphemisms

GOAL

The goal of this activity is to help you identify euphemisms and to consider whether to use them in your speeches.

TASKS

1. Form groups of three or four.
2. Identify the euphemisms in the following sentences.
3. As a group, rewrite each sentence in plain English, omitting euphemistic language.

   a. The restructured company kept everyone in a holding pattern.
   b. After passing away last fall, our beloved feline is now reposing in the pet cemetery.
   c. My brother told Mom and Dad about the pronounced concavities in the family car.
   d. Carl is between jobs.
   e. The synergistic couple decided to enter into a permanent domestic partnership.
   f. I am in a serious negative cash flow situation this month.
   g. The care facility reported negative patient care outcome.
   h. It was gratifying to know that I was not blamed for the inventory shrinkage.

OUTCOMES

Was your group successful at converting the statements into plain English? How did the rewritten sentences compare to the euphemistic ones? Were they more honest sounding? Were the revised statements easier to understand?

In social situations, euphemisms often are necessary. In writing and speeches, they can sound false or misleading.

❷ Clichés

<u>Clichés</u> are trite, overused expressions and phrases. Once clever or interesting, they have now become commonplace and boring. Examples are phrases like "tried and true," "better late than never," "meek as a lamb," and "late bloomer."

Avoid clichés or you will quickly lose your credibility as a speaker.

❸ Stereotypes

<u>Stereotypes</u> are oversimplified and often negative ways of defining a group of people without accounting for individual differences. You use stereotypes whenever you make assumptions about a person or group based on race, religion, culture, gender, national origin, occupation, sexual orientation, age, or economic status.

Stereotyping plays an important part in prejudice, racism, and many types of discrimination. Carefully avoid stereotypes in all types of speeches and speaking situations. If you offend, hurt, or anger members of your audience, you will quickly lose your credibility. The audience will stop listening seriously to what you have to say or may become downright hostile.

❹ Slang

<u>Slang</u> is popular speech, including informal non-standard English, new coined words and phrases that are known and used within a particular group, and new meanings for standard English words. Slang comes and goes quickly. Those who call things "cool" or who tell others to "chill out" (calm down) soon will be using new phrases themselves.

Don't use slang in a speech. Slang terms often are unknown outside specific geographic areas, occupations, ages, and cultures. If you use an unfamiliar slang term, you aren't communicating and you might lose credibility with the group.

❺ Incorrect Usage and Grammar

Spoken communication is less formal than written language. But it is equally important to use correct usage and grammar when you speak. Poor grammar or mistakes in usage can quickly diminish your credibility with a knowledgeable audience.

Usage

<u>Usage</u> refers to the conventional method of using words that are written or spoken. Some pairs of words that are commonly confused (and noticeable in speech) appear in the text box.

Use Words Correctly

affect, effect

Affect is usually a verb meaning "to influence or change." ("The 100° heat <u>affected</u> all of us.") *Effect* is typically a noun meaning "result" but may sometimes be a verb meaning "to accomplish." ("The speech had a shocking <u>effect</u>.")

among, between

In general, *among* is used when talking about three or more people, places, or objects. ("Who <u>among</u> us hasn't eaten cake for breakfast?") *Between* is used for relationships involving two people, places, or objects. ("Just <u>between</u> you and me, I didn't do my homework.")

can, may

Can refers to "ability." ("He <u>can</u> ride a unicycle, juggle, and whistle all at the same time.") *May* indicates "permission given." ("<u>May</u> I go with you to the blues festival?")

farther, further

Farther usually means "an additional distance" ("How much <u>farther</u> is it to the moon?") *Further* typically refers to "an additional amount of time, work, etc." ("This crazy idea needs <u>further</u> study.")

fewer, less

Fewer refers to separate, countable items, such as candy, problems, or credits. ("Why were you given ten <u>fewer</u> homework problems than I was?") *Less* refers to a general amount, such as calories, stress, or cash. ("Exercising helps me feel <u>less</u> stressed.")

good, well

Good is almost always an adjective. ("You did a <u>good</u> job trimming your bangs.") *Well* is usually an adverb. ("The two of you work <u>well</u> together.")

imply, infer

Imply means "to suggest." ("The program <u>implied</u> that we could sing along with the soloist.") *Infer* means "to conclude." ("I <u>infer</u> by your silence that you are mad at me.")

Grammar

Whether you are speaking or writing, using correct grammar is important. It shows your audience that you know the acceptable rules for speaking and writing. This section discusses some grammatical things to watch for when writing and giving a speech: dangling and misplaced modifiers, subject-verb agreement, compound subjects, indefinite pronouns, and pronoun-antecedent agreement.

Dangling and Misplaced Modifiers

A dangling modifier is a word, phrase, or clause that does not seem to relate to anything in the sentence.

In the sentence *"Arriving home a day early,* no one was there," "Arriving home a day early" is a dangling modifier.

Who arrived home early? The sentence doesn't say. The sentence might read: "Arriving home a day early, *Ben* found no one was there."

A misplaced modifier is one that is placed so far away from what it modifies that the effect is confusing.

"Nancy saw a bat, two eagles, and a raccoon *on a field trip."*

Just so no one thinks that the animals were on a field trip, the sentence could be revised to read:

"While on a field trip, Nancy saw a bat, two eagles, and a raccoon."

Subject-Verb Agreement

The subject and verb in a sentence must agree in number. Subject-verb agreement means that if the subject is singular, the verb must be singular; if a subject is plural, the verb must be plural. To make sure that your subjects and verbs agree, you must correctly identify the subject of the sentence.

"The free concert *tickets were* already given away." (*Tickets* and *were* both are plural.)

"My *grandmother likes* to do the tango." (*Grandmother* and *likes* both are singular.)

Sometimes identifying the correct subject of the sentence can get tricky.

"One of the dogs *is* missing." (*One* is the subject and not dogs. Since *one* is singular, *is* is the correct verb form.)

Compound Subjects

If a compound subject (two or more separate subjects) is joined by the word *and,* the verb is plural.

"Snowboarding <u>and</u> ice hockey are my two favorite winter sports."

If a compound subject is usually thought of as a single item, the verb is singular.

"Bacon and eggs is my standard breakfast."

If *or* or *nor* separates the two words in a compound subject, the verb agrees with the subject closest to it.

"If either the director or the *actors veto* the play, it will not be chosen."

"Neither the puppy nor the *boys seem* to know what happened to the cookies."

Indefinite Pronouns

Indefinite pronouns—such as *somebody, nobody, anybody, everybody, someone, no one, anyone, everyone, either, neither,* and *each*—don't refer to anyone or anything specific. Because they are singular pronouns, they require singular verbs.

"*Everybody* in the class *is* learning."

"*Everybody loves* Estelle."

"*Each* of the girls *thinks* she is the better musician."

Pronoun-Antecedent Agreement

Pronoun-antecedent agreement says that when a sentence with an indefinite pronoun contains other pronouns as well, those pronouns are also singular.

"*Everybody* in the orchestra thinks *he* or *she* (not *they*) should be first chair."

"*No one* did *his* or *her* (not *their*) best in the last swim meet."

Correct Common Language Problems

GOAL

The goal of this activity is to help you identify common problems discussed in this section, such as clichés, stereotypes, slang, and incorrect grammar and usage.

TASKS

1. Choose a partner.
2. Identify the clichés, stereotypes, slang, or incorrect grammar and usage in the following sentences.
3. Rewrite each sentence into strong, clear, and vivid language, free of these common problems.
    a. If you keep your eye on the prize, you're bound to succeed.
    b. To finish the term paper on time, sleep, relaxation, and fun were sacrificed.
    c. Men never want to ask for directions.
    d. There are many students who thinks that we can win the game on Friday.
    e. Each member of the family agree that the car is worth the money.
    f. Vacationers buy piñatas strolling through the village markets.
    g. The overall affect of the haircut was downright frightening.
    h. Everyone stuck to their story about how the window got broken.
    i. This is a really cool job that pays big bucks, so I hope they hire me.
4. Share your rewritten sentences with the class.

OUTCOMES

How accurate were you at finding problems? How did the rewritten sentences compare to the original sentences? Were they easier to understand? Were the revised statements more interesting to listen to?

How to Check Your Speech for Effective Language

Clarity

✓ Simple language (plain English, vivid phrases, active sentences)?

✓ Specific and concrete wording?

✓ Repetition of the main idea?

✓ Elimination of unnecessary words?

Emphasis

✓ Variety and contrast?

✓ Rhetorical questions?

✓ Language techniques (as appropriate)
  * Parallelism?
  * Antithesis?
  * Groups of three?
  * Inversion?
  * Order of climax?
  * Alliteration?
  * Repetition?

Figures of speech (as appropriate)

✓ Similes and metaphors?

✓ Personification?

✓ Hyperbole?

✓ Understatement?

✓ Irony?

Influence of other cultures

✓ Culturally sensitive?

Free from common language problems

✓ Euphemisms?

✓ Clichés?

✓ Stereotypes?

✓ Slang?

✓ Incorrect usage?

✓ Dangling and misplaced modifiers?

✓ Subject-verb agreement?

✓ Compound subjects?

✓ Indefinite pronouns?

✓ Pronoun-antecedent agreement?

Why Learn Public Speaking?

Sarah is an academic counselor at an important university. She is surprised that so many students who plan careers in education, journalism, management, sales, and other professions don't plan to take speech classes. They seem to think that teachers, managers, and salespeople just talk and that journalists just need to be able to write.

According to Sarah, they may be missing many crucial general job skills. She developed a brochure listing skills mastered in speech courses. Her list includes:

* Analytical skills
* Research skills
* Organizational skills
* Strategic skills
* Delivery skills
* Social skills
* Evaluation skills
* Writing and speaking skills
* Thinking skills

Sarah's efforts paid off. Many former students now thank her for steering them toward speech training. They attribute a good portion of their self-confidence, upward mobility, and career success to their speech education.

Wrap-up

Great speech writers such as Churchill, Kennedy, Roosevelt, and Martin Luther King, Jr., knew that effective speeches are clear, emphatic, vivid, and culturally sensitive. For clarity, they kept their wording simple, specific, and concrete. They repeated their main ideas and revised to eliminate wordiness. For emphasis, they made sure that their speeches include variety and contrast, rhetorical questions, and appropriate use of language techniques. For vividness, they employed figures of speech such as similes, metaphors, personification, hyperbole, understatement, and irony. They never offended their audiences through cultural insensitivity. And they made sure that their speeches were free of usage and grammatical errors.

abstract word—general idea, concept, feeling, or group of things.

alliteration—repetition of a consonant sound (usually an initial consonant) several times in a phrase, clause, or sentence.

antithesis—type of parallel structure in which the second part contrasts with the first.

clichés—overused, worn-out phrases that have lost their capacity to communicate effectively.

climax ordering—arrangement of ideas in a sentence, section, or the entire body of a speech from least important to most important; sometimes called emphatic order.

concrete word—object, an action, or a trait described in the most specific way possible.

emphasis—forcefulness of expression that gives importance to something.

euphemism—language that attempts to avoid the harsh reality of some truths by using more pleasant-sounding, overly "tactful" words.

figures of speech—expressions such as a metaphor or personification, in which a nonliteral and intensive sense of a word or words is used to create a forceful, dramatic, or illuminating image.

hyperbole—deliberate exaggeration for emphasis.

inversion—reversing the normal word order of a phrase or sentence.

irony—use of words to suggest the opposite of their usual sense.

metaphor—comparison between dissimilar things without the use of *like* or *as*.

parallelism—occurs when two or more phrases, clauses, or sentences have the same grammatical pattern.

personification—assignment of a human trait to a nonhuman thing.

repetition—deliberate repeating of important words or ideas to achieve emphasis.

restatement—repeating thoughts and ideas in different words and phrases.

rhetorical questions—questions posed by the speaker, who may or may not want an answer, to stimulate thinking and increase audience involvement.

simile—comparison between otherwise dissimilar things, using the word *like* or *as*.

slang—popular speech.

stereotypes—people, groups, or events that are grouped together with no regard for individual differences.

understatement—deliberate restraint for emphasis.

usage—conventional method of using written or spoken words.

CHAPTER 15

Delivering a Speech

In this chapter, you will consider:

- **What is the best method of delivery to use?**
- **What are the advantages and disadvantages of the various delivery methods?**
- **What is a good method for impromptu speaking?**
- **How will nonverbal cues influence your delivery?**
- **How should you prepare and use notes?**

If you are well grounded in speech delivery methods and techniques, you will speak with confidence and impact. In this chapter, you'll learn four methods for delivering a speech— the extemporaneous, manuscript, memorization, and impromptu methods. Next, since you convey as much as 65 percent of your message through nonverbal communication, you'll learn many techniques that will improve your personal delivery. These include important nonverbals such as appearance, facial expressions, voice, pauses, eye contact, gestures, and movement. You'll then discover how to use speaking resources and how to handle distractions and interruptions, as well as how to check your speaking environment, polish your delivery, and visualize a successful presentation.

Methods of Delivery

As a public speaker, your content and your words matter. But a strong delivery style determines whether you hold your audience or lose them.

There are several possible methods for delivering your speech. Which should you choose? That depends upon your content and goals. **Four** common methods for delivering speeches are the extemporaneous method, the manuscript method, the memorization method, and the impromptu method. Some speakers use a combination of these methods.

❶ Extemporaneous Method

In the __extemporaneous method__ of delivery, you talk through your speech, referring to key words and phrases on an outline or on note cards. An extemporaneous speech sounds natural and spontaneous. Use of notes also frees you to maintain eye contact with the audience.

Speakers use extemporaneous delivery in most speaking situations. Audiences prefer this method of delivery to a scripted or stiffly memorized delivery.

Advantages and Disadvantages

The extemporaneous method has several advantages. It:

* Stimulates you to "think on your feet."
* Allows for a conversational-sounding delivery.
* Takes less preparation time than other methods.
* Is flexible enough to allow last-minute changes and additions.

The only disadvantage of the extemporaneous method is that it requires you to be well-rehearsed. If you don't know your speech well, your delivery will be awkward rather than spontaneous.

Preparing an Extemporaneous Speech

To prepare your note cards, first write out your entire speech, word for word. Then reduce the speech to an outline. Finally, copy the outline onto 4 x 6 inch or 5 x 8 inch note cards.

Here are some tips for preparing your cards:

* Write the outline in keywords and phrases, using a black marker and large print.
* Leave wide margins and lots of white space between items.
* Use underlines, color coding, or hand-drawn boxes to emphasize your key points.
* Write out your speech's opening, all of your transitions, and your ending. This will help you to memorize these important passages.

Note Cards for
Extemporaneous Speaking

1

[Introduction]
Is Antarctica changing? Mountains of ice are
beginning to melt.
  Could this spell disaster for Mother Earth?

2

What is happening to the world's climate? Can
changes in climate alter the world's coastlines?
Scientists are working to discover answers to these
and other weather-related questions.

3

I. What's happening in Antarctica
    A. Continent at bottom of the world
       1. 700 miles from South America
       2. For 20 million years the coldest place on
          Earth
       3. But recently, heating up

Making Note Cards from an Outline

GOAL

The goal of this activity is to create clear note cards for delivering a speech.

TASKS

1. Locate a speech outline. If you haven't written one, write one now.

2. Rehearse the speech alone and make any final changes.

3. Obtain supplies—a pack of 4 x 6 inch or 5 x 8 inch note cards and a pen or marker with black ink.

4. Transfer your speech outline to note cards using the method described in this chapter.

5. Prepare your note cards according to the guidelines provided.

6. Practice giving your speech using these cards. Make any final adjustments you think necessary.

7. Choose a partner and deliver your speeches to each other, critiquing each other's delivery.

OUTCOMES

What changes did you make after practicing your speech? Did you find this method of delivery easy or difficult?

❷ Manuscript Method

With the **manuscript method** of delivery, you write out every word of a speech, and then read it to the audience. This delivery method is appropriate in situations that call for precise wording and perfect timing—contests, important government announcements, media broadcasts, and so forth. People in the public eye—such as corporate leaders, politicians, diplomats, and government representatives—often rely on manuscripts displayed in a teleprompter.

Advantages and Disadvantages

Manuscript delivery provides a secure safety net under what are potentially high-stress conditions. But it also has several disadvantages:

* A speech that is read aloud usually sounds formal and stilted.
* A speaker who is reading often can't maintain eye contact with the audience.
* A speech in manuscript form cannot be revised at the last minute.
* This type of speech requires a long preparation period.

Preparing a Speech Manuscript

Written language tends to be formal, so it can be hard to write a speech that sounds spontaneous. Therefore, you'll need to write several drafts. Your goal is clear content and natural, conversational language. Follow this procedure to prepare the manuscript:

1. Write a detailed topic outline of your script.
2. Talk through the speech using the outline. Tape record your words.
3. Write down the words that you used when talking through the speech.
4. Deliver the speech from the manuscript draft, tape recording it again. Revise as needed until you are satisfied that the speech sounds as spontaneous as possible. See Chapter 14 for tips on effective language.
5. Practice with an audience, asking for constructive feedback.
6. Continue to revise and practice until the speech sounds clear and natural.

Marking the Final Draft

After finalizing your text, prepare a clean, word-processed copy. You'll want to double-space the lines and to use a large font and boldface typeface. If you wish, use all capital letters. Set up your pages so that the type appears only on the top third of each page. This will help you to keep your head up while reading. Number your pages, making sure that each page ends with a complete sentence. Print out the manuscript on heavy paper that will be easy to grasp.

Now identify places that you'll want to pause, to breathe, or to emphasize a point. You can use symbols like the following.

* Use a slash (/) or dashes (—) to indicate a breath or pause.
* Mark vocal delivery cues such as (slow down) or (drop voice) above words or in the margins.
* **Boldface** and/or underline words that you want to emphasize.

Delivering the Speech

When reading a manuscript, it's easy to rivet your attention on the printed page, never pausing or looking up at the audience. Here are some suggestions on delivering your speech effectively:

* Create two stacks of paper on the lectern, one to read from and the other to hold used pages. Practice sliding finished pages noiselessly to the second stack after you read them.
* As you deliver the speech, be careful not to read too quickly. Vary your rhythm and inflection, using natural gestures for emphasis.
* Practice looking up often to make eye contact with the audience. Use your index finger to keep your place.

Reading a Manuscript

The goal of this activity is to use and understand how to use speaking cues and pause marks when delivering a speech by the manuscript method.

TASKS

1. Choose a partner.
2. Examine the manuscript below. A slash mark means a pause, and an underline means emphasize. If these marks don't seem natural to you, change them.
3. Take turns reading aloud the manuscript below, following the marks for pausing and emphasizing.
4. After reading it, discuss what you learned about reading a manuscript and using marks to help make a speech sound natural.

Manuscript

Is Antarctica changing? / Entire mountains of ice are melting and on the move. / Could this spell disaster for Mother Earth? //

(slow down, emphasis) What is happening to the world's climate? / Can changes in climate alter the world's coastlines? //

Scientists are working hard to discover answers—to these and other weather-related questions. /

What is happening to this ice sheet matters / to everyone in the world. (slightly faster) Antarctica sits at the bottom of the world, / 700 miles from South America. It is an entire continent cloaked in ice, // isolated from the rest of the world. / For 20 million years, Antarctica has been the coldest place on earth.

But now // things have changed. / Things are heating up. / In 1995, a huge iceberg separated from the Larsen ice shelf on Antarctica's coast. / A large portion of the ice shelf melted / (slower) in just a few days. /

—based on PBS NOVA TV program "Warnings from the Ice," aired April 21, 1998

OUTCOMES

Were the speaking cues natural to you? Did your partner's interpretation sound different from yours? Did you change the markings on the manuscript?

❸ Memorization Method

With the **memorization method** of speech delivery, you prepare a speech manuscript, memorize it, and then deliver it from memory. Speakers use this method mainly for contests, for speeches that entertain, or for general-interest speeches that will be delivered to many different audiences.

Committing your speech to memory frees you to use your dramatic talents to full effect. With the text set in memory, you can focus on your voice inflection, gestures, movement, and timing. If your script is written in a conversational style, your speech can sound spontaneous and natural.

Advantages and Disadvantages

The memorized method of delivery has several advantages:

* Eye contact can be maintained throughout the speech.
* You can move around the stage without worrying about notes or a manuscript.
* Delivery can be polished.
* Wording and timing can be perfected in advance.

However, the method also has disadvantages:

* Preparation time can be lengthy.
* Memorized speeches require acting ability as well as writing ability.
* Speech delivery can sound mechanical and uninspiring.
* A memorized speech can't be revised as you speak.
* Your memory needs to be 100 percent reliable, even under pressure.

Preparing a Memorized Speech

To prepare a memorized speech, follow the steps listed under the Manuscript Method. Then memorize your speech. As you write the speech, be sure to tape record your delivery and pay attention to feedback from your practice audiences.

❹ Impromptu Method

With the **impromptu method** of speech delivery, you give a speech or answer audience questions without prior preparation. Impromptu speeches are a surprise. But your audience usually will understand your predicament and will not expect a long or polished speech.

Here is a brief recap of points made in Chapter 11 about handling impromptu speeches.

When you're asked to make an impromptu speech, stay calm. Take a few minutes to focus on the situation. Mentally run through these steps. Write a few notes, if possible.

Step 1. Consider the Audience
* What do they already know about the topic?
* How do they feel about the topic?
* What is their mood?

Step 2. Organize Your Speech
* Identify your main point and two or three supporting points.
* Choose an appropriate organizational pattern (a chronological review of events, the pros and cons of each point, or order of interest, importance, complexity, or scope).

* Choose an interesting opening—a reference to a recent event, a personal reference, a preview of your main ideas, or a vivid description or metaphor.
* Plan your conclusion. Restate the topic or main idea, then conclude with a dynamic, upbeat ending sentence.

Step 3: Relax and Deliver the Speech
* Stand up, smile confidently, and make eye contact with your listeners.
* Don't panic or apologize for your lack of preparation.
* Talk to the audience as you would in conversation.

Personal Delivery

This section describes **three** aspects of personal delivery—nonverbal behaviors and personal style, speaking resources, and handling distractions and interruptions.

❶ Nonverbal Behaviors and Personal Style

When preparing to speak, you'll take great care in organizing your content and choosing your words. But spoken communication involves much more than words. Research shows that as much as 65 percent of a speaker's message is communicated through nonverbal behavior, or body language.

Research shows that an audience assesses a speaker's genuineness, honesty, and credibility partly through nonverbal language. Therefore, it's important that your actions support and reinforce your speech's message.

This section describes **six** important nonverbal aspects of personal delivery—appearance, facial expressions, voice, pauses, eye contact, and gestures and movement.

Appearance

Your appearance—the first thing an audience sees—is a key form of nonverbal communication. Like it or not, people initially judge you by how you look. Your appearance tells them how you feel about yourself, about them, and about the event.

Appropriate Dress

Deciding what to wear often is a problem. There are many factors in this decision. Think about the expected weather, the occasion, and the demographics of your audience. Ask the event's organizers what type of clothing is appropriate. If you're not sure, dress conservatively. Even a "business casual" audience expects you to dress as an outside consultant would, somewhat more formally. A jacket or a blazer is a good idea. If your audience is dressed very casually, you can always remove the jacket.

Everyday COMMUNICATION

First Impressions Count

Max, a high school sophomore, was part of an after-school program that offered drama classes and homework help. Because Max was enthusiastic and well-spoken, he was asked to speak to parents about the program.

The night of the presentation, everything went wrong. Tied up in a rehearsal, Max ran in ten minutes late. He hadn't changed clothes and was obviously stressed. He fumbled his note cards. His handouts weren't ready. When Max finally began, he was 15 minutes late.

Max began by apologizing and saying how nervous he was. But the audience didn't know about the rehearsal. All they saw was a nervous speaker in a torn sweatshirt and baggy shorts.

Before Max had even completed his clever opening, it was too late. Even though the audience wanted to react differently, Max had lost their respect due to his appearance, lateness, and lack of preparation. The time he'd spent preparing the speech was wasted.

This was a painful learning experience for Max. He learned that first impressions definitely count and that, in general, an audience judges a speaker immediately on the basis of his or her appearance, preparedness, credibility, and confidence.

Posture and Stance

Pay attention to your posture and your stance. Stand up straight, as if the top of your head were holding up the sky. Good posture communicates energy and health. It also aids your breathing.

Stand with your feet slightly separated, one foot a bit ahead of the other. If both feet have a slight outward angle, you'll be comfortable and ready to move easily to another position.

Facial Expressions

Your audience sees your face before they hear you speak. Because your facial expression reveals your thoughts, emotions, and attitudes, it makes a powerful first impression.

* Videotape yourself practicing your speech. Do your facial expressions project the tone you want, strengthen your message, and attract audience interest?
* Communicate your speech's tone through your expression. A serious speech calls for a thoughtful expression. An entertaining speech calls for a more pleasant expression.
* Smile as you speak, if appropriate. Your voice will sound more friendly and your audience will be more attentive. Smiling also helps you to relax.

Voice

As Monroe's study of speaker delivery showed, voice is a very important component of your delivery. Monroe's students identified a monotonous tone and a weak voice as highly annoying traits of ineffective speakers.

Think about what Martin Luther King, Jr.'s, vocal delivery added to his speeches. Truly, the voice is a crucial instrument. Powerful vocal delivery can rivet an audience just as poor vocal delivery can ruin a speech.

There are **five** vocal delivery components in public speaking: volume, articulation, pronunciation, pitch, and rate.

1. Volume

Volume is the loudness or softness of your voice. Your volume determines whether or not the audience hears you, so handling volume well is vital.

* A microphone can help you reach every member of the audience. A **lavaliere microphone** can be worn around the neck or clipped to a collar.
* Test a microphone by counting or asking the audience whether they can hear you. Never tap or blow into a microphone.
* Practice breathing from your diaphragm, the muscle below your rib cage. This will help you to control your volume and maximize your voice's quality.
* While practicing your speech, try dropping the volume of your voice to make an important point. Your audience will listen more carefully. However, be sure that everyone in the room can hear you.

2. Articulation

Articulation is the ability to form distinct speech sounds. If you're not articulating well, you are mumbling. Audiences cannot hear a speaker who mumbles, so good articulation is extremely important.

* Tape record your speech. Listen to the way you articulate words. Work on articulating those that you handle badly.
* Enunciate clearly. Don't slur or chop off words—for example, *wanna* for "want to," *dint* for "didn't," or *lemme* for "let me."

3. Pronunciation

Pronunciation is the ability to use the proper sounds to form words clearly and accurately. Mispronunciation signals a lack of education or sophistication, so take care to look up words that you're not sure of.

4. Pitch

Pitch refers to how high or how low your voice sounds. If you don't vary your pitch, you're speaking in a monotone. People often speak at a higher pitch when they're nervous. **Inflection** is the raising and lowering of pitch as you pronounce words and sounds. Inflection helps you project your meaning.

* Tape record your speech specifically to listen to variations in pitch and inflection.
* Mark up your speech with pitch and inflection in mind. Note when your pitch should be raised and lowered.
* End most sentences on a lower pitch. To signal a question, raise your voice at the end of a sentence.

5. Rate

The rate, or pace, of your speech should match the ideas you are conveying.

* Review your speech, marking places where you'll want to vary the pacing to emphasize key points or to convey excitement.
* Practice your rate changes with an audience. Ask listeners to comment specifically on this aspect of your speech.

Pauses

Pauses are temporary stops in your speech. If not overdone, they can be very effective.

* To stress an important point, make the point while looking directly at the audience, then pause. Your audience will repeat your point mentally.
* Don't use **vocalized pauses** such as "umm," "like," "er," "you know," and "uh." These can be very annoying to an audience.
* Be careful not to overuse pauses.

Eye Contact

Eye contact, or looking at the audience, is always high on the list of desirable speaker behaviors. Audiences love eye contact. Good eye contact gives listeners a sense that they're listening to a sincere, earnest human being. It establishes rapport, gives you credibility, builds listeners' interest, and allows you to gather feedback.

* Before starting your speech, make eye contact with the audience. This readies people to listen to you, as if you were in a conversation.

* Imagine that you're speaking to your best friend. Look directly at the audience when delivering your opening and closing statements. Smile if appropriate.
* Be sure to look at various people in the room as you speak. Don't focus on one friendly face and ignore everyone else. Practice turning your head slightly to address people in various parts of the room.

Gestures and Movement

Gestures and movement are two more aspects of the nonverbal part of your delivery.

Gestures

Gestures are movements of your limbs, body, or head that communicate emotions. As you become a more experienced speaker, your gestures will develop naturally.

When you wish to make a strong point, use **emphatic gestures,** such as pointing your finger, raising both hands, or striking the podium. If your emphatic gestures are natural to you, they will convey excitement and add to your believability.

Sometimes you'll use gestures to visually describe an object's shape or size. **Locative gestures** like these also can aid an audience in visualizing a location.

Here are guidelines to consider when you're thinking about gestures.

* Videotape your speech or perform it for a test audience. Critique your gestures carefully.
* Avoid repeating the same gesture over and over again. Think about what is appropriate to your content.
* Above all, be natural. Use gestures that express your personality and suit your speaking goals.

Movement

The Monroe study of speaker behavior, cited earlier in this chapter, suggested that audiences like speakers that move around. Movement, the shifting of your whole body from one spot to another, can make your speech more effective. You can use movement in several ways:

* To emphasize a new topic in your speech,
* To wake up the audience and redirect their attention to you, and
* To channel some of your own physical energy.

Your movements should appear to be natural, self-possessed, and calm. Don't overdo physical movement. If you move erratically or pace back and forth, the audience will become nervous.

Nonverbal Behavior in Speech Delivery

Appearance
✓ Appropriate dress

✓ Good posture and stance

Facial expressions
✓ Appropriate expressions

✓ Show interest and friendliness

Voice
✓ Volume

✓ Articulation

✓ Pronunciation

✓ Pitch and inflection

✓ Rate

Pauses
✓ Used effectively

✓ Avoid vocalized pauses—"uh," "er"

Eye Contact
✓ At key points in speech

✓ With all audience members

Gestures and movement
✓ Relaxed and natural

✓ Not distracting

✓ Flow from the message

✓ Avoid pacing

ACTIVITY

Evaluating Your Nonverbal Behavior

GOAL

The goal of this activity is to evaluate nonverbal behavior during speeches, using the Checklist in this chapter.

TASKS

1. Form groups of three to four.

2. Each person chooses and delivers a short speech that he or she already has written, paying particular attention to nonverbal behavior.

3. Others use the Nonverbal Behavior in Speech Delivery Checklist to evaluate the speaker.

4. After all have delivered their speeches, the group discusses each individual's performance, concentrating on constructive criticism. What are common problems?

OUTCOMES

What are the most challenging aspects of controlling nonverbal behavior during a speech?

❷ Speaking Resources

Along with nonverbal behavior, another key aspect of personal delivery is your speaking resources. These include your notes or manuscript and a lectern or speaking stand.

Using Notes or Manuscript

Earlier in this chapter you learned how to prepare your notes or your manuscript. To use them effectively, nothing succeeds like lots of practice. Here are some tips:

* Practice using your notes or reading your speech in a natural way, with good eye contact and appropriate gestures and movements.
* Do at least one run-through of your entire speech in the environment you're speaking in. If you'll be using a lectern, try it out.
* Make sure that your notes or manuscript pages are numbered and kept in order. Keep them with you until you speak.

Using a Lectern or Speaker's Stand

A **lectern** is a stand that supports a speaker's manuscript, books, or notes. Your lectern may be a freestanding floor unit with a microphone, clock, and speaker's light. Or it might be a small tabletop unit.

Here are some tips on using a lectern:

* Make sure that you have enough light to see your notes or your manuscript. Position the microphone so that you can speak into it comfortably.
* Evaluate your lectern's height. If you're barely visible behind it and can't comfortably read your notes or manuscript, ask for something to stand on.
* If you're reading a speech manuscript, make sure that your lectern is wide enough to comfortably fit two stacks of paper next to each other.
* Don't let the lectern block your contact with the audience. Stand next to it or move around it as you speak.
* Stock your lectern with supplies. You'll need a glass of water, a handkerchief, and at least one cough drop for emergencies.

❸ Handling Distractions and Interruptions

No one wants to be distracted or interrupted while making a speech. Sudden problems can be unnerving. But you can prepare for the unexpected by learning a few coping strategies ahead of time.

Sometimes you can sense audience problems by reading their body language. Think of audience members as friends whom you want to make comfortable. Respond to any needs that they express.

* If people start to fan themselves and wipe their brows, ask that someone open the doors or adjust the temperature.

* If people frown or lean forward, ask whether they can hear you. If not, increase your volume and speak very clearly.
* If the audience looks bored, increase your pace, your tone, and/or your pitch. Also consider simplifying any technical information you're delivering.
* If your audience looks puzzled or gets restless, ask whether further explanation is needed.

Handling Distractions

You can handle most distractions in a quiet, natural, and businesslike way. Stop speaking, solve the problem, and then proceed.

Handling Interruptions

Most interruptions from outside sources are minor and can be handled in a calm, professional manner.

Distraction	Solution
Watering eyes or runny nose	Say, "Excuse me," wipe your eyes or blow your nose, then continue.
Sweaty face	Use your handkerchief to wipe your face well.
Dry mouth	Take a sip of water, whenever you need it.
Need to cough	Stop speaking, say, "Excuse me," turn away from the microphone, and cough. Try drinking water or using a cough drop.
Interruption	**Solution**
A noisy audience	Stop, ask whether you may begin or continue, then wait for the talking to stop.
Outside noises— train whistles, sirens, machine sounds, airplanes, and so on.	Wait for the noise to end. If it continues, increase your volume and speak very slowly and clearly.
An audience question	Announce that you'll answer questions or comments after the speech.

Handling Interruptions

Bruce had dealt with many kinds of inter-ruptions in his long history as a technology conference presenter, but, at the time, this one felt like the worst. First, his room assignment was changed at the last minute. If that weren't bad enough, the new room was adjacent to an obviously popular soft drink machine.

"Innocent enough," recalled Bruce, "except that every time someone dropped money in the machine, it resulted in a power drain that caused the lights in my room to dim and a momentary loss of power in my microphone!

"In the end, you have to have a sense of humor," says Bruce. "The audience knew that I was dealing with something that was beyond my control. They had all been there themselves.

"I now know that a speaker can actually gain credibility by responding well to unexpected situations like this," explains Bruce. "If you completely lose your cool, get mad, or let it derail your presentation, you will lose your audience.

"If, on the other hand, you can acknowl-edge the problem, make a spontaneous joke about it (one that relates to your topic if possible!), and then move on, the audience will be right with you. They may notice the interruption each time it happens, and even chuckle, but they will also concentrate extra hard if for no other reason than to see your reaction! But, in the process, they actually become better listeners. They will join your team against the interruption."

Rehearsing a Speech

Rehearsing your speech has **three** aspects: checking the site of your speech, polishing your delivery, and visualizing your success.

❶ Checking the Site

To avoid unexpected trouble, visit the loca-tion of your speech *beforehand* to check out your route to the lectern, your exit route, the room itself, and other factors affecting your presentation.

Check Your Route to the Lectern

If possible, practice walking from the place where you will be sitting before the speech to the lectern. Look for obstacles, such as blocked aisles, rugs, or extension cords. Tripping as you walk to the lectern is not a good beginning for a speech.

Check Your Exit Route

If you aren't sure where to go when you finish, it will detract from the power of your speech. Make sure you know the return route back to your seat.

Check the Room Itself

Inspect the room environment, too. If you have control over the room's setup, you can help ensure that your presentation begins smoothly and proceeds without any surprises.

Here are some tips for creating a favorable environment:

* Make sure that any equipment and materials you've ordered are on site and working. Set up the equipment and run through your entire presentation with it.

* Check the room's seating arrangement. If possible, arrange seating in wide rows rather than in narrow ones. Arrange rows and chairs for audience comfort.

* Try your lectern. Make sure that the light and microphone work, that the lectern is wide enough for your manuscript, and that you can be seen standing behind it.

* Test the room acoustics and microphone level. Can someone sitting in the back row hear you easily? Can your visuals can be *read* by people in the back of the room? Make adjustments if necessary.

* Use the Environmental Checklist below.

Checklist

Environmental Checklist

Basic room and speaker setup

✓ Lectern proper height and width?

✓ Microphone and light tested and working?

✓ Audio levels adequate?

✓ Visual aids visible throughout room?

✓ Audience seating comfortable?

Equipment and tools

✓ All computer or projector/screen components delivered?

✓ Have extra extension cords, three-prong converters, spare bulbs, and so on?

✓ All equipment set up and tested?

✓ Speech rehearsed on site with equipment and visual aids?

✓ Handouts collated and ready?

Locate and know how to operate:

✓ Electrical outlets

✓ Heating, air conditioning, fan, and lighting

✓ Sound system volume controls

✓ Window blinds

Know locations of nearest

✓ Restrooms

✓ Telephones

✓ Stairs, elevators, emergency exits

❷ Polishing Your Delivery

Now it's time to polish your delivery. Here are some final tips.

* ***Gather what you need:*** note cards, manuscript, visual aids, handouts, extra equipment or extension cords, and any other supplies you'll need on the lectern.
* ***Do a final practice run,*** in the speech's real environment if possible. Videotape this rehearsal, if you can.
* ***Practice the delivery tips*** presented in this chapter.
* ***Check your speech's timing*** and revise if needed to keep within the required time limits.

❸ Visualizing Success

You finally are ready. Now you have nothing to do but wait for the event. But there's one more thing that you can do to assure an effective speech.

Before important events, professional athletes and other performers practice the art of visualizing their own success. They vividly imagine themselves walking through the entire upcoming event, from start to finish, exactly as they hope it will occur. This exercise helps dispel their fears and helps them to approach the event with a positive, upbeat attitude.

Instead of fearing what might go wrong with your speech, try visualizing it as a wonderful experience. Vividly imagine yourself on the day of your speech, dressed as you plan to dress (and looking terrific). Carrying all of your supplies, you walk into the room in which you'll speak. You perform your preliminary checks and watch the audience begin to gather. It's a large crowd and they seem pleased and excited. Finally, you see yourself being introduced and walking confidently across the stage to the lectern. You greet the person who introduced you, then turn to the audience and gaze at them in a friendly, open way.

Smiling, if appropriate, and using a conversational tone, you begin your speech, capturing the audience's attention with your introduction. You gather energy as you explain your topic, handling your notes and your visual aids with skill. Your delivery goes very smoothly and the audience listens attentively. You climax your speech with a resounding conclusion. The audience responds with enthusiastic applause, then audience members present some interesting and challenging questions, which you handle with confidence and knowledge. It's a great day and you go home happy. Your speech was a true success.

Wrap-up

Delivering a speech involves selecting a method of delivery, preparing nonverbal aspects of your personal delivery, and rehearsing your speech. Most speakers use the extemporaneous method of delivery, which is the most conversational and, therefore, has the greatest audience appeal. However, some occasions call for manuscript, memorized, and impromptu methods of delivery. Every speaker needs to be aware of nonverbal communication, which can account for more than 65 percent of the message. Attention to appearance, facial expressions, voice, pauses, eye contact, and gestures and movement also are crucial. Finally, take the time to review speaking resources, learn to handle distractions and interruptions, check your speech environment, polish your delivery, and visualize your success.

Speech

articulation—ability to make speech sounds clearly and distinctly.

emphatic gestures—movements that provide emphasis for spoken words.

extemporaneous method—method of speech delivery that uses a conversational tone and an outline or notes containing key words or phrases.

impromptu method—method of speech delivery that involves giving a speech without advance warning or preparation.

inflection—refers to the variation of the pitch of your voice; the raising and lowering of pitch as you pronounce words and sounds.

lavaliere microphone—microphone to amplify your voice. It either is clipped on the front of a shirt or dress or worn on a string around the neck.

lectern—stand that supports a speaker's manuscript, book, or notes.

locative gestures—movements that describe something.

manuscript method—method of speech delivery that requires you to write out every word of a speech and read it from a prepared text.

memorization method—method of speech delivery that requires you to prepare a manuscript and present it from memory.

pitch—refers to how high or low your voice sounds.

pronunciation—ability to use the proper sounds to form words clearly and accurately.

vocalized pauses—audible sounds that are not words, for example, "umm," "er," "you know," and "uh".

volume—loudness or softness of the voice.

CHAPTER 16

Evaluation and Feedback

In this chapter, you will consider:

- How can you identify your own areas for improvement?
- How should you go about critiquing your classmates' speaking efforts?
- What are the differences between evaluating speeches to inform and speeches to persuade?
- What is constructive criticism, and how should you give it?
- How can you learn to accept negative criticism without being hurt or becoming defensive?

For continuous improvement of your public speaking skills, you need evaluation and feedback. Through self-evaluation and peer evaluation, you will build on your strengths and correct problem areas. In this chapter, you'll find tools and tips for evaluating yourself and being evaluated by your peers. You'll also learn about the process and value of both formal and informal evaluation. You'll discover how to evaluate informative speeches and persuasive speeches, using general guidelines and evaluation forms that summarize all major points that a public speaker needs to master. Finally, you'll review samples of filled-in evaluation forms and get some tips for giving and accepting constructive criticism.

Evaluation

So far you have focused on speech preparation and delivery. However, giving a speech also involves results. When true communication occurs, something happens. During a speech to inform, the audience absorbs new information, learns a process, or considers new ideas. During a speech to persuade, listeners may decide to vote for you, to join a committee, or to buy your services.

What do you want your audience to do as a result of hearing your speech? Before giving your speech, define your audience action goal. If possible, make it something that can be measured or assessed.

How will you know whether your speech succeeds in this and other areas? You will learn this through self-evaluation and peer evaluation. Evaluation is the formal or informal process of judging your speech's content and delivery. Constructive evaluation can help you to chart your progress and to master the skill of public speaking.

Self-Evaluation

There are many talented public speakers, but they were not born knowing how to deliver great orations. Public speaking, like making a perfect jump shot, is learned.

Self-evaluation can help you determine your areas of strength and weakness in public speaking. Evaluate your speech before, during, and after giving it:

* **Before** your speech, identify your goals for the speech. Then picture yourself in the speaking situation, in the place of the audience. How would the audience view your words, your delivery, your supporting material? Ask for feedback when you practice for friends and family. Use evaluation forms, if you wish.

* **During** your speech, watch your listeners' body language and reactions. Are they positive and responsive? Or are they frowning, nodding off, squirming in their seats, and leaving? If you lost the audience, think about why. Adjust your speech to regain their attention.

* **After** your speech, score yourself with an evaluation sheet. Make notes on your strengths and weaknesses. Use this information, along with comments from others, to help you set goals for your next speech.

Elements of Self-Evaluation

When doing a self-evaluation, strive for goals such as those in the list below and in the self-evaluation form in this chapter.

* **Topic selection.** Your topic should be appropriate to the occasion and to your audience's needs and interests. It should fit your purpose of informing, persuading, or entertaining. It should be narrow enough that you can cover it well within the time limit of your speech.

* **Organization.** Your speech needs clear organization—an energetic, attention-getting introduction; a well-developed body; and a powerful conclusion. Strive for content that is developed simply and logically, with an appropriate organizational pattern and strong, interesting support material.

* *Support material.* Your support material should convince the audience. You should select it with this audience in mind, and it should be varied in type and represent typical examples. You should distinguish between fact and opinion, use current and credible sources, cite them properly, and employ your visual aids appropriately.

* *Delivery.* During delivery, your appearance should be appropriate to the occasion and the audience, your notes readable, your note-handling smooth, and your eye contact frequent and inclusive of all parts of the audience. Your body language should be appropriate and you should use the lectern in a way that doesn't block communication.

* *Language.* During a speech, your language needs to be suitable to the occasion and the audience. Your examples should be effective, and your vocal delivery and language usage should be appropriate and well-controlled.

* *Confidence.* You need confidence to speak well before an audience. Be sure to practice enough, to follow a solid pre-speech routine, and to do a thorough room check.

* *Overall assessment.* Consider your overall assessment of this speech. What was the best aspect of your presentation? What is your goal for next time? What one element do you intend to change?

Example of Self-Evaluation

Following is an example of a completed self-evaluation. You can create your own self-evaluation form, using this as a model.

Example

Self-Evaluation

Directions: After giving a presentation, evaluate yourself by writing comments after each topic.

Category	Comment
Topic Selection	Antarctica
Appropriate?	Yes. Audience is interested.
Relevant to purpose?	Need to focus on informing, not persuading.
Topic narrowed?	Should further narrow topic to focus on facts.
Within time limit?	Fit time perfectly.
Organization	
Introduction	
Attention-getting?	Yes, very.
Included objective?	Clarify my objective a little more.
Clear pattern?	Good—keep the chronological pattern.
Body	
Support material?	Need more vivid imagery, analogies, metaphors.
Transitions?	Add stronger transitions and summaries.
Conclusion	
Brief summary?	OK
To the point?	Yes, I stuck to my three main points.
Motivational?	Could have been more exciting.
Support Material	
Adequate?	Yes, enough information.
Appropriate to audience?	Yes
Varied types?	Need to vary support materials for three main points.
Representative?	Yes, examples are typical.
Fact vs. opinion?	OK, I have been clear about this.
Credible sources?	Yes, credible and current.

continues ▶

Self-Evaluation *continued*

Category	Comment
Visual aids	
Readable?	Need a bigger type or font.
Useful?	No. Cut out visuals with little information.
Integrated?	Yes, they were OK.
Presentation?	Smoothly presented.
Delivery	
Appearance?	Should dress more formally.
Notes readable?	OK
Note/MS handling?	Don't rustle pages. Otherwise OK.
Eye contact?	OK, but remember to look left.
Audience connection?	Smile while speaking.
Body language?	Generally supported points I was making.
Gestures?	Hand movements look awkward; practice.
Use of lectern?	Leaned on the side of lectern twice!
Language	
Suitable language?	Yes, no slang used.
Examples?	Personal anecdotes were very effective.
Voice	
Volume?	Voice soft, dropped volume at end of sentences.
Pace?	Vary pace a bit more.
Used pauses?	Taking time to pause helped my nervousness.
Fluent?	Eliminate "ers" and "uhs."
Usage	
Vocabulary OK?	Liven up word choices.
Grammar?	Good.
Pronunciation?	Generally good.
Passive/active?	OK
Confidence	
Enough practice?	Yes; next time videotape and time myself.
Pre-speech routine?	Don't speak on an empty stomach again!
Room check?	Make sure I have water available.
Overall Evaluation	
Strong points?	Content was strong and delivery was confident.
Goal for next time?	More practice of gestures.

Self-Evaluation

GOAL

The goal of this activity is to develop awareness of your strengths as well as the areas that need improvement.

TASKS

1. Record a speech (either audio or video) that you give for your class.

2. Use the evaluation form that your teacher uses to grade you and score your own speech.

3. Make a list of suggestions for improvement.

4. Use these suggestions to improve your speech and your presentation.

5. Re-record your revised speech and see whether you notice improvement.

OUTCOMES

Were you able to identify your strengths? Could you identify the areas that you need to improve? Did one area stand out as the most important one to fix?

Peer Evaluation

When your peers—your friends and fellow speech students—critique your speeches, you gain a valuable, new perspective. **Peer evaluation** can help you to perfect your content and delivery.

When you evaluate another's speech, you learn something, too. You sharpen your analytical skills, and you gain insight into the strengths and weaknesses of your own performances.

When giving a peer evaluation, follow the guidelines below.

* ***Set up evaluation criteria.*** Speeches differ in purpose, so use different criteria to judge them. You would judge a humorous extemporaneous speech differently than you would judge a 20-minute speech to inform. Before evaluating a speech, identify the criteria that you

will use. The evaluation forms in this book provide a large number of valuable criteria. Your teacher may also have guidelines for you. Sometimes school speech assignments focus on a specific element, such as visual aids or body language. If so, limit your feedback to those elements.

* ***Take your job seriously.*** Remember that your job is to help the speaker improve. Take the role seriously. Take notes during the speech to help you remember details—the examples that were especially moving, the irritating gestures, the great visual aids, and the rousing conclusion.

* ***Lead with the speaker's strengths.*** Always begin a critique by noting what a speaker did well. This gives the speaker something solid on which to build in

future speeches. It also makes it easier for him or her to listen to your criticisms. Identify important positive aspects of the speech, making sure that you are honest. For example, you might say, "Your organization was clear and logical," "Your charts were very easy to read," or "Your family stories were very interesting."

* **Cite concrete examples.** Vague, general comments, such as "I liked your speech" or "It needed improvement," don't help anyone. Refer to your notes for concrete details. Make specific comments, such as, "The story about your dog was very moving, especially with your voice inflection, the pause afterward, and good eye contact." Then add, "Think about videotaping your speech so you can work on making your gestures more natural."

* **Never get personal.** Even if you dislike the speaker or the speech topic, your job is to give a fair, helpful critique. Be objective. Communicate respect for the speaker. Instead of debating the speaker's argument, evaluate the argument's organization, logic, and evidence. To avoid sounding accusatory, biased, or bossy, be careful how you word your feedback. Avoid statements such as, "You didn't organize your ideas clearly." Instead, use "I" statements such as, "I had trouble following your train of thought."

* **Make constructive suggestions.** With each critical comment, give the speaker specific suggestions for improvement. In the example used above, you might say,

"To help the audience follow your train of thought, consider summarizing your main points more often."

* **Limit your comments.** Keep your comments brief and to the point. Focus on the most important areas of the speech rather than delivering a long, overwhelming list of minor criticisms. Ask yourself, "Which one or two areas, if changed, would improve this speaker's performance the most?" Concentrate on those areas.

* **Remember that everyone is learning.** Especially in a classroom setting, everyone is learning. Be reasonable in your expectations and empathetic in your feedback. The rule is simple: Treat your peers as you want to be treated. After all, you have been in their position—or you soon will be.

Evaluating Informative Speeches

When you give a speech to inform, your goal is to educate your audience. Your evaluation will help you to determine whether you succeeded. Did your listeners comprehend the information? Did they understand the process?

If possible, set concrete goals for the audience that will help you to measure your success. For example, you could set such goals as, "At least 30 people will take my business card" or "At least half of the audience will be able to search the Internet without help."

There are **two** general types of feedback: informal and formal.

Informal Feedback

Informal feedback is unstructured and often spoken. You'll gather informal feedback from both your practice audiences and your real audience. You can ask for comments during and after your speech. Body language is a form of informal feedback, too. An audience's body language and responses can show you when you need to speak louder, to take more time to explain a point, or to inject extra energy into your words.

Formal Feedback

Formal feedback is structured and organized. Fellow students, a teacher, or assigned judges give you this feedback in the form of completed evaluation forms, written comments, teacher critiques, or a letter grade. You can get formal feedback from your practice audiences by asking them to fill out evaluation forms. You'll usually get other formal feedback after your speech is completed.

Evaluation Form

A sample evaluation form for informative speeches is shown in the Handbook, on pages 362–363.

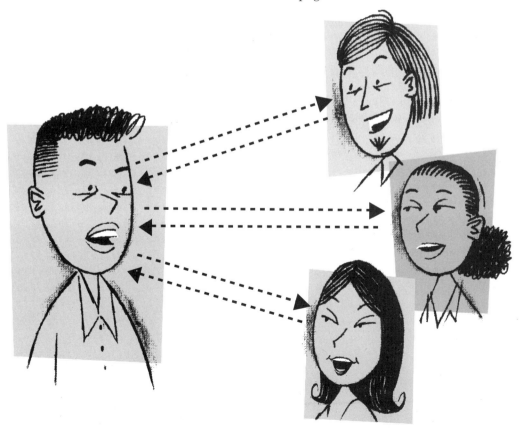

Evaluating Persuasive Speeches

With a persuasive speech, you want your audience to change an idea or attitude and to take some kind of action. It is important to define that desired action before your speech, along with a measurable way for you to determine whether or not you succeeded. For example, you might define your goal and the desired action as follows: "Thirty people will sign up for the workshop," or "I'll be elected class president by a landslide."

In a persuasive speech, evaluation addresses the areas that the Greek philosopher Aristotle defined as pathos (meeting listeners' needs), ethos (establishing your credibility), and logos (reasoning).

Pathos (Listeners' Needs)

Using pathos, a speaker excites a desired emotional response in the audience. Aristotle saw this as meeting listeners' needs. To succeed at a pathos appeal, your job is to know your audience and to target your speech to meet their expectations, needs, and interests. Informal and formal feedback can help you determine whether you have met that goal.

Before your speech, brief your practice audiences on the real audience that you will face—who they are and their attitude toward your topic: positive, neutral, apathetic, or opposed. Ask the practice audiences to listen to your speech as if they were this target audience.

During your real speech, watch your listeners' responses. If you wish, ask them for informal feedback.

After the speech, evaluation forms will help you to find out whether you convinced your listeners and met your goal. If you failed to move them, stop and think. Was the problem in your topic? Were you wrong about the audience's needs? Were your expectations for change unrealistic?

Ethos (Establishing Credibility)

Aristotle also suggested that a persuasive speaker could influence others through personal power or credibility. Speaker credibility is extremely important in persuasive speaking. From the time you walk to the lectern until you take your seat, all eyes will be on you. The audience determines your credibility from your personal appearance and from many aspects of your speech's content and delivery.

Before your speech, informal feedback about your credibility can be valuable—as long as your family and friends can put themselves in the place of the real audience. Formal feedback at the end of your speech will help you in the future. But, in general, when making an ethos appeal, planning ahead is the key. Once you begin, it is too late to change your clothes or your preparation.

Logos (Reasoning)

The third important persuasive speech element that Aristotle identified is logos, or reasoning. Speakers can't persuade in a responsible way without evidence. An evaluation of the logos aspect of a speech tries to determine whether the evidence was relevant, sound, sufficient, and logically presented.

Before you speak, ask practice audiences to critique your evidence. But whether or not you convince the real audience will remain a mystery until you get post-speech feedback. For this reason, the more time you spend constructing and fine-tuning your arguments beforehand, the better.

Evaluation Form

A sample evaluation form for persuasive speeches is shown in the Handbook, on pages 364–365.

Communication in Careers

Putting Feedback to Work

Ella Davis joined a large law firm right out of law school. Knowing that public speaking ability is crucial to succeeding in law, Ella devised a plan to help improve her speaking skills.

First, she volunteered on several occasions to write speeches for partners at her law firm. Noting the revisions that her colleagues made, she improved her own speeches by including more anecdotes and using more vivid language. She also learned about delivery techniques by listening to her colleagues present her material.

Second, Ella read books about public speaking. Finally, she scheduled speaking engagements for herself every few months by signing up with the speakers' bureaus of her local bar association, the Chamber of Commerce, and several civic organizations. Formal and informal audience feedback helped Ella improve her speaking abilities.

In part because of her self-evaluation efforts, her career soared, and she became a highly visible and successful lawyer in her community.

Constructive Criticism

Evaluation feedback that is positive and helpful rather than personal, negative, or mean-spirited is **constructive criticism**. It is useful for teaching and learning.

A constructive evaluation follows the guidelines given earlier in this chapter for peer evaluation. Here is a summary of those guidelines:

1. Set up evaluation criteria.
2. Take your job seriously.
3. Lead with the speaker's strengths.
4. Cite concrete examples.
5. Never get personal.
6. Make constructive suggestions.
7. Limit your comments.
8. Remember: everyone is learning.

Example of Good Criticism

In the evaluation that follows, Jenny Wright reviewed Derek Williams's speech, "Basketball Is the Best Sport." It is a good example of a constructive evaluation.

Put yourself in Derek's place as you read:

* How would you feel overall?
* What changes could you easily make?
* What goals might you set for your next speech as a result of Jenny's constructive criticism?

Example

Evaluation: Speech to Inform

Speaker	<u>Derek Williams</u>
Topic	<u>Basketball Is the Best Sport</u>

Category	**Comment**
Topic Selection	
Appropriate?	Yes, great!
Narrow topic?	Yes, you didn't try to discuss all sports.
Within time limit?	3 minutes over, but I didn't care.
Introduction	
Attention-getting?	Nervous at start—try more eye contact.
Builds interest?	The basketball prop made me curious!
Previews topic?	Yes, you were clear about what you were going to say.
Organization	
Logical and well-organized?	Yes, very.
Appropriate organizational pattern?	Yes, time pattern of organization worked well.

Easy to follow?	Yes.
Repeats information?	No, but seemed OK.
Smooth transitions?	Stronger transitions needed—triangle offense lost me.

Supporting Materials

Sufficient number?	Great stories! I liked the one about your camp coach.
Variety?	No, I would have liked things in addition to anecdotes.
Up-to-date?	I tallied evidence in every stage of life you discussed.
Visuals effective?	No visuals. Could have drawn some plays.
Well-researched?	Yes.
Sources properly cited?	No. Need source for opening quote.

Language

Word choice?	You are a natural storyteller!
Grammar/sentence structure?	No problems.
Appropriate?	Yes. Garrett liked the story that involved him!

Speaker Credibility

Dress and grooming?	Clever to wear your uniform!
Established credibility?	No problem since you're our star forward.
Enthusiasm?	Yes, you obviously like basketball.
Smooth delivery?	I felt the transitions were a little rocky, but overall fine.

Delivery

Conversational?	Yes.
Distracting mannerisms?	Holding and twirling the ball was distracting to me.
Enunciation and diction?	Not always clear. You looked down a lot.
Gestures/facial expressions?	I would have liked more gestures.
Eye contact?	I recommend more eye contact, especially at first.
Volume and pace?	Speak up. I couldn't hear in the back of the room.
Smooth use of notes?	No, papers were distracting. I recommend note cards.

Conclusion

Brief summary?	Yes.
Motivational?	Yes.
Purpose clear?	Without a doubt!

Overall Effectiveness

Message	Very clear.
Purpose	Overall, yes, except for connection with audience.

Evaluator   Jenny Wright

Example of Nonconstructive Criticism

Following is another student's review of the same speech. Again, put yourself in the speaker's place. How would you respond to this evaluation?

* Is this form more or less helpful to you than the criticism by Jenny? Why or why not?
* Does it motivate you to set new goals for improvement? Why or why not?
* What would you have liked that wasn't included?

Evaluation: Speech to Inform

Speaker	Derek Williams
Topic	Basketball Is the Best Sport

Category	**Comment**
Topic Selection	
Appropriate?	No, I don't like basketball.
Narrow topic?	Narrowed down too much on basketball.
Within time limit?	OK.
Introduction	
Attention-getting?	Not really. This topic doesn't interest me.
Builds interest?	Not me!
Previews topic?	Yes.
Organization	
Logical and well-organized?	Yes and no.
Appropriate organizational pattern?	I think so.
Easy to follow?	Not sure.
Repeats information?	Not really.
Smooth transitions?	I don't think so.
Supporting Materials	
Sufficient number?	Yes. Told a few good stories.
Variety?	No, not really.
Up-to-date?	I guess.
Visuals effective?	Ball OK, I guess.
Well-researched?	I guess so.
Sources properly cited?	Don't remember.

Language

Word choice?	He could have used different words.
Grammar/sentence structure?	Seemed OK.
Appropriate?	No.

Speaker Credibility

Dress and grooming?	OK.
Established credibility	Yes, he's a basketball player.
Enthusiasm?	Yes.
Smooth delivery?	All right.

Delivery

Conversational?	Yes.
Distracting mannerisms?	Yes.
Enunciation and diction?	No. Not all the time.
Gestures/facial expressions?	No.
Eye contact?	No.
Volume and pace?	No.
Smooth use of notes?	No.

Conclusion

Brief summary?	Not really.
Motivational?	Maybe.
Purpose clear?	Yes and no.

Overall Effectiveness

Message	Sort of.
Purpose	I still don't like basketball, so I guess not.

Evaluator   <u>Marlin Waters</u>

Accepting Constructive Criticism

Everyone loves praise, but what a beginning speaker needs is truthful feedback. Public speaking is a complex skill, and you can't improve without guidance from others.

A form full of positive feedback won't necessarily help you. There always are areas where you can improve. The most useful evaluations contain both positive and negative comments.

As a speaker you need to learn how to accept criticism gracefully and to incorporate suggestions into your next speech. Here are **five** ways to handle constructive feedback.

❶ Avoid Becoming Defensive

Negative comments can be hard to accept. However, if you view yourself as someone who is learning, you won't dismiss constructive criticism as "stupid," "mean," or "unfair." View your evaluators as people who can help you. Keep an open, positive attitude. You don't have to agree with every comment. Just try to hear them in a nondefensive way.

❷ Listen Carefully

Practice your best listening skills. Consciously hold back your own responses and personal views so that you can fully take in the evaluators' comments without interruption. Try above all to understand precisely what each evaluator is saying. Take notes for later reference.

❸ Learn to Paraphrase

Focus on paraphrasing what you think the evaluator said. Paraphrasing requires careful listening. In general, evaluators will respect you for listening openly to criticism and for your positive attitude.

❹ Evaluate the Comments

You don't have to accept all feedback and suggestions for changes. However, be sure to sift through the comments and weigh them carefully. In evaluating a comment, consider these points:

* *Do you understand the comment?* If not, ask for clarification.
* *Have you heard this criticism before?* Do the reviewers agree on this point, or does one reviewer stand alone? You may choose not to follow through on isolated opinions.
* *Does the criticism match* what you have been taught about effective public speaking?

❺ Put the Feedback to Work

The most heartfelt feedback won't help you if you ignore it. Try putting some of your evaluators' comments into action. Just say to yourself, "What if I did everything they suggested?" That's the only way to find out whether the suggestions will work for you. With this type of thoughtful, determined effort, you are likely to see major improvements in your speaking ability.

Accepting Constructive Criticism

Sales manager Vincent Aguilar had his first annual job appraisal. At Burns Electric, employees do a self-evaluation and also are evaluated by the supervisor. Then the two sit down and compare notes.

At Vincent's evaluation, the supervisor began with Vincent's strong points and praised him highly. Vincent was very pleased. But when she started talking about areas where Vincent was weak, he got upset. He didn't expect these negative comments. Instead of listening, he reacted defensively. He even interrupted the supervisor to defend himself.

As a result, Vincent missed the supervisor's explanation of areas she wanted

Vincent to prioritize during the following year. She had put them in writing, but when Vincent read them later, he wasn't sure what she expected him to do. He got upset all over again.

If Vincent had put his personal reactions on hold, he could have heard her explanations and asked her questions. Because he didn't accept this constructive criticism well, Vincent's progress within the company was slower than he'd hoped.

Vincent realized that he'd hurt himself in this situation. He finally attended a seminar on communication in the workplace. At this session, he learned not to take criticism personally and to use the information to establish a plan for improvement.

Peer Evaluation

GOAL

The goal of this activity is to help you and your classmates become helpful evaluators.

TASKS

1. Form groups of four or five.
2. Each person in the group gives a short practice speech.
3. Listeners complete an evaluation form for each speech. Use appropriate forms for speeches to inform and speeches to persuade.

4. Speakers receive feedback in the form of discussion (oral feedback) and in written evaluation form(s).
5. Repeat the process until everyone in the group has had a chance to speak.

OUTCOMES

What did you learn from your evaluations? What changes will you make to your speech based on the feedback? Were you able to use active listening skills and resist taking negative comments personally? Were evaluators able to focus on the speech and refrain from personal comments?

Refocusing a Speech

If your speech is heavily criticized, try not to get depressed. You can't take it personally. You're new at public speaking, and you're trying to learn.

Take stock of the situation. Use your failures and disappointments as learning experiences. Valid suggestions and criticisms can help you refocus your efforts. Set goals for your next speech and work to implement them. Success in anything stems from the will to improve.

Use Feedback to Refocus Your Speech

GOAL
The goal of this activity is to use the information from self-evaluation and peer evaluation to refocus a speech that you plan to give for a class assignment.

TASKS
1. Gather all feedback and evaluations that you have done and have received from peers and the teacher.
2. Create an organized list of criticisms.
3. After each criticism, write what you will do to solve this problem.
4. Incorporate these changes in any speech on which you're still working. Use this as a personal checklist for all future speeches.

OUTCOMES
On what areas did you focus to improve? What changes did you make to your presentation? Did these changes improve your speech? Did you practice before a mirror, a group of friends or family, or a video camera or tape recorder? What shift did you see in your performance?

Wrap-up

Speakers learn to improve through evaluation and feedback. Speeches are judged by how well you've defined the situation, determined your purpose, considered the needs of your audience, researched and gathered information, and chosen a delivery method. They also are judged by the quality of your delivery and your results. To improve your public speaking skills, it is important to evaluate yourself as well as to become a helpful peer evaluator. Because the goals of informative and persuasive speeches are different, these speeches are evaluated by somewhat different criteria. In all instances, however, criticism needs to be constructive and to serve as a teaching tool for the speaker. Learning to accept and utilize constructive criticism is important to every speaker's growth.

Speech Words to Know

constructive criticism—evaluation of a performance that provides feedback that will assist the speaker in improving.

peer evaluation—feedback process in which classmates identify strengths and areas that need improvement.

self-evaluation—process in which you judge yourself and become aware of your strengths and areas that need improvement.

Handbook

Parliamentary Procedure

Parliamentary procedure is a set of procedures for conducting fair and orderly meetings. These rules originated in England's Parliament, which was founded in the thirteenth century. Now used by groups ranging from student governments to the U.S. Congress, parliamentary procedure helps leaders to run meetings in a way that is orderly, fair, democratic, and efficient.

Since there are several published sources on parliamentary procedure, any group using this system should adopt a standard text to use as a reference for procedural questions. One of the best known sources is *Robert's Rules of Order*, which was written in 1876 by Henry M. Robert, a U.S. Army general. The updated version is called *Robert's Rules of Order, Newly Revised* (9th edition, Perseus Books, 1991).

Fundamental Principles of Parliamentary Procedure

Here are some of the basic principles of parliamentary procedure:

* To prevent minority rule, a quorum, or a certain percentage of the membership, must be present for the group to make valid decisions.
* A fair and impartial president or Chair runs the meetings.
* No member can speak unless the Chair recognizes him or her. A member can speak only once on a question if others haven't yet spoken.
* The body addresses only one issue at a time.
* The group holds open discussions, in which every member's opinion is respected and treated equally.
* Each member has a single vote and all votes have equal value.
* The majority rules.

Rules of Conduct

Parliamentary procedure specifies many rules of conduct designed to cover any situation that may arise. Among the basic rules are:

1. **Respect for the Chair and for other members.** Under the rules of parliamentary procedure, members address other members and the Chair as "my esteemed colleague," "Madame Chairperson," or "Mr. Lopez." (First names and "you" are not used.)
2. **Permission to speak.** Anyone wishing to speak must ask the Chair for the "floor." Once given permission, that person alone may speak. Other members of the group are expected to listen carefully and politely.

3. **Interrupting a speaker.** To speak while another member has the floor, a member must ask the Chair for permission. The Chair then asks the current speaker, "Will the speaker yield" (allow an interruption)? Yields are either temporary or permanent. A temporary yield returns the floor to the first speaker after the second speaker finishes. In some groups, once a member has the floor, he or she may keep it indefinitely. This is sometimes done to prevent a vote on an issue. The act of holding the floor indefinitely is called a filibuster.

The Leadership

In groups that use parliamentary procedure, the two required leaders are a president, or Chair, and a secretary. Other officers may include a vice-president, recording secretary and a corresponding secretary, a treasurer, a parliamentarian, a historian (who maintains an ongoing record of the group's activities and membership), and a sergeant at arms (who maintains order at meetings).

The president or Chair presides over the meeting, restores order if the meeting becomes disorderly, decides who is allowed to speak, decides who "has the floor," and votes in case of a tie. The vice-president fills in when the Chair is absent or when he or she wishes to make a motion or join a floor debate. Usually this role is temporary.

The secretary (or clerk) records and reads the "minutes" of the meeting, takes attendance, and signs most documents for the group. The treasurer signs checks and accounts for the group's funds.

The Order of Business

Parliamentary procedure outlines a basic format for "the order of business," or a meeting's agenda.

1. The Chair calls the meeting to order, often using a gavel.
2. A quorum is called for.
3. The minutes of the last meeting are read, corrected as needed, then approved by the members.
4. Any preliminary matters— announcements, agenda changes, and so on—are discussed.
5. Reports by officers, boards, standing (that is, ongoing) committees and special (usually short-term) committees are delivered.
6. Old business—unfinished agenda items from previous meetings—is discussed.
7. New business—new agenda items—is discussed.
8. Members make short announcements and informal requests—such as asking the date of the next meeting.
9. The Chair adjourns the meeting, usually by another tap of the gavel.

Making Decisions

Parliamentary procedure provides an efficient and democratic way for a group to consider issues and take action. The process includes **four** steps: a motion, a second to the motion, the discussion, and the vote.

❶ The Motion

Anyone wishing to propose an action to the group may make a motion at an appropriate point in the agenda. After being recognized by the Chair, a member says, "I make a motion that. . . ." The motion should be short and its wording should be specific.

❷ The Second

In many groups, a second is needed ("I second the motion") before the motion can be discussed by the group. This ensures that at least two people are interested in a discussion of this motion.

Once a motion is made, secondary motions also may be made. Possible secondary motions include the following:

1. Motion to amend, to change the first motion's wording.

2. Motion to table, to temporarily delay action on the first motion, often because of a lack of time or information.

3. Motion to refer to committee, which transfers the first motion to a smaller group for further study or rewording. Members make this motion when the original motion is too confusing, long, or complex for the group to act upon quickly.

4. Motion to limit discussion, which closes debate on the issue. This helps to move the process along when discussions become repetitive.

5. Call for the question, a formal request to the Chair that the vote be taken.

6. Motion for secret ballots, usually enacted when an issue causes heated conflict or debate.

❸ The Discussion

After a motion has been seconded, members discuss the issue, respectfully taking turns as recognized by the Chair. When discussion is finished and there are no secondary motions or requests, the Chair repeats the motion and then asks for the final time, "Is there any further discussion?"

❹ The Vote

If there is no further discussion, the Chair says, "Hearing none, I'll now call for the [voice or secret ballot] vote."

If this group uses a voice vote, the Chair calls for the vote by saying, "All in favor say, 'Aye.'" And "All opposed say, 'Nay.'"

The Chair then announces the outcome of the vote, saying, "The 'ayes/nays' have it. The motion is carried/defeated." If the Chair is unsure about whether the motion has passed, he or she may ask for a show of hands, a standing vote, a secret ballot, or some other way of counting members' votes.

Some noncontroversial issues may be decided without a vote, by unanimous consent. For example, a member may say, "Mr./Madam Chairperson, I ask unanimous consent that I be allowed to excuse myself at 11:00 to attend a funeral." The Chair then says, "Without objection," or asks, "Are there any objections?" If not, the Chair says, "So ordered." If there is an objection, the matter must be put to a vote.

During this process, a member who has a question about a possible breach of parliamentary procedure—a "point of order"—may make a "parliamentary inquiry." This means that the member may interrupt the speaker and ask the Chair about the rule, saying, "Point of order, Mr./Madam Chairperson. . . ."

Running a Meeting Efficiently

To assure that meetings run efficiently, the Chair can take the following steps.

Before a meeting, the Chair should:

* Send members the agenda and other important information, so they can consider their views and prepare questions.
* Contact committee chairs to confirm that they will attend and provide reports.
* Encourage members to write out wording of any motions that they plan to make. A well-written motion answers the questions what, when, how, and how much (time and money). Carefully worded motions are less likely to be reworded or sent to committee.

During a meeting, the Chair should:

* Manage agenda items so that the meetings end on time.
* Remind members that issues cannot be discussed without a motion being made and seconded.
* Keep the discussion moving and take votes without waiting for "the question" to be called.
* Strictly enforce rules that prevent any one member from monopolizing discussion or debate.
* Educate members about parliamentary procedure by explaining procedures and rulings.

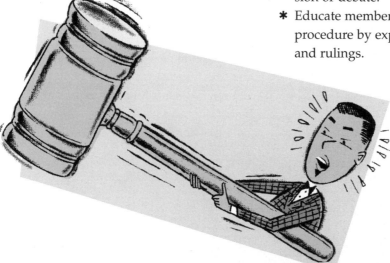

Presentation Aids

Presentation aids include pictures; objects; models; graphs, charts, and diagrams; slides, overhead transparencies; video; and audio CDs and tapes. You can give a highly effective speech without presentation aids, but many audience members will focus and comprehend better if they see information in addition to hearing it.

Presentation aids can serve several important functions in your speech. Presentation aids:

* Focus the audience's attention.
* Introduce new concepts and reinforce main ideas.
* Set a mood and stimulate emotional involvement.
* Heighten listeners' grasp and recall of new or complicated concepts, models, and statistical data.
* Add interest, humor, or a visual break.

Use presentation aids in a well-planned, coherent way. Make sure that they add to rather than detract from your speech. Remember that your presentation aids won't work unless you begin with a top-notch speech.

Types of Presentation Aids

Presentation aids often are divided into two groups—those that do not change during a presentation and those that do change. Static presentation aids include pictures; objects; models; graphs, charts, and diagrams; slides; and overhead transparencies. Dynamic presentation aids include videotapes and audio CDs and tapes. Both types of presentation aids can enhance a speech, and both have drawbacks. Static presentation aids are easy to create and use but lack the energy and excitement of video and audio. Video and audio can dazzle an audience and make points effectively, but they require longer preparation time, more equipment, and more careful handling on stage.

Pictures

The term *pictures* refers to a whole range of static visuals—drawings, photographs, blueprints, floor plans, and more. Pictures can instantly clarify ideas that may be difficult to explain in words. They can clarify a concept or situation, help you to compare items, establish a mood, and introduce a realistic context.

How can pictures help your speech? Read through your outline, thinking visually. Photos could help you to compare features of new SUVs or to show New York streets in 1910. Floor plans could help you explain your upcoming renovation project. Or children's artwork could vividly illustrate your points about childhood fears. With a small audience, hold up pictures mounted on cardboard. With a larger group, present them through a computerized graphics program.

Be sure that pictures you use are relevant to your topic and visible to all audience members. Think twice before using clip art from popular software packages, because it tends to be overused and may not make the impression you had hoped.

Objects

When you want people to know what something actually looks like, consider using an object or prop. Objects are the "real thing"—for example, a Civil War uniform. Objects and models can be fascinating to an audience. They also have great power to communicate.

Think about how an object might add drama to your speech. In talking about home fire safety, you could bring in home firefighting equipment or child sleepwear that does not meet safety standards. In discussing popular toys, you can bring in the toys themselves.

Objects and props have some disadvantages. They can be hard to transport and awkward to handle. You'll also want to show or demonstrate an object only when you're discussing it. Then move it out of sight so it doesn't distract the audience.

Models

Models are three-dimensional replicas of a real thing, such as an architect's scale model of a building. Models reproduce something on a smaller scale. Like other objects, they're interesting and provide detail that isn't possible in other types of visual aids. They liven up a speech and make a memorable impression.

Models are difficult to construct and are not appropriate to every type of speech. But when discussing world political hotspots, you can spin a globe dramatically to find each new location. When talking about the Space Shuttle or types of aircraft, you can produce realistic toy replicas. Models often work best when you are attempting to show something not yet completed, such as a new sports stadium or skyscraper.

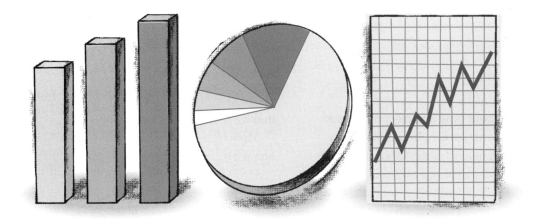

Graphs, Charts, and Diagrams

Graphs, charts, and diagrams are visual representations of numerical information. Because they show relationships, they make it easy for an audience to understand numerical comparisons and contrasts, upturns and downturns, results, and trends over time. These visual images give the audience information quickly, freeing you to comment on specific key points.

Graphs and charts collapse large amounts of complicated numerical information into graphic representations. Bar graphs use horizontal or vertical bars, often in contrasting colors, to show comparisons. You might use a bar graph to compare the rising SAT scores of high school juniors over the past three years. Line graphs show how items compare over time. You might use a line graph to show decreasing crime statistics over months, years, or decades. Pie charts are divided into wedges like a real pie and show 100 percent of anything divided up into those wedges. You might use a pie chart to show your school population by grade level.

A diagram is a visual representation of an idea, process, plan of action, or a place. Speakers often use diagrams to illustrate abstract ideas that are difficult to understand or follow. Diagrams may illustrate a building interior, a proposed city park, or a new freeway interchange. Diagrams also can help to describe complicated mechanisms or steps in a procedure. You might use a diagram of the heart to explain different types of rhythmic heart problems. Or you could use a flowchart to show the relationships and sequence of steps in a process or in a computer program.

Slides

In general, audiences like slides if they are used well. Slides can magnify the effect of a speaker's words, especially during speeches with emotional impact. They are large, colorful, and easy to see. Slides show a variety of images, including pictures, diagrams, and charts.

Slides are compact, easy to store, and easy to transport. It's also relatively easy to bring your own slide projector to a presentation. But using slides also can present problems. Film and processing costs can add up, and slides require you to lower the lights during your presentation, which makes it harder for you to see your audience and for them to see you.

Overhead Transparencies

Overhead transparencies are popular with speakers because they are easy to prepare and use. Transparencies can be created by hand or with a computer and printer. Speakers sometimes use them to accompany an entire talk.

Transparencies can be useful in classroom speeches. For example, you can use a transparency map in a speech on world hunger, marking each location with a transparency pen as you discuss it. Color overlays can help you show changing information, as in a speech on shrinking rain forests. If an overhead projector is available, transparencies can provide a handy backup for a computer program that doesn't work.

Follow these guidelines when using transparencies:

* Use a simple, consistent design with a single idea on each sheet.
* Make sure that each transparency is well-worded and error-free.
* Use large, neat lettering so that everyone in the room can read the words.
* Project the transparencies to either side of the podium—not to the center where the speaker will stand.
* When there is nothing on the screen, turn off the lamp so the audience does not have to stare at a brightly lit blank screen.
* Keep transparencies organized and neat by placing each one in a numbered cardboard frame or file folder with text notes on each.
* Practice using them until your delivery is smooth.
* As you speak, face the audience, as opposed to turning your back on it and looking at the screen.

Videotapes

The moving images and powerful sound of video can greatly energize a presentation. You can use video to educate an audience, explain complex processes, show historical progressions, illustrate a point, and share real-life examples and events.

Business presenters use video clips for celebrity and customer testimonials and for product demonstrations. Doctors use videotape to demonstrate new procedures to students. Special events organizers feature biographical or historical videos to capture listeners' attention and stir their emotions.

You can edit recorded videotapes or shoot your own videos. Home videos might capture an interview, show how to prepare a recipe, or present a real-world scene.

Although video has many advantages, it also has a few drawbacks. Video requires lowered lights that make you lose touch with your audience. You also need special equipment with compatible software, extension cords, lighting flexibility, and a large enough screen for everyone to see. Some studies also suggest that videotape causes the brain to go into passive rather than active mode, making what is seen on video hard to recall.

Audio CDs and Tapes

Audio CDs and tapes can energize a speech and emphasize important ideas. Music can supply an illustration, underscore a main point, create a mood, or add emotional impact.

Audiotapes or CDs can add real emotional power to a speech. For example, if you're talking about Martin Luther King, Jr.'s, famous "I Have a Dream" speech, don't read the words yourself. Instead, play a tape of Dr. King delivering the speech. If you're speaking about hip hop music, why try to describe it? Play songs by popular hip hop artists. If it's appropriate, use upbeat, catchy music to wake up your audience or play solemn music to set a serious tone. You can use music anywhere in your speech—before, during, or after—depending on your purpose.

Designing and Using Presentation Aids

Here are some guidelines for choosing, designing, and using presentation aids:

1. Start with a well-planned speech. Then find places that may be enhanced or improved with presentation aids or points you want to emphasize.

2. Decide which presentation aids would be most effective and best serve your purpose. Ask yourself, "Does this presentation aid clarify, amplify, or simplify a concept or idea?"

3. Limit the presentation aids, so they will not overwhelm the audience. Everything you use must enhance your speech.

4. For visual aids, use a simple design, consistent format, and large print. Experts recommend using five or six lines per visual with no more than six words per line. Use simplified graphics and symbols to show numerical data.

5. Proofread all visual aids and use meaningful titles. Limit video clips and sound clips to short, relevant segments that support your speech rather than distract from it.

6. Give yourself plenty of time to create, proof, and finalize your materials.

7. Test any necessary equipment on site.

8. Practice using your presentation aids until you can use them smoothly.

9. Make sure that the entire audience can see your visuals and video and hear your audio.

High-Tech Presentations

Today's high-quality computer-assisted presentations are accessible to all, amateurs and professionals alike. When choosing from the many user-friendly presentation tools, start by considering the goal of your presentation, the audience, the environment, your computer expertise, and the time you have available for preparation.

Two types of technology-assisted presentations are common. Both types are speaker-controlled. The first presents attractive text and graphics that follow and illustrate the points that a speaker is making. The second type uses additional media—text, graphics, animated sequences, video, sound, and branching hypertext.

New high-tech presentation packages appear frequently, and revisions of popular programs often offer exciting new features. Watch for new developments and innovations in this field, at trade shows, in trade journals, and through Web sites.

Projection Options

Speakers have many different viewing options for any type of technology-assisted presentation. One of the most common viewing setups is a laptop computer attached to an LCD display unit sitting on a traditional overhead projector. Whatever is displayed on the computer screen is projected from the LCD to a screen or on the wall.

This simple LCD unit can be joined by sophisticated but easy-to-use video projection monitors. They display whatever is on the computer screen as well as the multimedia elements that involve moving images and sound. These assets make possible the full integration of the multimedia elements in a sophisticated presentation. The clarity, color, and sound quality of these units has continued to improve over the last several years.

Text and Graphics Presentation Packages

Features and Capabilities

Text and graphics presentation packages offer many options to speakers. They help you in putting together the written text of a presentation and then enhance it with many different types of images—photos, drawings, diagrams, graphs, illustrations, and flowcharts. These packages are limited to visuals and text only. You provide the sound and narration, using text and images to amplify and reinforce your message.

Most text and graphics presentation packages have templates that are easy for a beginner to use, yet include advanced drawing and other custom features for an expert user. The programs allow a speaker to import, scan, size, and alter images.

The most sophisticated programs first help you to organize your ideas. Then you can create the presentation itself in outline form as a series of "slides." Each slide may contain text, graphics, and other still images. You can easily sort slides and make changes in the sequence when needed, adding changes in the narration, new transitions, or animation. Because editing is so simple, you may continuously refine a presentation to make it more effective or to target it to a specific audience. You also may create handouts, if desired.

Uses in Presentations

Imagine a speech demonstrating a company's new software. A text/graphics presentation program that includes drawing, spreadsheet, and word processor tools would allow a speaker to present screen shots from the program, diagrams of the navigational choices, photos of the program, sample pages of the product, and a spreadsheet to show financial projections. The presentation program can pull them all together in a slide show presentation.

Designing Your Presentation

As with any other type of presentation aid, consistency of design is very important. Fortunately, many presentation programs provide templates, or pre-designed formats, that enable speakers to create professional slides and Web pages with a consistent look. The speaker can select a theme template that helps to standardize titles, fonts, bullets, backgrounds, and formats throughout a presentation.

When selecting templates, it is important to consider the audience and the purpose of the speech or presentation. Some templates are playful or lighthearted, appropriate for a less serious speech or a young audience. Other templates are suitable to more formal-looking multimedia presentations. You should choose the template with features that best fit the audience, mood, and purpose.

Multimedia Presentation Packages

Features and Capabilities

Integrated multimedia presentation packages expand your media possibilities. In addition to text and graphics, they allow use of animation, video, and sound (voice narration, music, and sound effects). These media can be integrated into a single presentation.

Multimedia programs allow graphics, text, sound, and video to be combined in endless ways. You can edit short movies, download graphics, capture images using a digital camera, access information on the Internet, and much more. Best of all, everything is contained within one program. Since multimedia presentation programs include sound and moving video, your live narration can be interspersed with other narrators, sound effects, and music.

Uses in Presentations

Multimedia tools are used in schools, businesses, and at home to create business plans, multimedia reports, Web sites, sales presentations, resumes, training modules, and more. Job applicants now send multimedia portfolios and resumes over the Web. College applicants can submit financial aid information and even multimedia admissions materials. Many business consultants, training professionals, and public relations specialists use multimedia presentations for a number of their speeches.

Designing Your Presentation

When designing a multimedia presentation, you use the software's authoring program to create, select, retrieve, insert, and edit material used in the final product. You decide which material to download and insert, which movie clips to edit and use, and which images to create and place into the text.

When you plan a multimedia presentation, keep your purpose clearly in mind. Focus on adding interest to and clarifying the main points of your speech. Be careful not to overwhelm the presentation. Multimedia should be subordinate to the main ideas of the speech.

Images and Other Media Materials

Where do you find multimedia materials? Consider it a research project. You will find useful material in libraries and databases. You also can purchase CD-ROMs that are specifically designed for multimedia presentations. These offer still images, video clips, sound clips, and animations. Even though you also can find images on the Web, note that these usually are copyrighted and cannot be used without licensing fees.

Digital cameras and image enhancement programs have made it easy to integrate photos into any presentation. Using a digital camera, you can take pictures of a new project or a new building and then can attach the camera to your computer and download the images without film processing. Using image enhancement programs, you can then alter the images, layer them with text, and add special effects.

Scanners also can be useful for creating computer image files from text documents, photos, drawings, and printed materials. Scanners vary in price, quality, and features. Any image that is placed on the scanner bed can be captured and become an image file on the computer. This image can be further enhanced by graphic program tools and integrated into a text/graphics or multimedia presentation.

Display and Sound

Viewing options for multimedia include LCD displays and video projection monitors. The latter is best suited to handle the diversity of multimedia elements. The screen can be a white wall, a pull-down screen, a large monitor, or a group of monitors. Especially with video, the clarity of the image will be affected by the quality of these pieces of equipment. The important thing is that the audience can easily see the screen. The size of the room and the screen's position will help to determine the type of viewing option to use. Experts suggest that for any presentation made to more than about six people, the monitor or viewing space should be at least 35 inches.

Your audience shouldn't have to strain to hear you or the multimedia elements of your presentation. Video projection monitors generally have reasonably high-quality speakers. If you are using a display that relies on an attached or built-in speaker, you might want to use stand-alone speakers to enhance the sound.

Remember that computers and display units can create a formidable physical barrier. Try not to let them get between you and the audience. Keep your back to the screen. Try setting up one monitor to face you, placing the large monitor or screen to face the audience. That way, you can talk directly to the audience and still see what is being projected on the large screen.

Emerging Multimedia Materials and Tools

Presentation tools and materials continue to evolve, increasing in power, flexibility, and ease of use. Here are some of the emerging options:

* Multiple screen images
* Sound editing
* Ability to move around easily within programs in all stages of development
* Multilingual presentation and editing capabilities
* Two-way Internet interface and interactive capability in real time

Using Technology Tools to Create a Presentation

If you decide to use technology with your presentation, one of your first choices will be what software package to use.

Text and Graphic Presentation Packages

Text and graphic presentation packages provide step-by-step help information to assist you in putting elements together into a presentation. These well-developed programs easily integrate a spreadsheet, a drawing, and a screen of text into the slide show tool and then sequence it and present it with pauses and different options for speaker control.

The presentation tools of these packages help you to customize your presentation. Text templates allow a speaker to create a presentation with the same "look" throughout. Wizards function as minitutorials to help you set up a presentation in small steps. At the end of a tutorial, you have, in fact, created a presentation of your own.

The best advice is simply to try out a presentation program. You will probably find using it easier than you would expect.

Multimedia Presentation Packages

Multimedia presentation packages also include online help. Since the options are more varied and sophisticated, effective, self-paced tutorials help you through the process. Some publishers offer free interactive training courses for all levels of users. Some packages also provide research-based guidelines on what is both effective and ineffective in multimedia presentation design and delivery.

As user-friendly as many of these new packages are, you still will need to invest time in learning how to use the tools and features effectively. The desire to "get in and get done" quickly can result in a mediocre, low-tech presentation.

Managing the Presentation

You can manage your high-tech presentation in a number of different ways. Be aware that high-tech equipment can interfere with the speaker-audience connection that is so essential to effective public speaking.

If you want to stay close to the computer and to manage screen changes manually, set up your equipment so that your audience can see you. For greater freedom of movement, use sequence controls in the program so that it plays automatically, leaving silent spaces for your speech. With enough practice, this will work well and free you to make eye contact with the audience. Another option is a laser (infrared) or radio-controlled device that enables you to move the mouse from a distance. You also can use a laser pointer to send a light beam to the screen to highlight different elements and help listeners focus their attention on specific points.

Skillful use of these tools takes time and practice. When giving a speech, nervousness sometimes kicks in, and even the simplest mouse operation on a mouse pad becomes challenging. Many presenters have found that a shaky or sweaty hand can send the mouse into the hinterlands of the screen, completely disappearing at the worst possible moment.

When using a mouse or laser pointer, practice with it until you can control it.

Critical Listening

Listening is a two-way exchange between speaker and listener. It is a form of communication. There are **three** main types of listening:

1. Active listening
2. Informational listening, and
3. Critical listening.

All three types are important, but active listening is appropriate mainly in conversations with one other person or in small groups. Informational and critical listening are more relevant to speechmaking.

Whenever your purpose in listening is to learn, you are engaging in informational listening. In this passive form of listening, you simply gather information without responding, evaluating, or judging it.

In critical listening, you also attempt to listen and understand, but you go one step further. You analyze, evaluate, and draw conclusions about what you hear, judging its quality and truth.

When you evaluate a speech, you become a critical listener. You listen for a speaker's strengths but you also listen for inaccuracies and inconsistencies. Your attitude is questioning. You assess whether the information that you hear is accurate, whether you agree with it, whether it's logical, and whether it's relevant to the topic. Critical listening is particularly useful when you listen to persuasive speeches.

Strategies for Critical Listening

Critical listening is a skill that takes practice. Here are **six** critical listening strategies:

1. **Find out about the speaker's background and qualifications.** Can you identify anything that might cause the person to be biased or self-serving?

2. **Shelve your prejudices and biases.** Prepare yourself to listen openly but critically.

3. **Hear the speaker's message.** Understand exactly what is being said. Don't over-react, either positively or negatively, or jump to premature conclusions.

4. **Focus on the main idea.** What is the speaker driving at? What ideas and evidence is the speaker using to build his or her case? Does the evidence seem logical and credible? Is it up-to-date?

5. **Separate facts from opinions.** As you hear new information, do a check to make sure that you are still listening openly.

6. **Take note of any faulty reasoning used.**

Faulty Reasoning

When people speak, you might assume that their conclusions always follow from identifiable facts and logic. This is not always the case. Many times, speakers use logical fallacies, or false methods of reasoning, to convince listeners. This may be due to lazy thinking in preparing the presentation, or it may be because compelling facts and other solid evidence do not exist. As a critical listener, you need to pay attention to the flow of an argument and to watch for faulty reasoning.

The two types of faulty reasoning—logical fallacies and propaganda— are discussed in Chapters 3 and 10.

Checklist

A Good Critical Listener

☑ Prepares to listen attentively.

☑ Identifies the speaker's biases and assumptions.

☑ Connects new information to what he or she already knows.

☑ Keeps an open mind and can even change an opinion on the basis of sound evidence and reasoning.

☑ Distinguishes fact from opinion by listening for fallacies.

☑ Can identify:

 * Unsubstantiated statements
 * New information that doesn't seem to fit logically
 * Contradictions and opposing arguments

☑ Identifies good logic, sound reasoning, and common sense in a new idea, opinion, or way of thinking about a subject.

☑ Recognizes that there can be more than one valid conclusion or solution to a problem.

Evaluation Rubrics

Evaluation and feedback encourage steady improvement of your public speaking skills. Through your own evaluations and those done by peers and other listeners, you will find ways to build on your strengths and correct problem areas in your speaking.

Formal evaluation tools help evaluators by focusing attention on the specifics of what to listen for. Evaluation rubrics are one type of formal evaluation tool. They supply an organized and systematic way to judge a speech. They list major categories of speechmaking as well as specific criteria in each category.

Though there are common elements in every type of speech, following are different evaluation rubrics for self-evaluation and for speeches to inform and to persuade. Use these forms to check your own speeches and to objectively judge the speeches of others.

How to Use Rubrics

Evaluation rubrics are useful both to speakers and evaluators. For speakers, they are helpful checklists. For evaluators, they supply an objective framework for judging a speech.

When evaluating another student's speech, remember these guidelines from Chapter 16:

1. **Start by identifying the criteria** that you will use. Use criteria appropriate to the type of speech being given.

2. **Take your job seriously.** Stay focused and take notes.

3. **Always begin a critique by noting what a speaker did well.**

4. **Cite concrete examples.** Avoid vague, general comments, such as "I liked your speech" or "It needed improvement."

5. **Never get personal.** Even if you dislike the speaker or the speech topic, give a fair, helpful critique. Communicate respect for the speaker.

6. **Try not to argue.** Instead of debating the speaker's argument, evaluate its organization, logic, and evidence.

7. **Word feedback carefully.** Don't use accusatory "you" statements such as, "You didn't organize your ideas clearly." Instead, use nonblaming "I" statements such as, "I had trouble following your train of thought."

8. **Make constructive suggestions.** With each critical comment, give the speaker specific suggestions for improvement.

9. **Limit your comments.** Focus only on the most important areas of the speech.

10. **Remember that everyone is learning.** Be reasonable in your expectations and empathetic in your feedback.

Self-Evaluation Rubric

Example

Self-Evaluation

Directions: After giving a presentation, evaluate yourself by writing comments after each topic.

Category	Comment

Topic Selection
Appropriate?
Relevant to purpose?
Topic narrowed?
Within time limit?

Organization
Introduction
Attention-getting?
Included objective?
Clear pattern?
Body
Support material?
Transitions?
Conclusion
Brief summary?
To the point?
Motivational?

Support Material
Adequate?
Appropriate to audience?
Varied types?
Representative
Fact vs. opinion?
Credible sources?
Visual aids
Readable?
Useful?
Integrated?
Presentation?

Delivery

Appearance?

Notes readable?

Note/MS handling?

Eye contact?

Audience connection?

Body language?

Gestures?

Use of lectern?

Language

Suitable language?

Examples?

Voice

Volume?

Pace?

Used pauses?

Fluent?

Usage

Vocabulary OK?

Grammar?

Pronunciation?

Passive/active?

Confidence

Enough practice?

Pre-speech routine?

Room check?

Overall Evaluation

Strong points?

Goal for next time?

Speech to Inform
Evaluation Rubric

Example

Evaluation: Speech to Inform

Speaker _____

Topic _____

Category   **Comment**

Topic Selection

Appropriate?   _____

Narrow topic?   _____

Within time limit?   _____

Introduction

Attention-getting?   _____

Builds interest?   _____

Previews topic?   _____

Organization

Logical and well-organized?   _____

Appropriate organizational

pattern?   _____

Easy to follow?   _____

Repeats information?   _____

Smooth transitions?   _____

Supporting Materials

Sufficient number?   _____

Variety?   _____

Up-to-date?   _____

Visuals effective?   _____

Well-researched?   _____

Sources properly cited?   _____

Language

Word choice?

Grammar/sentence structure?

Appropriate?

Speaker Credibility

Dress and grooming?

Established credibility?

Enthusiasm?

Smooth delivery?

Delivery

Conversational?

Distracting mannerisms?

Enunciation and diction?

Gestures/facial expressions?

Eye contact?

Volume and pace?

Smooth use of notes?

Conclusion

Brief summary?

Motivational?

Purpose clear?

Overall Effectiveness

Message?

Purpose?

Evaluator

Speech to Persuade
Evaluation Rubric

Evaluation: Speech to Persuade

Speaker _____

Topic _____

Category   **Comment**

Situation

Appropriate for occasion?   _____

Within time limit?   _____

Introduction

Attention-getting?   _____

Builds interest?   _____

Previews topic?   _____

Needs of Listeners (Pathos)

Identified audience attitude?   _____

Met audience needs?   _____

Common ground of agreement?   _____

Acknowledged other views?   _____

Stated audience action?   _____

Appeals appropriate?   _____

Personal Credibility (Ethos)

Appearance appropriate?   _____

Knew subject?   _____

Credible/current evidence?   _____

Well-organized and prepared?   _____

Shared interests and concerns?   _____

Provided personal information?   _____

Appeared truthful/sincere?   _____

Spoke with conviction/enthusiasm?   _____

Reasoning and Evidence (Logos)

Good organizational pattern? _____

Clear central argument? _____

Evidence quality/relevance? _____

Enough evidence? _____

Argument sound? _____

Arguments convincing? _____

Delivery

Extemporaneous? _____

Distracting mannerisms? _____

Enunciation and diction? _____

Gestures and facial expressions? _____

Eye contact? _____

Volume and pace? _____

Use of notes? _____

Use of visual aids? _____

Language

Word choice? _____

Grammar/sentence structure? _____

Appropriate to audience? _____

Nontechnical language? _____

Conclusion

Adequate? _____

Effective? _____

Overall Effectiveness

Message? _____

Purpose? _____

Evaluator

Informative Speech

President Franklin Delano Roosevelt successfully communicated with the American public throughout his tenure as president (1932–1945). His frank and eloquent manner of speech set many people at ease during the desperate years of the Depression and World War II. FDR's First Inaugural Address is an exemplary informative speech. It describes clearly and concisely the unfortunate state of the country and convincingly promises better days to come.

Model

Franklin Delano Roosevelt

First Inaugural Address, Washington D.C., March 4, 1933

I am certain that my fellow Americans expect that on my induction into the Presidency I will address them with a candor and a decision which the present situation of our nation impels. This is preeminently the time to speak the truth, the whole truth, frankly and boldly. Nor need we shrink from honestly facing conditions in our country today. This great nation will endure, will revive, and will prosper. So, first of all, let me assert my firm belief that the only thing we have to fear is fear itself—nameless, unreasoning, unjustified terror which paralyzes needed efforts to convert retreat into advance. In every dark hour of our national life a leadership of frankness and vigor has met with that understanding and support of the people themselves which is essential to victory. I am convinced that you will again give that support to leadership in these critical days.

In such a spirit on my part and on yours, we face our common difficulties. They concern, thank God, only material things. Values have shrunken to fantastic levels; taxes have risen; our ability to pay has fallen; government of all kinds is faced by serious curtailment of income; the means of exchange are frozen in the current of trade; the withered leaves of industrial enterprise lie on every side; farmers find no market for their produce; the savings of many years in thousands of families are gone.

More important, a host of unemployed citizens face the grim problems of existence and an equally great number toil with little return. Only a foolish optimist can deny the dark realities of the moment.

Yet our distress comes from no failure of substance. We are stricken by no plague of locusts. Compared with the perils which our forefathers conquered because they believed and were not afraid, we still have much to be thankful for.

Persuasive Speech

Mohandas K. Gandhi is known and respected around the world for his commitment to nonviolence. This nationalist leader of India spoke tirelessly and persuasively about passive resistance, and, as a result, helped to secure his country's peaceful independence from England. In the following persuasive speech presented to an English court, Gandhi expresses facts and personal values as evidence of the need to reform India's corrupt government.

Model

Mohandas K. Gandhi

Ahmadabad, India, March 23, 1922

"Non-violence is the article of my faith."

Non-violence is the first article of my faith. It is the last article of my faith. But I had to make my choice. I had either to submit to a system which I considered has done an irreparable harm to my country or incur the risk of the mad fury of my people bursting forth when they understood the truth from my lips. I know that my people have sometimes gone mad. I am deeply sorry for it; and I am therefore, here, to submit not to a light penalty but to the highest penalty. I do not ask for mercy. I do not plead any extenuating act. I am here, therefore, to invite and submit to the highest penalty that can be inflicted upon me for what in law is a deliberate crime and what appears to me to be the highest duty of a citizen. The only course open to you, Mr. Judge, is, as I am just going to say in my statement, either to resign your post or inflict on me the severest penalty if you believe that the system and law you are assisting to administer are good for the people. I do not expect that kind of conversion. But by the time I have finished with my statement you will, perhaps, have a glimpse of what is raging within my breast to run this maddest risk which a sane man can run.

Gandhi then read his statement to the court.

I owe it perhaps to the Indian public and to the public in England, to placate which this prosecution is mainly taken up, that I should explain why from a staunch loyalist and cooperator I have become an uncompromising disaffectionist and Non-Cooperator. To the court too I should say why I plead guilty to the charge of promoting disaffection towards the Government established by law in India.

My public life began in 1893 in South Africa in troubled weather. My first contact with British authority in that country was not of a happy character. I discovered that as a man and an Indian I had no rights. On the contrary I discovered that I had no rights as a man because I was an Indian.

continues ▶

But I was not baffled. I thought that this treatment of Indians was an excrescence upon a system that was intrinsically and mainly good. I gave the Government my voluntary and hearty cooperation, criticizing it fully where I felt it was faulty but never wishing its destruction.

Consequently when the existence of the Empire was threatened in 1899 by the Boer challenge, I offered my services to it, raised a volunteer ambulance corps and served at several actions that took place for the relief of Ladysmith. Similarly in 1906 at the time of the Zulu revolt I raised a stretcher-bearer party and served till the end of the 'rebellion'. On both these occasions I received medals and was even mentioned in dispatches. For my work in South Africa I was given by Lord Hardinge a Kaiser-i-Hind Gold Medal. When the war broke out in 1914 between England and Germany I raised a volunteer ambulance corps in London consisting of the then resident Indians in London, chiefly students. Its work was acknowledged by the authorities to be valuable. Lastly in India when a special appeal was made at the War Conference in Delhi in 1917 by Lord Chelmsford for recruits, I struggled at the cost of my health to raise a corps in Kheda and the response was being made when the hostilities ceased and orders were received that no more recruits were wanted. In all these efforts at service I was actuated by the belief that it was possible by such services to gain a status of full equality in the Empire for my countrymen.

The first shock came in the shape of the Rowlatt Act, a law designed to rob the people of all real freedom. I felt called upon to lead an intensive agitation against it. Then followed the Punjab horrors beginning with the massacre at Jallianwala Bagh and, culminating in crawling orders, public floggings and other indescribable humiliations. The Punjab crime was white-washed, and most culprits went not only unpunished but remained in service and some continued to draw pensions from the Indian revenue, and in some cases were even rewarded. I saw too that not only did the reforms not mark a change of heart, but they were only a method of further draining India of her wealth and of prolonging her servitude.

I came reluctantly to the conclusion that the British connection had made India more helpless than she ever was before, politically and economically. A disarmed India has no power of resistance against any aggressor if she wanted to engage in an armed conflict with him. So much is this the case that some of our best men consider that India must take generations before she can achieve the Dominion status. She has become so poor that she has little power of resisting famines. Before the British advent, India spun and wove in her millions of cottages just the supplement she needed for adding to her meager agricultural resources. The cottage industry, so vital for India's existence, has been ruined by incredibly heartless and inhuman processes as described by English witnesses.

Little do town-dwellers know how the semi-starved masses of Indians are slowly sinking to lifelessness. Little do they know that their miserable comfort represents the brokerage they get for the work they do for the foreign exploiter, that the profits and the brokerage are sucked from the masses. Little do they realize that the Government established by law in British India is carried on for this exploitation of the masses. No sophistry, no jugglery in figures can explain away the evidence the skeletons in many villages present to the naked eye. I have no doubt whatsoever that both England and the town-dwellers of India will have to answer, if there is a God above, for this crime against humanity which is perhaps unequalled in history. The law itself in this country has been used to serve the foreign exploiter. My unbiased examination of the Punjab Martial Law cases has led me to believe that at least ninety-five per cent of convictions were wholly bad. My experience of political cases in India leads me to the conclusion that in nine out of every ten the condemned men were totally innocent. Their crime consisted in love of their country. In ninety-nine cases out of a hundred, justice has been denied to Indians as against Europeans in the Courts of India. This is not an exaggerated picture. It is the experience of almost every Indian who has had anything to do with such cases. In my opinion the administration of the law is thus prostituted consciously or unconsciously for the benefit of the exploiter.

The greatest misfortune is that Englishmen and their Indian associates in the administration of the country do not know that they are engaged in the crime I have attempted to describe. I am satisfied that many English and Indian officials honestly believe they are administering one of the best systems devised in the world and that India is making steady though slow progress. They do not know that a subtle but effective system of terrorism and an organized display of force on the one hand and the deprivation of all powers of retaliation or self-defense on the other have emasculated the people and induced in them the habit of simulation. This awful habit has added to the

continues ▶

ignorance and the self-deception of the administrators. Section 124-A under which I am happily charged is perhaps the prince among the political sections of the Indian Penal Code designed to suppress the liberty of the citizen. Affection cannot be manufactured or regulated by law. If one has no affection for a person or thing one should be free to give the fullest expression to his disaffection so long as he does not contemplate, promote or incite to violence. But the section under which Mr. Banker and I are charged is one under which mere promotion of disaffection is a crime. I have studied some of the cases tried under it, and I know that some of the most loved of India's patriots have been convicted under it. I consider it a privilege, therefore, to be charged under it. I have endeavored to give in their briefest outline the reasons for my disaffection. I have no personal ill-will against any single administrator, much less can I have any disaffection towards the King's person. But I hold it to be a virtue to be disaffected towards a Government which in its totality has done more harm to India than any previous system. India is less manly under the British rule than she ever was before. Holding such a belief, I consider it to be a sin to have affection for the system. And it has been a precious privilege for me to be able to write what I have in the various articles tendered in evidence against me.

In fact I believe that I have rendered a service to India and England by showing in Non-Cooperation the way out of the unnatural state in which both are living. In my humble opinion, non-cooperation with evil is as much a duty as is cooperation with good. But in the past, non-cooperation has been deliberately expressed in violence to the evildoer. I am endeavoring to show to my countrymen that violent non-cooperation only multiplies evil and that as evil can only be sustained by violence, withdrawal of support of evil requires complete abstention from violence. Non-violence implies voluntary submission to the penalty for non-cooperation with evil. I am here, therefore, to invite and submit cheerfully to the highest penalty that can be inflicted upon me for what in law is deliberate crime and what appears to me to be the highest duty of a citizen. The only course open to you, the Judge and the Assessors, is either to resign your posts and thus dissociate yourselves from evil if you feel that the law you are called upon to administer is an evil and that in reality I am innocent, or to inflict on me the severest penalty if you believe that the system and the law you are assisting to administer are good for the people of this country and that my activity is therefore injurious to the public weal.

Eulogy

Jawaharlal Nehru worked closely with famed Indian leader Mohandas K. Gandhi. Gandhi's death in 1948 was a powerful blow to people around the world, who, like Nehru, had revered him. Nehru's eulogy pays homage to Gandhi's life and enduring legacy, sincerely conveying feelings of sorrow and loss.

Model

Jawaharlal Nehru

Delhi, India, January 30, 1948

"The light has gone out of our lives."

Friends and comrades, the light has gone out of our lives and there is darkness everywhere. I do not know what to tell you and how to say it. Our beloved leader, Bapu as we called him, the father of the nation, is no more. Perhaps I am wrong to say that. Nevertheless, we will not see him again as we have seen him for these many years. We will not run to him for advice and seek solace from him, and that is a terrible blow, not to me only, but to millions and millions in this country, and it is a little difficult to soften the blow by any other advice that I or anyone else can give you.

The light has gone out, I said, and yet I was wrong. For the light that shone in this country was no ordinary light. The light that has illumined this country for these many years will illumine this country for many more years, and a thousand years later that light will still be seen in this country and the world will see it and it will give solace to innumerable hearts. For that light represented the living truth . . . the eternal truths, reminding us of the right path, drawing us from error, taking this ancient country into freedom.

All this has happened when there was so much more for him to do. We could never think that he was unnecessary or that he had done his task. But now, particularly, when we are faced with so many difficulties, his not being with us is a blow most terrible to bear.

continues ▶

Eulogy *(continued)*

Model

A madman has put an end to his life, for I can only call him mad who did it, and yet there has been enough of poison spread in this country during the past years and months, and this poison has had effect on people's minds. We must face this poison, we must root out this poison, and we must face all the perils that encompass us and face them not madly or badly but rather in the way that our beloved teacher taught us to face them. The first thing to remember now is that no one of us dare misbehave because we are angry. We have to behave like strong and determined people, determined to face all the perils that surround us, determined to carry out the mandate that our great teacher and our great leader has given us, remembering always that if, as I believe, his spirit looks upon us and sees us, nothing would displease his soul so much as to see that we have indulged in any small behavior or any violence.

So we must not do that. But that does not mean that we should be weak, but rather that we should in strength and in unity face all the troubles that are in front of us. We must hold together, and all our petty troubles and difficulties and conflicts must be ended in the face of this great disaster. A great disaster is a symbol to us to remember all the big things of life and forget the small things, of which we have thought too much.

Impromptu Speech

Sojourner Truth toiled as a slave for much of her life and was relentless in her pursuit of freedom and women's rights. Despite her lack of education, Truth spoke wisely and demonstrated her skill at impromptu speech. In this speech, she makes her point on women's rights absolutely clear, supports it with details, and uses illustrative metaphors.

Model

Evangelist Sojourner Truth

Ohio Women's Rights Convention, 1851

"And ain't I a woman? Look at me!"

Well, children, where there is so much racket there must be something out of kilter. I think that 'twixt the Negroes of the South and the women at the North, all talking about rights, the white men will be in a fix pretty soon. But what's all this here talking about?

That man over there says that women need to be helped into carriages, and lifted over ditches, and to have the best place everywhere. Nobody ever helps me into carriages, or over mud puddles, or gives me any best place! And ain't I a woman? Look at me! Look at my arm. I have plowed and planted, and gathered into barns, and no man could head me! And ain't I a woman? I could work as much and eat as much as a man—when I could get it—and bear the lash as well! And ain't I a woman? I have borne thirteen children, and seen them most all sold off to slavery, and when I cried out with my mother's grief, none but Jesus heard me! And ain't I a woman?

Then they talk about this thing in the head; what's this they call it? Intellect, someone whispers. That's it, honey. What's that got to do with women's rights or Negro's rights? If my cup won't hold but a pint, and yours holds a quart, wouldn't you be mean not to let me have my little half-measure full?

Then that little man in black there, he says women can't have as much rights as men, 'cause Christ wasn't a woman! Where did your Christ come from? Where did your Christ come from? From God and a woman! Man had nothing to do with him.

If the first woman God ever made was strong enough to turn the world upside down all alone, these women together ought to be able to turn it back, and get it right side up again! And now they is asking to do it, the men better let them.

Obliged to you for hearing me, and now old Sojourner ain't got nothing more to say.

Preparing a Speech

In the midst of an economic recession and Republican policy-making, Democrat Mario Cuomo spoke candidly at the 1984 Democratic National Convention about America's decline and potential to rise again. In the following speech, Cuomo identifies a problem, states his objective, and suggests ways to attain the desired end. His words are both inspiring and motivating and are made all the more credible by the inclusion of facts and personal anecdotes.

Mario Cuomo

San Francisco, July 16, 1984

"Make this nation remember how futures are built"

Ten days ago, President Reagan admitted that although some people in this country seemed to be doing well nowadays, others were unhappy, and even worried, about themselves, their families and their futures.

The President said he didn't understand that fear. He said "Why, this country is a shining city on a hill."

The President is right. In many ways we *are* "a shining city on a hill."

But the hard truth is that not everyone is sharing in this city's splendor and glory.

A shining city is perhaps all the President sees from the portico of the White House and the veranda of his ranch, where everyone seems to be doing well.

But there's another part of the city, the part where some people can't pay their mortgages and most young people can't afford one, where students can't afford the education they need and middle-class parents watch the dreams they hold for their children, evaporate.

In this part of the city there are more poor than ever, more families in trouble, more and more people who need help but can't find it.

Even worse: there are elderly people who tremble in the basements of the houses there.

There are people who sleep in the city's streets, in the gutter where the glitter doesn't show.

There are ghettos where thousands of young people, without an education or a job, give their lives away to drug dealers every day.

There is despair, Mr. President, in faces you never see, in the places you never visit in your shining city.

In fact, Mr. President, this nation is more a "tale of two cities" than it is a "shining city on a hill."

Maybe if you visited more places, Mr. President, you'd understand.

Maybe if you went to Appalachia where some people still live in sheds, and to Lackawanna where thousands of unemployed steel workers wonder why we subsidized foreign steel while we surrender their dignity to unemployment and to welfare checks, maybe if you stepped into a shelter in Chicago and talked with some of the homeless there: maybe Mr. President, if you asked a woman who'd been denied the help she needs to feed her children because you say we need the money to give a tax break to a millionaire or to build a missile we can't even afford to use–maybe then you'd understand.

Maybe, Mr. President.

But I'm afraid not.

Because, the truth is, this is how we were warned it would be.

President Reagan told us from the beginning that he believed in a kind of social Darwinism, survival of the fittest. "Government can't do everything," we were told, "so it should settle for taking care of the strong and hope that economic ambition and charity will do the rest. Make the rich richer and what falls from their table will be enough for the middle class and those trying to make it into the middle class."

The Republicans called it trickle-down when Hoover tried it. Now they call it supply side.

It is the same shining city for those relative few who are lucky enough to live in its good neighborhoods.

But for the people who are excluded–locked out–all they can do is to stare from a distance at that city's glimmering towers.

It's an old story. As old as our history.

The difference between Democrats and the Republicans has always been measured in courage and confidence.

The Republicans believe the wagon train will not make it to the frontier unless some of our old, some of our young, and some of our weak are left behind by the side of the trail.

The strong will inherit the land!

We Democrats believe that we can make it all the way with the whole family intact.

We have. More than once.

Ever since Franklin Roosevelt lifted himself from his wheelchair to lift this nation from its knees, wagon train after wagon train. To new frontiers of education, housing, peace. The whole family aboard, constantly reaching out to extend and enlarge that family. Lifting them up into the wagon on the way. Blacks and

continues ▶

Hispanics, people of every ethnic group, and native Americans–all those struggling to build their families and claim some small share of America.

For nearly fifty years we carried them to new levels of comfort, security, dignity, even affluence.

Some of us are in this room today only because this nation had that confidence.

It would be wrong to forget that.

So, we are here at this convention to remind ourselves where we come from and to claim the future for ourselves and for our children.

Today our great Democratic Party, which has saved this nation from depression, from Fascism, from racism, from corruption, is called upon to do it again . . . This time to save the nation from confusion and division, from the threat of eventual fiscal disaster and most of all from a fear of a nuclear holocaust . . . .

We must win this case on the merits.

We must get the American public to look past the glitter, beyond the showmanship . . . to reality, to the hard substance of things. And we will do that not so much with speeches that sound good as with speeches that are good and sound . . . .

We must make the American people hear our "tale of two cities."

We must convince them that we don't have to settle for two cities, that we can have one city, indivisible, shining for *all* its people. . . .

To succeed we will have to surrender small parts of our individual interests, to build a platform we can all stand on, at once, comfortably–proudly singing out the truth for the nation to hear, in chorus, its logic so clear and commanding that no slick commercial, no amount of geniality, no martial music will be able to muffle it.

We Democrats must unite so that the entire nation can. Surely the Republicans won't bring the convention together, their policies divide the nation . . . into the lucky and the left-out, the royalty and the rabble.

The Republicans are willing to treat that division as victory. They would cut this nation in half, into those temporarily better off and those worse off than before, and call it recovery.

We should not be embarrassed or dismayed if the process of unifying is difficult, even at times wrenching.

Unlike any other party, we embrace men and women of every color, every creed, every orientation, every economic class. In our family are gathered everyone from the abject poor of Essex County in New York, to the enlightened affluent of the gold coasts of both ends of our nation.

And in between is the heart of our constituency, the middle class . . . The people not rich enough to be worry free but not poor enough to be on welfare. Those who work for a living because they have to. White collar and blue collar. Young professionals, men and women in small business desperate for the capital and contracts they need to prove their worth.

We speak for the minorities who have not yet entered the mainstream.

For ethnics who want to add their culture to the mosaic that is America.

For women indignant that we refuse to etch into our governmental commandments the simple rule "Thou shalt not sin against equality," a commandment so obvious it can be spelled in letters . . . ERA!

For young people demanding an education and a future.

For senior citizens terrorized by the idea that their only security . . . their *social* security . . . is being threatened.

For millions of reasoning people fighting to preserve our environment from greed and stupidity and fighting to preserve our very existence from a macho intransigence that refuses to make intelligent attempts to discuss the possibility of nuclear holocaust with our enemy. Refusing because they believe we can

pile missiles so high that they will pierce the clouds and the sight of them will frighten our enemies into submission. . . .

That struggle to live with dignity is the real story of the shining city. It's a story I didn't read in a book, or learn in a classroom. I saw it, and lived it, like many of you.

I watched a small man with thick calluses on both hands work fifteen and sixteen hours a day. I saw him once literally bleed from the bottoms of his feet, a man who came here uneducated, alone, unable to speak the language, who taught me all I needed to know about faith and hard work by the simple eloquence of his example. I learned about our kind of democracy from my father. I learned about our obligation to each other from him and from my mother. They asked only for a chance to work and to make the world better for their children and to be protected in those moments when they would not be able to protect themselves. This nation and its government did that for them.

And that they were able to build a family and live in dignity and see one of their children go from behind their little grocery store on the other side of the tracks in South Jamaica where he was born, to occupy the highest seat in the greatest state of the greatest nation in the only

continues ▶

world we know, is an ineffably beautiful tribute to the Democratic process.

We Democrats *still* have a dream. We *still* believe in this nation's future.

And this is our answer—*our* credo.

We believe in *only* the government we need but we insist on all the government we need.

We believe in a government characterized by fairness and *reasonableness*, a reasonableness that goes beyond labels, that doesn't distort or promise to do what it knows it can't do.

A government strong enough to use the words "love" and "compassion" and smart enough to convert our noblest aspirations into practical realities.

We believe in encouraging the talented, but we believe that while survival of the fittest may be a good working description of the process of evolution, a government of humans should elevate itself to a higher order, one which fills the gaps left by chance of a wisdom we don't understand.

We would rather have laws written by the patron of this great city, the man called the "world's most sincere democrat"—St. Francis of Assisi—than laws written by Darwin.

We believe, as Democrats, that a society as blessed as ours, the most affluent democracy in the world's history, that can spend trillions on instruments of destruction, ought to be able to help the middle class in its struggle, ought to be able to find work for all who can do it, room at the table, shelter for the homeless, care for the elderly and infirm, hope for the destitute.

We proclaim as loudly as we can the utter insanity of nuclear proliferation and the need for a nuclear freeze, if only to affirm the simple truth that peace is better than war because life is better than death.

We believe in firm but fair law and order, in the union movement, in privacy for people, openness by government, civil rights, and human rights.

We believe in a single fundamental idea that describes better than most textbooks and any speech what a proper government should be. The idea of family, mutuality, the sharing of benefits and burdens for the good of all. Feeling one another's pain. Sharing one another's blessings. Reasonably, honestly, fairly–without respect to race, or sex, or geography or political affiliation.

We believe we must be the family of America, recognizing that at the heart of the matter we are bound one to another, that the problems of a retired schoolteacher in Duluth are *our* problems. That the future of the child in Buffalo is *our* future. The struggle of a disabled man in Boston to survive, to live decently is *our* struggle. The hunger of a woman in Little Rock, *our* hunger. The failure anywhere to provide what reasonably we might, to avoid pain, is *our* failure.

For fifty years we Democrats created a better future for our children, using traditional Democratic principles as a fixed beacon, giving us direction and purpose, but constantly innovating, adapting to new realities: Roosevelt's Alphabet programs; Truman's NATO and the GI Bill of Rights; Kennedy's intelligent tax incentives and the Alliance for Progress; Johnson's Civil Rights; Carter's Human Rights and the nearly miraculous Camp David Peace Accord.

We will have America's first woman Vice-President: the child of immigrants, a New Yorker, opening with one magnificent stroke a whole new frontier for the United States.

It will happen–*if we make it happen.*

I ask you–ladies and gentlemen, brothers and sisters–for the good of all of us–for the love of this great nation, for the family of America–for the love of God, please, make this nation remember how futures are built.

Special Occasion Speech

In the following special occasion speech, President John F. Kennedy marks the death of poet Robert Frost with eloquence and care. He acclaims Frost for both his contribution to the literary world and to society at large. He uses Frost's example to illustrate the value and power of art in all aspects of life.

John F. Kennedy

Amherst College, Amherst, MA, 27 October 1963

... This day, devoted to the memory of Robert Frost, offers an opportunity for reflection which is prized by politicians as well as by others and even by poets. For Robert Frost was one of the granite figures of our time in America. He was supremely two things—an artist and an American.

A nation reveals itself not only by the men it produces but also by the men it honors, the men it remembers.

In America our heroes have customarily run to men of large accomplishments. But today this college and country honors a man whose contribution was not to our size but to our spirit; not to our political beliefs but to our insight; not to our self-esteem but to our self-comprehension.

In honoring Robert Frost, we therefore can pay honor to the deepest sources of our national strength. That strength takes many forms, and the most obvious forms are not always the most significant.

The men who create power make an indispensable contribution to the nation's greatness. But the men who question power make a contribution just as indispensable, especially when that questioning is disinterested.

For they determine whether we use power or power uses us. Our national strength matters; but the spirit which informs and controls our strength matters just as much. This was the special significance of Robert Frost.

He brought an unsparing instinct for reality to bear on the platitudes and pieties of society. His sense of the human tragedy fortified him against self-deception and easy consolation.

"I have been," he wrote, "one acquainted with the night."

And because he knew the midnight as well as the high noon, because he understood the ordeal as well as the triumph of the human spirit, he gave his age strength with which to overcome despair.

At bottom he held a deep faith in the spirit of man. And it's hardly an accident that Robert Frost coupled poetry and power. For he saw poetry as the means of saving power from itself.

When power leads man toward arrogance, poetry reminds him of his limitations. When power narrows the areas of man's concern, poetry reminds him of the richness and diversity of his existence. When power corrupts, poetry cleanses.

For art establishes the basic human truths which must serve as the touchstones of our judgment. The artist, however faithful to his personal vision of reality, becomes the last champion of the individual mind and sensibility against an intrusive society and an officious state.

The great artist is thus a solitary figure. He has, as Frost said, "a lover's quarrel with the world." In pursuing his perceptions of reality, he must often sail against the currents of his time. This is not a popular role.

If Robert Frost was much honored during his lifetime, it was because a good many preferred to ignore his darker truths.

Yet in retrospect we see how the artist's fidelity has strengthened the fiber of our national life. If sometimes our great artists have been the most critical of our society, it is because their sensitivity and their concern for justice, which must motivate any true artist, makes him aware that our nation falls short of its highest potential.

I see little of more importance to the future of our country and our civilization than full recognition of the place of the artist. If art is to nourish the roots of our culture, society must set the artist free to follow his vision wherever it takes him.

We must never forget that art is not a form of propaganda; it is a form of truth. And as Mr. MacLeish once remarked of poets, "There is nothing worse for our trade than to be in style."

In free society, art is not a weapon and it does not belong to the sphere of polemics and ideology. Artists are not engineers of the soul.

It may be different elsewhere. But democratic society—in it—the highest duty of the writer, the composer, the artist is to remain true to himself and to let the chips fall where they may.

In serving his vision of the truth, the artist best serves his nation. And the nation which disdains the mission of art invites the fate of Robert Frost's hired man—"the fate of having

continues ▶

Model

nothing to look backward to with pride and nothing to look forward to with hope."

I look forward to a great future for America—a future in which our country will match its military strength with our moral restraint, its wealth with our wisdom, its power with our purpose.

I look forward to an America which will not be afraid of grace and beauty, which will protect the beauty of our national environment, which will preserve the great old American houses and squares and parks of our national past and which will build handsome and balanced cities for our future.

I look forward to an America which will reward achievement in the arts as we reward achievement in business or statecraft.

I look forward to an America which will steadily raise the standards of artistic accomplishment and which will steadily enlarge cultural opportunities for all of our citizens.

And I look forward to an America which commands respect throughout the world not only for its strength but for its civilization as well.

And I look forward to a world which will be safe not only for democracy and diversity but also for personal distinction.

Robert Frost was often skeptical about projects for human improvement. Yet I do not think he would disdain this hope.

As he wrote during the uncertain days of the Second War:

Take human nature altogether since time
    began. . . .
And it must be a little more in favor of man,
Say a fraction of one percent at the very
    least. . . .
Our hold on the planet wouldn't have so
    increased.

Because of Mr. Frost's life and work, because of the life and work of this college, our hold on this planet has increased.

Special Occasion Speech

Richard Nixon was the only president of the United States to ever resign from office. Facing certain impeachment as a result of his involvement in the Watergate scandal, Nixon left the White House in disgrace. He and many members of his administration had fallen out of favor with the majority of Americans who had become disillusioned by both Watergate and by the way in which he had run the country. Just before leaving the White House, Nixon addressed his staff to extend a heart-felt good-bye.

Model

Richard Nixon

Washington, DC, 9 August 1974

'Au revoir'

You are here to say goodbye to us, and we don't have a good word for it in English—the best is *au revoir*. We will see you again.

I just met with the members of the White House staff, you know, those who serve here in the White House day in and day out, and I asked them to do what I ask all of you to do to the extent that you can and, of course, are requested to do so: to serve our next president as you have served me and previous presidents—because many of you have been here for many years—with devotion and dedication, because this office, great as it is, can only be as great as the men and women who work for and with the president. . . .

And so it is with you. I look around here, and I see so many on this staff that, you know, I should have been by your offices and shaken hands, and I would love to have talked to you and found out how to run the world—everybody wants to tell the president what to do, and boy, he needs to be told many times—but I just haven't had the time. But I want you to know that each and every one of you, I know, is indispensable to this Government.

I am proud of this Cabinet. I am proud of all the members who have served in our Cabinet. I am proud of our sub-Cabinet. I am proud of our White House Staff. As I pointed out last night, sure, we have done some things wrong in this Administration, and the top man always takes the responsibility, and I have never ducked it. But I want to say one thing: We can be proud of it—five and a half years. No man or no woman came into this Administration and left it with more of this world's goods than when he came in. No man or no woman ever profited at the public expense or the public till. That tells something about you.

Mistakes, yes. But for personal gain, never. You did what you believed in. Sometimes right, sometimes wrong. And I only wish that I were a wealthy man—at the present time, I have got to find a way to pay my taxes—(laughter)—and

continues ▶

Model

if I were, I would like to recompense you for the sacrifices that all of you have made to serve in government.

But you are getting something in government–and I want you to tell this to your children, and I hope the Nation's children will hear it, too–something in government service that is far more important than money. It is a cause bigger than yourself. It is the cause of making this the greatest nation in the world, the leader of the world, because without our leadership, the world will know nothing but war, possibly starvation or worse, in the years ahead. With our leadership it will know peace, it will know plenty.

We have been generous, and we will be more generous in the future as we are able to. But most important, we must be strong here, strong in our hearts, strong in our souls, strong in our belief, and strong in our willingness to sacrifice, as you have been willing to sacrifice, in a pecuniary way, to serve in government. . . . We think sometimes when things happen that don't go the right way; we think that when you don't pass the bar exam the first time–I happened to, but I was just lucky; I mean, my writing was so poor the bar examiner said, 'We have just got to let the guy through.' We think that when someone dear to us dies, we think that when we lose an election, we think that when we suffer a defeat that all is ended.

Not true. It is only a beginning, always. The young must know it; the old must know it. It must always sustain us, because the greatness comes not when things go always good for you, but the greatness comes and you are really tested, when you take some knocks, some disappointments, when sadness comes, because only if you have been in the deepest valley can you ever know how magnificent it is to be on the highest mountain.'

Credits

181 "I have nothing to offer but blood, toil, tears and sweat" (made in London on 13 May 1940) by Sir Winston S. Churchill. Reproduced with the permission of Curtis Brown, Ltd., on behalf of the Estate of Sir Winston S. Churchill. Copyright Winston S. Churchill. 266 "I Have a Dream" by Martin Luther King, Jr., August 28, 1963, Washington,D.C. Reprinted by arrangement with The Heirs to the Estate of Martin Luther King, Jr. c/o Writers House, Inc. as agent for the proprietor. Copyright 1963 by Martin Luther King, Jr., copyright renewed 1991 by Coretta Scott King. 374 Speech "Make this nation remember how futures are built" by Mario Cuomo, San Francisco, July 16, 1984. Mario M. Cuomo, three-term Governor of New York State. Reprinted by permission. 385 "Nelson Mandela's Address on his Release from Prison," February 11, 1990, Cape Town, South Africa. Copyright © 1990. Reprinted by permission of the African National Congress.

Index